CRITICAL INSIGHTS

Good and Evil

CRITICAL INSIGHTS

Good and Evil

Editor

Margaret Sönser Breen

University of Connecticut

SALEM PRESS

A Division of EBSCO Publishing

Ipswich, Massachusetts

Library of Congress Cataloging-in-Publication Data
Good and evil / editor, Margaret Sönser Breen.
    p. cm. -- (Critical insights)
  Includes bibliographical references and index.
  ISBN 978-1-4298-3736-1 (hardcover) -- ISBN 978-1-4298-3784-2 (ebook) 1. Good and evil in literature. 2. English literature--19th century--History and criticism. 3. English literature--20th century--History and criticism. 4. American literature--19th century--History and criticism. 5. American literature--20th century--History and criticism. I. Breen, Margaret Sönser.
  PR468.G66G66 2012
  820.9'353--dc23
                              2012018999

Contents_____

Resources

About This Volume _____

Margaret Sönser Breen

Good and evil is one of the great themes of literature. But what are good and evil, and how do we distinguish one from the other? Should we regard them as one and the same? Are they abstractions that help us to order our lives? Are they embodied: can people personify good or *be* evil? Are good and evil moral absolutes, or are they relative terms, historically and culturally determined? What is literature's relationship to dominant cultural, political, and religious definitions of good and evil; how does literature encode these definitions or resist them? What, after all, can literature teach us? These are some of the questions that the sixteen essays in this volume ask.

Critical Insights: Good and Evil is divided into four sections: an introduction that includes this preface as well as an opening essay; a section titled "Critical Contexts," comprising four essays that lay out different methodological approaches for analyzing literature's treatment of the theme of good and evil; a section titled "Critical Readings," consisting of eleven essays that analyze works ranging from Shakespeare's *King Lear* to J. K. Rowling's *The Prisoner of Azkaban*; and, finally, a bibliographic section that provides suggestions for further reading.

Even as contributors have written primarily with an American undergraduate audience in mind, we understand that our readers belong to a varied and complex group. One does not have to be an English major (let alone an American!) to love literature and to learn from it and write about it. While most of the contributors are literature professors, some specialize in other disciplines: one is an art historian, another a historian, and yet another a librarian. By reading literature we encounter all kinds of situations and people from whom we might otherwise have been separated. The act of reading allows strangers to become deeply familiar, and, sometimes, those who on the surface seem so much like us to prove to be alien.

This volume is meant to challenge and provoke. Its essays emphasize the importance of the *activity* of reading. Implicitly, they ask us who we are and who we have and will *become* through the reading of literature. Literature has the potential to change our perceptions of ourselves as well as of the world; it calls upon us to recognize our power and responsibility. As readers we participate in interpretive acts that allow us to see anew, to revise and revitalize our relationship with ourselves and others. Such imaginative engagement lets us realize our own agency; reading literature makes us understand that our actions carry not only personal but also social, political, ethical, and moral weight.

So, reading literature is fundamentally "about" our capacity to do good and evil. Stories, poems, plays, novels, and essays require that we identify, cross, and remake the moral, social, political, cultural, and familial boundaries of our lives. Consider *Good and Evil* an invitation—an invitation to read widely and wildly, well beyond the limits of this collection, in order to develop your own ability to recognize and understand the possibilities and patterns of good and evil and your relationship to them.

This invitation begins with my own introduction, which focuses on four texts (Primo Levi's memoir *Survival in Auschwitz*, Dorothy Allison's novel *Bastard Out of Carolina*, Mark Doty's poem "Difference," and Alice Walker's essay "In Search of Our Mothers' Gardens") and explores the transformative potential of storytelling. In each case storytelling functions as a narrative good, one that, like welcome physical touch, humanizes and dignifies the storyteller. In the wake of various forms of violation, storytelling allows writers, narrators, speakers, and characters (and, by extension, readers) the possibility to resist oppression and claim—or reclaim—authority and integrity.

Following this introductory essay is the "Critical Contexts" section, the first essay of which focuses on the relationship between literary criticism and literature. In "Good and Evil in the Modern Critical Tradition," Mena Mitrano begins by meditating on a horrifying image from Primo Levi's *Survival in Auschwitz*: the image of the *Muselmann* (literally, "the Muslim"), a man whom the Holocaust concentration camp has produced, a man who is no longer a man. The Muselmann embodies the cost of the Holocaust's evil. How, Mitrano asks, has literary criticism since World War II responded to the twinned issue of good and evil? By way of answer, she examines various critical schools, including formalism, structuralism, deconstructionism, feminism, and theory. For her, "the problem of good and evil has shaped [literary criticism's] very course."

Questions of good and evil also inform a historical approach to literature. In "Good and Evil: Inclusion and Exclusion in Life and Literature," Sherri Olson points to the problem of bias in the making of histories. She reminds us that "history," for all its ostensible objectivity, is never far from "story," in this case the subjective sway of cultural prejudice. So, for example, she observes that throughout Western history, dominant groups have invoked the biblical story of Noah's curse in order to sanction violence against other peoples. Historical bias and, more broadly, the cultural context for the making of history need to be kept in mind, Olson argues, when we read literature and its representations of good and evil. Her cases in point include interpretations of Roman emperor and Stoic philosopher Marcus Aurelius's *Meditations*, Jane Austen's novels *Emma* and *Mansfield Park*, and Harriet A. Jacobs's *Incidents in the Life of a Slave Girl*.

Linked to Olson's is Robert Deam Tobin's comparative approach, which considers literary texts from three distinct historical periods. In "World without Evil? Faust's Fortunes through the Centuries," Tobin compares and contrasts three well-known versions of the Faust myth, which tells of a man who gains power and fame by selling his soul to the devil. Christopher Marlowe's Renaissance tragedy *Doctor Faustus*, Johann Wolfgang von Goethe's Enlightenment/romantic play (or plays) *Faust*, and Thomas Mann's "post-Holocaust novel" *Doctor Faustus* "provide very different takes on evil." Nonetheless, Tobin argues, "each of these literary texts has great sympathy with Faust and implies that even in the most dire situations, evil might actually lead to good and thus not be evil at all."

The final essay in the "Critical Contexts" section is Frederick S. Roden's "Decadence and *Dorian Gray*: Who's Afraid of Oscar Wilde?" In part, this essay engages the question of the Faustian bargain that Wilde's character Dorian Gray makes. More broadly, by paying attention to the ways in which Wilde's writings both formally and thematically encode transgressive possibilities, the essay offers a queer methodological approach for interpreting the great Victorian Anglo-Irish poet and writer's life and work. For Roden, "inversion," which is the term that Victorians used to describe "the sexual 'deviance' that shaped Wilde's own identity," is "the central metaphor in Wilde's thinking—and living"; it is also "a means to comprehend [Wilde's] thought." For Roden, Wilde is a surprising and important "theologian of good and evil" whose life and work "dramatize the danger of transgression, even as they celebrate the pleasure of forbidden fruit."

The "Critical Readings" section constitutes the core of this volume. Even though the essays here follow a basic chronological order, readers will recognize the thematic overlap of many of these pieces. The first two pieces focus on two great works of the seventeenth century. Gregory Kneidel's "Bonds, Needs, and Morals in *King Lear*" considers Shakespeare's play in terms of its central questions: "How do we measure our obligations to others? And how then do we value their lives over our luxuries?" Important for Kneidel is not only how Shakespeare takes up these questions in the tragedy but also how we can apply the lessons of *Lear* to our own lives. Mitchell M. Harris's essay follows Kneidel's. In "John Milton's *Paradise Lost* and the Problem of Evil," Harris also asks readers to learn from the text. Harris examines the poem's engagement with "the problem of evil." Citing key scholarly debates, Harris demonstrates that the questions that *Paradise Lost* provokes—"is God good or is God bad?" and "where does evil originate?"—have no neat and ready answers. Perhaps, Harris argues, "the answers to such questions lie not in the text but in our own reading experience." If so, then we as readers must determine "whether we are willing to entertain those questions and, more importantly, whether we are prepared to answer those questions and be accountable to our answers."

The next three essays in this section examine British and American works written in the nineteenth century. Mark Kipperman's "Driven by Demons: 'The Rime of the Ancient Mariner'" is a close reading of Samuel Taylor Coleridge's 1798 poem. For Kipperman, "Rime" is "one of literature's most haunting narratives of moral terror." The poem does not "show us *how* a corrupt will can turn to faith and love." It does, however, "conjure a fearsome vision of what happens when we fail."

Texts such as Coleridge's influenced both romantic and Victorian writers greatly. Charlotte Brontë's novel *Jane Eyre*, the subject of Katie R. Peel's essay, echoes "Rime" insofar as Jane, over the course of her development, learns to self-regulate and so to value moral restraint over passionate impulse. Yet, in "The Inadequacy of Closure in Charlotte Brontë's *Jane Eyre*; or, Why 'Reader, I Married Him' Is One of the Most Disappointing Sentences in Victorian Literature," Peel reads against the conventional interpretation that celebrates Jane's marriage at the novel's end as a triumph of self-control over passion. Peel's feminist and postcolonial analysis measures the novel's "happy" ending in terms of the various transgressions against women and minorities on which Jane's love story depends. For Peel, "the 'good' resolution of the text . . . is not enough to counter or compensate for the numerous evils that create the book's conflicts."

Though published a few years after the Victorian *Jane Eyre*, Nathaniel Hawthorne's *The Scarlet Letter* is itself a romantic text. In "Hawthorne's Pearl: The Origins of Good and Evil in *The Scarlet Letter*," Karen J. Renner turns our attention to the child, the figure who preoccupied so many romantics. For Hawthorne, the child was not, as she was for romantics such as William Wordsworth, a figure of innocence and purity. Instead, as Renner demonstrates, Hawthorne links the child Pearl's "strange and sometimes disconcerting behavior back to her treatment by both the community that estranges her and the mother for whom, like the scarlet letter itself, she is a constant reminder of shame." Hawthorne's Pearl reflects his belief that evil "is not an inherited quality but a psychological response."

This concern with the psychology of evil intensified by the end of the nineteenth century. In his comparative essay "'The Accurst, the Tainted, and the Innocent': *The Strange Case of Dr. Jekyll and Mr. Hyde* and the Fragmentation of Personality in Late Victorian and Edwardian Scottish Fiction," Tom Hubbard examines the psychological preoccupation of four nineteenth- and twentieth-century Scottish novels: Robert Louis Stevenson's *The Strange Case of Dr. Jekyll and Mr. Hyde* and *The Master of Ballantrae*, George Douglas Brown's *The House with the Green Shutters*, and John MacDougall Hay's *Gillespie*. The first of these novels provides the most notable example of a late Victorian exploration of the disintegration of personality, whereby good and evil split into distinct identities embodied by one person. As Hubbard explains, Freudian psychology proves an apt lens for understanding these texts' explorations of the inner workings of evil.

Literary explorations of violent conflict and genocide in the mid-twentieth century are the focal points of the next three essays in the collection. In "From Mice to *Mickey* to *Maus*: The Metaphor of Evil and Its Metamorphosis in the Holocaust," Pnina Rosenberg examines the image of the mouse in two illustrated texts, Horst Rosenthal's *Mickey Mouse in Gurs Internment Camp*, which he created while himself imprisoned in the World War II camp, and Art Spiegelman's *Maus*, which narrates the story of Spiegelman's father's life before, during, and after the Holocaust. Rosenberg demonstrates that with their illustrated texts, Rosenthal and Spiegelman engage and invert wartime anti-Semitic propaganda, which portrayed Jews as vermin; the writers transform "the emblem of all evil" into a sympathetic and compelling "symbol of victims as well as survivors" of Nazi extermination.

In "Understanding Communal Violence: Khushwant Singh's *Train to Pakistan*," Patrick Colm Hogan turns readers' attention to one writer's exploration of the extensive violence that took place between religious groups at the time of the 1947 partition of the Indian subcontinent into India and Pakistan. "Though much less extensive than the Holocaust in its human devastation," Hogan writes, "the Partition is comparably baffling, seemingly 'unnarratable' in the sense of resisting a coherent causal account." With the novel *Train to Pakistan*, Hogan continues, Singh gives himself "the task of depicting how and explaining why, over the course of a few weeks in late 1947, enduring communal harmony . . . was destroyed in a small Indian village."

A decade earlier, in the Dominican Republic, tens of thousands of Haitians and people of Haitian descent were massacred. Edwidge Danticat makes this event the subject of one of her novels. As Katharine Capshaw Smith demonstrates in "Unfinished Evil and Benevolent Community in Edwidge Danticat's *The Farming of Bones*," the novel searches to understand "the political and social forces that create the conditions for genocide."

"Critical Readings" ends with essays that analyze non-historically based popular-culture texts. In "Revisiting the Gothic: *Buffy the Vampire Slayer* and *Angel* as Contemporary Gothic," Erin Hollis considers the two television shows in terms of the genre that they modify and update for a late twentieth- and early twenty-first-century viewing audience. Hollis contends that the shows "represent a contemporary approach to the gothic," one that requires that viewers engage in a "nuanced exploration" of good and evil.

Vera J. Camden's essay, "The Touch of Evil and the Triumph of Love in Harry Potter," rounds out the section. Here, Camden argues that "the victory Harry enjoys at the end of [the] epic saga is itself premised on a moral psychology that has been explicated throughout the series, but nowhere more powerfully than in the third novel, *Harry Potter and the Prisoner of Azkaban*." In the process, Camden explains, author J. K. Rowling "has created a contemporary mythology for the generation that has come of age with Harry Potter"—a mythology that offers "this generation" a narrative safeguard both "from their individual traumas" and from "the terrors of their own troubled times."

The "Resources" section completes the volume. Richard J. Bleiler's suggestions for further reading include lists of primary as well as secondary works that take up questions of good and evil.

This collection is by no means comprehensive. *Good and Evil* rather embodies an occasion for learning and discovery. We hope that our essays provide readers with the opportunity to explore new as well as familiar texts and experience, in the process, the pleasure and wisdom—the powerful imaginative good—that literature has to offer.

On Good and Evil

Margaret Sönser Breen

1. Introduction

How are we to understand good and evil? Are the terms polar opposites? Are they historically and culturally specific, or are they transcendent, universal? Do they overlap: should one speak of the good of evil and the evil of good? Are good and evil one and the same? These are just some of the kinds of questions that any study of good and evil provokes.

This essay cannot possibly offer a comprehensive examination of good and evil and their tangled relationships across histories and cultures. What this essay does provide is an introduction to how literature engages the concepts of good and evil, specifically through the theme of human connection. By considering four different texts (three American and one Italian) from a fairly discrete historical period (the latter half of the twentieth century), with each text representing a distinct literary genre, I hope to show two things. First, the stories that literature tells have the capacity to transform our understanding of good and evil; it is no accident that storytelling itself is often at the heart of literature's exploration of the struggle to apprehend and name good and evil. Second, literary form shapes meaning. Form affects the kinds of questions that literature asks regarding good and evil and particularly regarding our capacity to welcome (or estrange) those whose identities or experiences differ from our own.

Literature is an especially powerful medium for the study of good and evil and the accompanying dynamic of connection and disconnection. Profoundly concerned with the making and remaking of meaning, literature allows for the questioning, resisting, and refiguring of good and evil, and it does so on the levels of content and form. Literature's effects resonate: they are not only intellectual but also sensuous, and they can be immediate as well as long-lasting. Literature engages us with ourselves, with each other, and with the world beyond us, even when other means for understanding experience cannot. Accordingly, literature can provide oppressed groups, whose voices may well be silenced within other cultural and social contexts, with a crucial vehicle for the articulation of social justice issues.

Particularly fascinating are those literary texts that challenge historically and culturally determined assumptions about the interplay of good and evil and the attendant theme of connection. Primo Levi's memoir *Survival in Auschwitz*, Dorothy Allison's novel *Bastard Out of Carolina*, Mark Doty's poem "Difference," and Alice Walker's essay "In Search of Our Mothers' Gardens" all reveal the at times dehumanizing price of adhering to prevailing definitions of good and evil. In each work the writer explores the transformative possibilities of human connection. Both storytelling and touch play a crucial role in this regard. Mena Mitrano has written that "modern theories of meaning have hinged on the sense of touch" (11). In these texts, physical touch serves to demarcate the border between good and evil, between welcoming embrace and dehumanizing rejection. Storytelling itself might also be understood as touch. It allows the writer (or, as the case may be, the narrator, the remembered self, the character, the speaker, the reader, or the auditor) to *grasp* his or her situation and, if only fleetingly, alter or handle it. Through the narrative touch of storytelling, he or she can lay claim to an authority and agency otherwise unavailable. Storytelling becomes a means of effecting social change—of engaging the meaning of good and evil and, in the process, identifying strategies for survival and empowerment. Storytelling is, as Allison has written, "the thing needed" (*Two* 3).

2. Primo Levi: Testimony, Touch, and Translation
In his Holocaust memoir *Survival in Auschwitz* (*Se questo è un uomo*, 1958), Primo Levi (1919–87) examines the evil of the Nazi concentration and extermination camp complex Auschwitz, to which he was deported in 1944. (Outside the United States, English-language ver-

sions have been published under the title *If This Is a Man*, reflecting the original Italian title.) Evil, in terms of the camp system, meant the denial of millions of human beings' status as human. As historian Doris L. Bergen has written, many groups proved to be Nazi targets: Jews, Roma and Sinti (Gypsies), people of African and Slavic heritage, people with disabilities, Jehovah's Witnesses, Freemasons, communists and other political opponents of Nazism, and gay men and lesbians (typically grouped, along with other social undesirables, in the general category of "asocials") (3). By 1942, however, Jews had become the subjects of genocide. In that year, German officials began the implementation of the "Final Solution," the systematic extermination of European Jewry (Dwork and van Pelt 280–84). Over the course of World War II, approximately six million Jews, two-thirds of the Jewish population in Europe, were killed, most of them outside the concentration camps. Levi's memoir describes his ten-month internment in Auschwitz. By focusing on particular moments and aspects of his experience of imprisonment, his testimony emphasizes that the world of the camp—what writer and activist David Rousset has called "l'univers concentrationnaire"—turned on disconnection: the systemic denial that prisoners, particularly Jewish prisoners, were human beings.

A chemist and a member of the Italian Resistance, Levi was captured by Fascist forces in December 1943. In his memoir Levi records that he mistakenly thought he would stand a better chance of surviving if he identified himself as an "Italian citizen of Jewish race" rather than as an opposition fighter (*Survival* 13). Levi was sent to a detention camp in northern Italy, and soon thereafter Nazi soldiers arrived and determined that all Jewish internees were to be deported.

Levi the memoirist takes readers into the narrative present of his remembered past. From the moment of his transport in an overcrowded goods train, Levi the prisoner realizes that he and his fellow internees are not prisoners in any conventional sense of the term; they are treated not as people but as objects. As he and others are being loaded onto the train, Levi hears an officer call out *"Wieviel Stück?"*—literally "how many pieces?" (16). The question's dehumanizing import is literalized once the transport arrives in Auschwitz and the prisoners are separated from each other on the basis of their gender, age, health, and general fitness for work. Levi's training as a chemist, which allows him to be attached to a specialized work detail, undoubtedly contributes to his survival. The prisoners have their belongings taken from them, are given ill-fitting clothing, and have their heads shaved. A number is tattooed on each prisoner's arm; rather than a name (such as Primo), a number (in Levi's case, 174517) becomes the means whereby the prisoners identify themselves to camp officials.

One of the most powerful examples of Levi's own objectification occurs at the end of the "Chemical Examination" chapter, when he describes how a Kapo (or prisoner-overseer) "[w]ithout hatred and without sneering . . . wipes his hand on my shoulder, both the palm and the back of the hand, to clean it" (108). Here, Levi's body is no more than a piece of cloth, an animate handkerchief that the Kapo uses to clean himself. So often in the memoir, physical touch signals a disavowal of human connection.

Levi the memoirist's use of German in an Italian-language text (or, for American readers, an English-language text) contributes to the alarming realization that people have been reduced to things. German terms and phrases recur throughout the memoir. The camp is a *Lager*, a prisoner is a *Häftling*, and prisoners are divided into work details or *Kommandos*. When a thirsty Levi asks a guard who has grabbed an icicle from him and thrown it away *"warum"* ("why"), he is told, *"Hier ist kein warum"* ("there is no why here") (29). Perhaps most disturbing in this unreasonable and unreasoning world of the concentration camp is the figure of the *Muselmann* (literally "the Muslim"), the camp's term for the man "in decay" of whom "in a few weeks nothing will remain . . . but a handful of ashes" (89). "[I]f I could enclose all the evil in our time in one image," Levi writes, "I would choose this image which is familiar to me: an emaciated man, with head dropped and shoulders curved, on whose face and in whose eyes not a trace of a thought is to be seen" (90). As a memoirist, Levi offers a sense of that annihilation through his use of German words and, specifically, camp terminology. These words signal the kind of cognitive disorientation and disintegration that non-German-speaking prisoners underwent in the camp. In his posthumously published *The Drowned and the Saved* (1988), Levi makes the point that native German speakers who were imprisoned in the camps suffered their own special linguistic torture (135).

If German words serve to disorient and alienate, so too does the "Babel" of languages spoken by the prisoners. Of the Auschwitz-Buna camp where he was imprisoned, Levi writes:

> The Buna is as large as a city; . . . forty thousand foreigners work there, and fifteen to twenty languages are spoken. . . .
> The Carbide Tower, which rises in the middle . . . was built by us. Its bricks were called *Ziegel, briques, tegula, cegli, kamenny, mattoni, téglak.* . . . [The tower is] like the Tower of Babel, and it is this that we call it: — *Babelturm, Bobelturm. (Survival* 72–73)

The "Babel" of languages signals people's separation and their confusion—their descent into linguistic incoherence.

Language—the ability to communicate—is core to people's understanding of themselves and each other as human. Ultimately, Levi can only describe Auschwitz by locating its evil beyond the limits of language: "our language lacks words to express this offence, the demolition of a man," he writes (27). Auschwitz's exacting of linguistic disconnection, then, was a powerful means of dehumanizing prisoners in relation to non-prisoners, each other, and themselves.

How then, Levi asks implicitly, was the prisoner to maintain his sense of dignity: starving, diseased, brutalized, and brutal and desperately selfish, was he really a man? (Levi's question is gender specific; with few exceptions, the people he encountered were men.) *Survival in Auschwitz* does not answer the question in the affirmative. Instead, the memoir offers example after example of the Nazi assault on manhood.

At times Levi and others manage to resist and in the process assert their (as well as others') humanity. These instances, though, are fleeting. *Survival in Auschwitz* offers no comforting assurance that good ultimately triumphs over evil. On the contrary, good or goodness occupies only moments of experience both in Auschwitz and in Levi's postliberation memory of Auschwitz—moments to be recollected and held on to in the hope that one can survive with some sense of personal humanity intact. So, for example, Levi offers a few sentences to memorialize his best friend, Alberto, who did not survive. Alberto "did not become corrupt. I always saw, and still see in him, the rare figure of the strong yet peace-loving man against whom the weapons of night are blunted" (57).

A little more than halfway through the memoir, the "Canto of Ulysses" chapter describes Levi's literary example of an attempt to resist dehumanization. In this chapter Levi recounts how he and a young man, Jean, share the task of collecting the soup rations for their work detail. Jean, who speaks German and French fluently, has asked Levi to teach him Italian. While the two men awkwardly balance a large soup pot on poles, Levi begins to recite, as well as translate into French, lines from the great Italian poem *The Divine Comedy*, written by Dante. The lines, which are from canto 26 of *Inferno* (the poem's extended meditation on hell), describe Dante's encounter with the mythic figure of Ulysses, who explains how his actions have led to his placement in hell. Ulysses foolishly urged his men to sail beyond the known limits of the ancient world, and as a result they all drowned. Levi wants to convey the sense of Ulysses' error (or sin), but even more so he wants Jean to understand the meaning of Ulysses' speech:

> Think of your breed; for brutish ignorance
> Your mettle was not made; you were made men,
> To follow after knowledge and excellence. (113)

Ulysses praises his sailors' heroism and celebrates their manhood. The lines affect Levi (though perhaps not Jean) powerfully. Levi cannot remember all the words, and his French is not fluent enough for him to render the canto effectively. Even so, the attempt at translation proves a moment for affirming his connection with Jean and, more specifically, their shared claim to manhood. Levi the memoirist recalls that in this moment he understood that "tomorrow [Jean] or I might be dead, or we might never see each other again, I must tell him . . . about . . . something gigantic that I myself have only just seen, in a flash of intuition, perhaps the reason for our fate, for our being here today" (115).

This moment, in which Levi cites a key passage from Italian literature in order to affirm his and Jean's manhood, is short-lived. Soon, they reach the line for the soup and can no longer talk. Literary critic Lawrence L. Langer has cautioned against being swayed by the aesthetic appeal of the "Canto of Ulysses" chapter and so reading Levi's translation attempt as an example of the triumph of the human spirit (45). Even though Levi recalls how he thought "I would give today's soup to know how to connect . . . the last lines [of the canto]" (*Survival* 114), he closes the chapter by mixing the announcement of soup with the poetry from Dante that signals the death of the sailors: "'*Kraut und Rüben . . . Choux et navets. Kaposzta és répak.*' 'And over our heads the hollow seas closed up'" (115). The moment of literary connection with its comforting touch of translation passes; the camp's reality of linguistic—and, more broadly, human—breakdown remains.

In *The Drowned and the Saved*, Levi observes that he wrote *Survival in Auschwitz* "for Italians, for my children, for those who did not know, those who did not want to know, those who were not yet born, those who, willing or not, had assented to the offense . . . [and] its true recipients, those against whom the book was aimed like a gun . . . the Germans" (168). Levi identifies his work as, above all, a testimony to a historical atrocity that readers are to know and, knowing, not forget. His comment also prompts a question: what kind of gun is a memoir? This is an important question since the memoir provides a record of violence, of evil, as seen through the lens of Levi's personal experience. The memoir testifies to German accountability; the evil of Auschwitz is necessarily a part of history with which Germans especially must reckon. In this, *Survival in Auschwitz* acts as a kind of literary sentry that guards a record of evil and, in effect, delineates the border between an evil society and a society that would stand for good. The latter society can only be achieved if readers learn to recognize the inexpressible costs of human suffering—of disconnection—to which Levi's memoir proves witness.

3. Dorothy Allison: Abuse, Pleasure, and Storytelling

Dorothy Allison (b. 1949) is an American writer and sexuality activist. Her 1992 novel *Bastard Out of Carolina* is a semiautobiographical work that draws on Allison's own experiences of sexual abuse at the hands of her stepfather. Like Levi's memoir, Allison's novel recounts suffering. Obviously, the scale and circumstances of the perpetuation of evil that the two works detail differ significantly; however, the possibilities for survival and resistance that the vehicle of storytelling affords are far greater in Allison's text than in Levi's. In part, this is because an individual rather than a regime perpetrates the evil that storytelling combats within the novel. Even more important are the authors' differing conceptions of writing's relation to evil. Both Levi and Allison describe evil actions and hold those who commit them accountable. Yet, while *Survival in Auschwitz* is primarily concerned with recording evil, *Bastard Out of Carolina* is ultimately committed to transforming it. Levi is bound to report events, such as his attempt at translating Dante, as he remembers them. Allison has more flexibility. The novel form allows her to draw not only on memory but also on fictional possibility; it facilitates her exploration of storytelling as a means of transformation and healing.

In a novel (even an autobiographical one), there are distinctions between author, narrator, and character that allow the author to create and develop meanings across different layers of text. In this way, the formal features of a novel have a greater capacity to create meaning than do those of a memoir. So, for example, the protagonist of *Bastard Out of Carolina* is a young girl nicknamed Bone, who is also the narrator. Allison's naming of her heroine is important: "Bone" simultaneously conveys the girl's toughness and her vulnerability. It is also significant that Allison decided to write Bone's story in the first person; she could, for instance, have used a third-person narrator. If she had done so, however, the novel's pattern of meaning and the meaning itself would have been different. The first-person narration allows the readers to understand the physical and sexual abuse that Bone endures from *her* perspective. Bone is not only the main character but also the mediator between readers and the story. Moreover, as a teenage narrator Bone exercises an authority that directly answers the victimization that she experiences as a young girl who is beaten and violated by her stepfather between the ages of five and thirteen. (The novel includes several descriptions of instances of physical and sexual abuse that build to a graphic account of her rape by Daddy Glen.) As the narrator, Bone, in effect, reverses the power relation between her and Daddy Glen. Storytelling is Bone's means of integrating the experiences of violence into her self-understanding and, furthermore, her vehicle for connecting to a larger world beyond herself. *Bastard Out of Carolina* is a coming-of-age novel in which coming-of-age means, in part, claiming the right to tell one's own story and have that story count.

Reading and storytelling are Bone's principal means for surviving her stepfather's violence. "I talked to no one and kept my face buried in books," she recalls (118). Books provide her with an alternate reality; they offer her a temporary escape, even as they point to an eventual way out. Storytelling proves similarly empowering:

> I would make up stories in my head. My cousins loved my stories. . . . My stories were full of boys and girls gruesomely raped and murdered. . . . I got to be very popular as a baby-sitter; everyone was quiet and well-behaved

while I told stories, their eyes fixed on my face in a way that made me feel like [I was] casting a spell. (118–19)

Bone's stories are marked by violence and pleasure—in this case, the violence of the story line and the pleasure of the storytelling itself. Bone's attempt to confront the evilness of her stepfather's actions through storytelling (the stories that she as the protagonist reads and tells her cousins and the stories that she as the narrator recounts for her readers) should be understood as essential to her emotional, ethical, and intellectual development.

Also part of Bone's coming-of-age is her sexual awakening, and within that awakening, the experiences of danger and desire are intertwined as well. Bone's sexual fantasies are themselves a kind of storytelling, and they are especially suited to responding to the memory of Daddy Glen's assaults:

> I imagined people watching while Daddy Glen beat me. . . . When I was safe and alone, I would imagine the ones who watched. . . . In my imagination I was proud and defiant. I'd stare back at him with my teeth set. . . . Those who watched admired me and hated him. I pictured it that way and put my hands between my legs. It was scary, but it was thrilling too. Those who watched me, loved me. (112)

She continues:

> I was ashamed of myself for the things I thought about when I put my hands between my legs, more ashamed for masturbating to the fantasy of being beaten than for being beaten in the first place. . . .
> Yet it was only in my fantasies with people watching me that I was able to defy Daddy Glen. (112–13)

In these fantasies, the experience of sexual desire answers the memory of physical violation and revises it. Bone the protagonist cannot, however, accept that sexual fantasies involving danger and violence could be "good." Instead, she finds them shameful. In this, the young Bone resembles some early critics of the novel who misread Bone's sexuality as a pathological extension of trauma. Bone's fantasies should rather be understood as part of her attempt to rewrite a story of sexual violence as one of sexual desire or, again, to *displace* a story of violence with one of desire. In her fantasies, she is heroic and admirable; in them, the excitement of sexual touch overcomes the memory of beating, of pain and helplessness. Within the realm of her sexual storytelling, even her transference to herself of what should be Daddy Glen's shame suggests a degree of agency and authority that she does not possess in the other aspects of her life.

Bone's story of physical and sexual abuse is part of a larger story that, set in Greenville, South Carolina, during the 1950s and 1960s, explores what it means to live on the margins of southern society. Bone is a member of the Boatwright family, the members of which Allison characterizes as "white trash." They are poor and at times hungry and un- or underemployed; Bone's uncles are often in trouble with the law. Bone herself is illegitimate (hence the "bastard" of the novel's title), and her birth status speaks to the larger cultural illegitimacy of her family. Their behavior is, by conventional standards, improper and dangerous; it is tough, promiscuous, and wild. Yet, as Vincent King has pointed out, the Boatwrights' distance and disconnection from social propriety also prove to be the basis of their goodness—the vitality and generosity of the family's spirit in the midst of poverty (136). (Significantly, it is Raylene, the lesbian aunt who makes a living gathering and reselling "trash"—objects that people have discarded—who comes to take care of Bone at the novel's end.) It is the strength of her "bastard" family that Bone learns to recognize and identify with in order to overcome the experience of her stepfather's assaults and the legacy of shame and self-loathing that it inflicts. Aunt Raylene's touch, which is as much emotional and cognitive as physical, answers the "restless" (*Bastard* 62) and "impersonal" (70) hands that have violated

Bone: "When Raylene came to me, I let her touch my shoulder, let my head tilt to lean against her, trusting her arm and her love. I was who I was going to be, someone like her, like Mama, a Boatwright woman" (309). It is Bone's connectedness to her family's strength that marks her storytelling strategies for survival.

For Allison, returning to the memory of her stepfather's abuse is crucial to understanding the possibilities for her own narrative and sexual authority. In her memoir *Two or Three Things I Know for Sure* (1995), she writes,

> I am no longer a grown-up outraged child but a woman letting go of her outrage, showing what I know: that evil is a man who imagines the damage he does is not damage, that evil is the act of pretending that some things do not happen or leave no mark if they do, that evil is not what remains when healing becomes possible. (44)

These words might well be applied to *Bastard Out of Carolina*. Ultimately, for Bone, recounting Daddy Glen's evil proves to be an act of healing. Storytelling, including sexual storytelling, offers her a means of agency and resilience.

4. Mark Doty: Imagery, Metaphor, and Contact

Like Allison, Mark Doty explores life at the social and sexual margins. In his case, those margins are often gay specific or gay inflected, and they are sites of not only loss and vilification but also beauty and fragility. Doty (b. 1953) is an American poet and memoirist whose work has been profoundly shaped by the AIDS crisis, and his work from the 1980s and 1990s may be fruitfully read from this perspective.

In the early 1980s, AIDS (acquired immunodeficiency syndrome) was known as GRID (gay-related immune deficiency), an acronym that spoke to both the disease's relatively high incidence among gay men and the cultural mainstream's homophobic equation of homosexuality with pathology. Given the prejudices that gay men and lesbians faced in the United States of the 1980s, prejudices that continue to a lesser degree today, it is sadly unsurprising to realize that AIDS research met with little funding. Thousands of people did not receive treatment, such as there was, and died because of widespread indifference to the lives, more specifically the *value* of the lives, of those infected. Indeed, as poet and critic Deborah Landau has noted, some religious and political leaders even spoke of the disease as a kind of divine judgment being meted out against gay people (13). From this viewpoint, insofar as homosexuality was deemed a moral evil, AIDS acted as a kind of biblical scourge, a necessary if deadly agent of good. The AIDS crisis proved a crucial turning point for gay and lesbian (and, more broadly, queer) activism in the United States and elsewhere. Groups such as the Gay Men's Health Crisis (GMHC), ACT UP, and, later, Queer Nation formed not only to fight the epidemic but also, more generally, to combat and overturn pervasive homophobic attitudes.

Doty's early work, such as his award-winning collection *My Alexandria* (1993), may be understood as an example of literary activism, poetic pushback against narrow-minded and bigoted attitudes and actions that have dismissed the worth of gay lives. Poet Mark Wunderlich has called Doty's *My Alexandria* "perhaps the finest in-depth literary investigation of the AIDS crisis" (186). The poem "Difference" offers a moving example of Doty's ability to transform a gay-inflected image of something typically reviled, something dismissed as worthless, into something beautiful and desirable, something that ultimately proves to be an invitation to creativity, an impetus for human contact and connection.

"Difference" begins with the image of a bloom (or group) of jellyfish. Beachgoers typically try to avoid jellyfish and keep them at a distance. At worst, jellyfish can be dangerous: they sting on contact, and in some cases, they are even lethal. At best, they are unimportant, sticky and gross, marginal to the experience of a seaside visit. For the speaker, though, they are markedly different. The jellyfish touch him not physically but metaphorically. Each one is unique; each reminds him of something in particular. Even as they are all "elaborate sacks / of nothing" (lines 6–7), one resembles "a balloon" (14), another "a breathing heart" (17), and yet another a "pulsing flower" (18). As the jellyfish float in the bay, they change shape. For the speaker these transformations taken together constitute a kind of artistry: they are a "submarine opera" (23) and a "ballet" (56).

In the poem, the jellyfish are beautiful. So, too, are the sounds—the patterns and repetitions (the assonance and consonance) and the meter (the rhythm)—of the words that the speaker uses to describe the jellyfish. The jellyfish are also inspiring. They are

> nothing but something
> forming itself into figures
> then refiguring,
> sheer ectoplasm
> recognizable only as the stuff
> of metaphor. (28–33)

For the speaker, the sight of the jellyfish not only invites a series of metaphors based on their individual shapes but also allows him to reflect on how their moving, reforming bodies are themselves metaphors for poetic creation.

This poetic process is, importantly, inflected with a gay sensibility. One might say of poetry in general that the production (or reproduction) of meaning proceeds differently from that of other literary forms. It need not rely on fact or reason. Perhaps more so than in any other literary genre, the making of meaning in poetry stems from aesthetic and sensuous concerns. Moreover, the power of metaphors depends upon a creative economy that both simultaneously insists on and collapses rhetorical distance, that turns on the ironic acknowledgement that things so different from us are in fact the same as us. Thus, in a general sense, one might speak of the queer dynamics of poetic signification. More specifically, "Difference" has many gay-specific markers of meaning. Doty's metaphors for the jellyfish, for example, recall male genitalia as well as those clichés of gay male artistic engagement, opera, dance, and drag. So, one jellyfish looks like "a rolled condom" (19). As "elaborate sacks" (6), jellyfish might evoke an image of testicles that "shrink" (37) and "swell" (37). The bloom also suggests "a marine chiffon: / a gown for Isadora" (41–42), where "Isadora" could stand for Isadora Duncan, one of the founders of modern dance, or even, perhaps, recall the stage name of a drag queen performer. Taken together, these metaphors reflect the poem's gay sensibility—a sensibility with "alien grace" (51) that, though it might be avoided or met with fear, is nonetheless wondrous, vital, and creative.

Even more so, the jellyfish and the images they conjure remind the speaker of the transformative work of poetry. "Difference" closes with the speaker's admission of his yearning for others. The impetus for poetry, he realizes, is contact:

> Hear how the mouth,
> so full
> of longing for the world,
> changes its shape? (57–60)

The speaker's lips, tongue, and teeth touch each other again and again. They make and remake shared stories of good and evil and, in so doing, expand the possibilities for human connection for speaker, poet, and reader alike.

5. Alice Walker: Material Reality and Creative Expression

Literature's explorations of good and evil necessarily deepen and complicate our understanding of those terms. This is especially the case when writers consciously reflect on the power of storytelling within their work. In telling their own story, in juxtaposing their representation of reality with another, often socially dominant one, writers such as Levi, Allison, and Doty in effect move, if only momentarily and within the world of the text, from a position of marginality to one of authority—from a position of disconnection to one of connection with themselves and with readers. *Survival in Auschwitz, Bastard Out of Carolina*, and "Difference" all affirm the possibility for an oppressed individual or group to assert authority by engaging and countering conventional definitions of good and evil.

For both readers and writers, literature offers the opportunity to claim one's integrity. Insofar as this is so, we would do well to ask two related questions: who is not afforded this opportunity, and, taking this exclusion into account, how then are we to define literature? These are questions that Alice Walker takes up in her 1974 essay "In Search of Our Mothers' Gardens."

Alice Walker (b. 1944) is an American writer best known for her award-winning novel *The Color Purple* (1982), a work profoundly shaped by the social justice movements of the 1960s and 1970s and itself part of the rich body of literature produced by women of color during the 1980s. *The Color Purple* shares with Levi's, Allison's, and Doty's texts a thematic concern with good and evil; like them, Walker's novel attests to the power of storytelling. Yet, it is her essay "In Search of Our Mothers' Gardens" that directly examines the social limits placed on storytelling: issues such as how a lack of access to time, money, materials, and education, along with a history of gender and racial oppression, prevents some individuals and groups from writing stories and having their stories count as literature.

Part of a collection bearing the same title, "In Search of Our Mother's Gardens" may be read as a revision of famed British modernist writer Virginia Woolf's 1929 landmark essay *A Room of One's Own*. In that essay, Woolf examines how gender-specific restrictions (including various cultural, economic, educational, legal, and social barriers) and prescriptions (such as marriage and motherhood) have severely limited the possibilities for women's independence and self-expression. These very real limitations, regulating women's activity not only on the level of society but also on the level of body, Woolf argues, have prevented the emergence of any great tradition of women writers. For these reasons, "a woman must have money and a room of her own if she is to write fiction" (4); until quite recently, very few women in either Great Britain or the United States have had as much.

Throughout her essay, Walker returns to Woolf's premise and reworks it. In order to understand the possibilities for African American women's creative expression, she explains, one must recognize not only the gender limitations but also the experience and legacy of slavery that African American women have faced. Even the term "writer" was for many centuries not a legal possibility, since "for most of the years black people have been in America, it was a punishable crime for a black person to read and write" (234). Thus, in order to begin to conceptualize a tradition of African American women's writing, one must begin with terms broader (yet, arguably, more profound) than "writer" and "literature": "artist" or "creator" and "art" or "creative expression." The lack of money and a room of one's own that, according to Woolf, (white) women writers have historically encountered pales in comparison to the lack of freedom that black women artists faced for much of American history. The root meaning of "essay" is "attempt"; Walker's essay attempts to comprehend the possibilities for creative expression available to "our mothers and grandmothers," whom she evocatively describes as "exquisite butterflies trapped in an evil honey" (232).

The twinned evils of racism and sexism require that any discussion of African American women's literature take the material possibilities for creative expression into account. Material conditions (whether economic privilege or relentless poverty, educational opportunity or inescapable illiteracy, or the luxury of time and space to think or the struggle for bare subsistence) determine the tools, form, and frequency of artistic production. So, Walker explains, "We have constantly looked high, when we should have looked high—and low" (239). For Walker, for whom writing and activism often "work together" (Lauret 224), a tradition of African American women's writing includes not only the poetry of eighteenth-century slave Phillis Wheatley and the novels of Harlem Renaissance figure Nella Larsen but also the music of blues singer Bessie Smith and the quilt-making of "an anonymous Black woman in Alabama, a hundred years ago" ("In Search" 239). Unknown women are especially important for understanding a tradition of African American women's writing. Walker explains, "Our mothers and grandmothers have, more often than not anonymously, handed on the creative spark, the seed of the flower they themselves never hoped to see: or like a sealed letter they could not plainly read" (240).

Walker understands herself as part of this artistic lineage, and significantly, she identifies her mother as her direct literary forebear. Her mother is a compelling storyteller for whom "the telling . . . came . . . as naturally as breathing" (240). Yet, Walker realizes, her mother's gardens have proven her most powerful means of storytelling. For much of her life, Walker's mother was a sharecropper who "labored" from "before sunup . . . until late at night" (238). The materials available to her—seeds and hoe and soil—were her tools. Walker describes her mother's art:

> She planted ambitious gardens . . . with over fifty different varieties of plants that bloom profusely from early March until late November. Before she left home for the fields, she watered her flowers, chopped up the grass, and laid out new beds. When she returned from the fields she might divide clumps of bulbs, dig a cold pit, uproot and replant roses, or prune branches from her taller bushes or trees—until night came and it was too dark to see. . . .
>
> Because of her creativity with her flowers, even my memories of poverty are seen through a screen of blooms—sunflowers, petunias, roses, dahlias, forsythia, spirea, delphiniums, verbena . . . and on and on. (241)

Walker recognizes her mother as an embodiment of transcendent goodness: she is a "Creator: hand and eye" (241). She is an artist whose aesthetic touch is powerful enough to rewrite her daughter's "memories of poverty." Mother has bequeathed daughter "a legacy of respect . . . a respect for the possibilities—and the will to grasp" her own and her literary foremothers' capacity for creation (241–42).

Walker's essay underscores the idea that literary production is necessarily tied to material conditions. It lets readers understand this connection and, accordingly, appreciate more fully individual writers' struggles to revise the experiences of want and suffering and oppression that they have faced. Yet, the essay facilitates something even more profound. In insisting that a quilt-maker and a gardener be recognized as writers, Walker allows readers to claim and connect with forms of self-expression that would otherwise not be identified as artistic, let alone literary. The story she tells of literature and literary tradition constitutes a methodological good, one that pays tribute to and participates in a history of artists, known and unknown, whose creative touch has recorded, even as it has resisted and attempted to reform, the lived reality of evil.

6. Conclusion

Primo Levi, Dorothy Allison, Mark Doty, and Alice Walker all teach readers that personal accountability and artistic integrity are necessarily linked to literature's transformative potential, a potential realized through the act of storytelling. As Allison explains, "The story of what happened, or what did not happen but should have—that story can become . . . a tool" (*Two* 3). Storytelling proves a crucial vehicle for memory, advocacy, and resilience; it empowers marginalized individuals and groups to speak out, to grasp and, if possible, remake their relationship to good and to evil. It grants the oppressed visibility and voice, agency and authority, and the opportunity to connect with larger systems of meaning that they might otherwise not have. Storytelling heals. It is "the thing needed" (*Two* 3).

Works Cited

Allison, Dorothy. *Bastard Out of Carolina*. New York: Plume, 1993.

_____. *Two or Three Things I Know for Sure*. New York: Plume, 1996.

Bergen, Doris L. *War and Genocide: A Concise History of the Holocaust*. Lanham: Rowman, 2003.

Doty, Mark. "Difference." *My Alexandria*. Urbana: U of Illinois P, 1993. 52–54.

Dwork, Debórah, and Robert Jan van Pelt. *Holocaust: A History*. New York: Norton, 2002.

King, Vincent. "Hopeful Grief: The Prospect of a Postmodernist Feminism in Allison's *Bastard Out of Carolina*." *Southern Literary Journal* 33.1 (2000): 122–40.

Landau, Deborah. "'How to Live. What to Do': The Poetics and Politics of AIDS." *American Literature: A Journal of Literary History, Criticism, and Bibliography* 68.1 (1996): 193–225.

Langer, Lawrence L. *Holocaust Testimonies: The Ruins of Memory*. New Haven: Yale UP, 1991.

Lauret, Maria. *Alice Walker*. New York: Macmillan, 2011.

Levi, Primo. *The Drowned and the Saved*. Trans. Raymond Rosenthal. New York: Random, 1989.

_____. *Survival in Auschwitz*. Trans. Stuart Woolf. New York: Touchstone, 1996.

Mitrano, G. F. [Mena]. "Introduction: The Sense of an Equality of Things." *The Hand of the Interpreter: Essays on Meaning after Theory*. Ed. Mitrano and Eric Jarosinski. Bern: Lang: 2009. 11–38.

Rousset, David. *L'univers concentrationnaire*. Paris: Éditions du Pavios, 1946.

Walker, Alice. *The Color Purple*. New York: Harcourt, 1982.

_____. "In Search of Our Mothers' Gardens." *In Search of Our Mothers' Gardens*. New York: Harcourt, 1983. 231–43.

Woolf, Virginia. *A Room of One's Own*. New York: Harcourt, 1989.

Wunderlich, Mark. "About Mark Doty." *Ploughshares* 25.1 (1999): 183–89.

CRITICAL
CONTEXTS

Good and Evil in the Modern Critical Tradition_____

Mena Mitrano

1. Good *and* Evil

Good and evil. We often pronounce the words in the same breath. The word "and" should join the two abstract nouns in coordination; instead, it draws out their remarkable opposition. More than concepts, they come forward as mutually annihilating energies. To speak of "good and evil" means first of all to feel the pressure of an unfathomable dualism. For this reason, the eighteenth-century poet William Blake described good and evil as a "fearful symmetry."

Literature has responded to this unfathomable dualism by relaying it as question worthy of pursuit. In the Bible, language has played the important task of streamlining the fearful symmetry in stories, images, and parables that protect us from a shattering encounter and, by indirection, remind us of good and evil's centrality to the human experience. Good and evil has been a favorite theme of literary classics. By posing questions without easy answers, such texts make us confront the unfathomable quality of the dualism: Why does King Lear, a respected statesman, exact adulation? Why is Ahab obsessed with the white whale? Why does Victorian society abuse innocent children such as Oliver Twist? Why does Emily Dickinson, who lived a sheltered life in a quiet Massachusetts town, speak of herself as a loaded gun? Against whom? Against what?

Literature's thematic engagement of the struggle between good and evil has meant the transliteration of this struggle from religious or universal terms to historic and secular ones. Thus, for instance, *Hamlet* is not about the evil of power in general. It is about the persistence of an old form of medieval power that becomes particularly destructive in the midst of an emergent Renaissance order of which Hamlet, the younger leader who chooses his intellect over the sword, is the embodiment. As for contemporary modernity, the most enduring evidence of the defeat of good at the hands of evil remains the Nazi concentration camp prisoner. Primo Levi's *Survival in Auschwitz* (*Se questo è un uomo*, 1958) includes the striking description of the *Muselmann* (literally "the Muslim"): "[I]f I could enclose all the evil in our time in one image, I would choose this image which is familiar to me: an emaciated man, with head dropped and shoulders curved, on whose face and in whose eyes not a trace of a thought is to be seen" (90). In Levi's narrative, the Muselmann features as the living symbol of oppression. Through this character, Levi testifies to a specifically modern form of evil, the violent severance of a human being from the life of the mind. "All the evil of our time" is for Levi summed up in this exile from thinking.

If literature has responded thematically to good and evil, what about that other half of the literary universe, literary criticism? It has always been possible, of course, to produce critical commentaries on good and evil regarding a particular author or work. But here we are concerned with something different from critical propositions about good and evil. We wish to ask what the impact of good and evil has been on the practice of literary criticism. How has literary criticism felt the pressure of the unfathomable dualism?

The aim of literary criticism is to facilitate our understanding of literature, to offer guidance as to the best and most productive ways of receiving a text. It would perhaps be better for our purpose to speak of literary reception, because it evokes more closely the act of receiving. Literary reception is akin to welcoming, to being open to something, to being hospitable. In the following overview of key figures and critical approaches, we will discover that, far from being peripheral to literary criticism, the problem of good and evil has shaped its very course since World War II. We shall find out that its modern development coincides with the will to repair the violent nakedness to which Levi's man was abandoned.

In this essay we shall consider some of the major critical approaches that have arisen in the recent past: Russian formalism, structuralism, deconstruction, feminism, and theory. These approaches form a historical heritage of modern criticism, which they have enabled to become a discipline in its own right. All the while, we shall look closely at how some of the leading critics read; this exercise can offer useful tools to the student who wishes to approach literary analysis in an informed way.

2. The Work of Art after Auschwitz

Even the most cursory glance at the modern critical tradition will reveal that the reception of art and literature was irreversibly transformed by the Holocaust and, particularly, by the emergence of concentration and death camps such as Auschwitz. Before Auschwitz, art invited the viewer's admiring contemplation. It reconnected the viewer to ideals of social harmony and functioned to reinsert him or her into a world otherwise marred by exploitation, class struggle, and all sorts of misery and suffering. After Auschwitz the aesthetic attitude is no longer possible. The beauty of art can no longer hope to heal the fragile link of the individual to the social community. The devastating realization that evil buttresses progressive and enlightened rationality results in a prohibition of beauty.

One of the strongest proponents of this prohibition was Theodor W. Adorno (1903–69), a German philosopher and social critic. In his essay "Cultural Criticism and Society," he writes: "To write poetry after Auschwitz is barbaric" (210). The statement is intended as a condemnation of traditional views of beauty and harmony. In his work, Adorno demands that art address itself to what is dissonant, excluded, or rejected. But just as authentic art must opt for ugliness and participate in the unmasking of a false or evil reality, so criticism must throw off the false veil of harmony and beauty. "Critical intelligence," writes Adorno, "cannot be equal to this challenge as long as it confines itself to self-satisfied contemplation" (210). The duty of the interpreter is to denounce art whenever it, whether seeming to be consolatory or rebellious, predisposes us to accept reality or, in Adorno's words, "the materialistic transparency of culture."

Any act of creation or interpretation after Auschwitz seemed to be caught in a loathsome commercial network. The pursuit of meaning and the pleasure of forms became equally offensive and paralyzing options for the interpreter. The fear of advancing technology further decreed the disorientation and the speechlessness of the receiver (Virilio 27). Modern criticism rose to counter this stupefying state of speechlessness.

3. Formalist Defamiliarization, or Literature as the Good Technology

Steeped in an acute awareness of historical evil, modern criticism tries to overcome the impasse that Adorno describes by defending its autonomy as a new science (Eichenbaum; Jakobson, "On Realism"). The post–World War II period is marked by an interest in the formal makeup and the structures of the work of art. This interest reflects the attempt to disengage literature from totalitarian ideologies and prevent it from being used in the service of falsely universalist messages. The critical movement known as Russian formalism began a radical transformation of literary criticism from *causerie*, or a random collection of appreciative remarks taken from discourses as disparate as psychology, philosophy, politics, and so on, to a conceptual system with a precise terminology (Jakobson, "On Realism" 38).

Formalist interpretation was driven by the search for the specificity of the literary material or, again, by the quest to discover what makes literature literature. The "formal method" consisted not so much in a specific methodology as in the formulation of theoretical principles derived directly from the close reading of specific literary works and their peculiarities. Rather, it "was governed by the principle that the study of literature should be made specific and concrete" (Eichenbaum 7).

It would be hard to grasp formalism and its offspring, structuralism, as responses to historical evil if one did not take into account the geography of ideas in the twentieth century. The most influential formalist criticism was produced in the first half of the twentieth century, during the first decade or so after the October Revolution in Russia in 1917. It was the offspring of the futurism of Vladimir Mayakovsky and Velimir Khlebnikov. Like these writers, the formalist critics wanted to emancipate poetic language from philosophical and religious discourse (7). Formalism was disseminated to Western Europe and the United States only beginning in the 1960s. This geographical migration of ideas from Eastern Europe erased the chronological gap; the ideas nurtured by the Russian Revolution felt like a fresh beginning and afforded a credible alternative to Adorno's bleak vista of silence and commercialism.

The formalist assumption that literary language is different from social and cultural uses proved especially appealing in the wake of historical trauma. The formalists reclaimed a more authentic connection to the world and assigned to art the task of making us see reality as if for the first time. Leading critic Victor Shklovsky (1893–1984) writes: "After we see an object several times, we begin to recognize it. The object is in front of us and we know about it, but we do not see it—hence we cannot say anything significant about it. Art removes objects from the automatism of perception" (21). Shklovsky envisions the study of literature as a new science that repairs and heals the damaged fragile connection between the external world and human beings. He wants interpretation to register nothing less than art's capacity to transform the viewer so that he or she "may recover the sensation of life" (20). But this therapeutic program can be carried out only by discovering the laws of literary creation.

For Shklovsky literature is technique—device, artifice. This technical nature is best summed up by the concept of defamiliarization (*otstranenie*), the core of the creative process, which Shklovsky explains as follows: "The technique of art is to make objects 'unfamiliar,' to make forms difficult, to increase the difficulty and length of perception because the process of perception is an aesthetic end in itself and must be prolonged" (20). Defamiliarization favors the unusual duration of perception; it jolts the receiver out of the stupor of habitual knowledge and helps restore his or her capacity to perceive. Concretely, the procedure consists in the transfer of the traits or properties of an object to another object so that the object described is made unfamiliar (21). Shkovsky mentions the Russian writer Leo Tolstoy's description of a flogging. Tolstoy lingers on particularly cruel details of the act. These details deflect attention from the factual act of flogging—they make it "unfamiliar"—revealing the perverse pleasures that underlie the act. Defamiliarization unhinges the object from a familiar network of perceptions and causes a reaction akin to shock in the perceiver. For these reasons it is also a social procedure: it serves to "touch consciousness" (22). The view of literature as artifice or device develops from a modernist sense of alienation, which manifests itself as a general loss of meaning in the face of advancing technology. By contrast, in Shklovsky's account, literature becomes the good technology that heals and changes the world.

We can begin to understand why the resurfacing of Russian formalism in the post–World War II era gave new hope and new impetus to the pursuit of meaning. The formalists were concerned with the viewer's incapacity to move from sensuous apprehension to insight. This concern spoke directly to the postwar climate and to Levi's image of a man severed from thought and language.

4. Wakefulness: Roman Jakobson and Roland Barthes

Formalist ideas gave rise to a new critical movement called structuralism. The emblem of this movement was a refugee, Roman Jakobson (1896–1982). Between the two world wars, Jakobson taught in Czechoslovakia, where, under the pseudonym Olaf Jansen, he wrote his polemics against Nazi falsifiers of Czech and Slavic history. When the country was invaded by the Nazis in 1938, he fled to Scandinavia and then, in 1941, to the United States. Jakobson was charismatic and cosmopolitan. The scientific approach he went on to develop, with its strong emphasis on structures, may be seen as a strategy of defense against the attempt to use literature in the service of totalitarian ideologies.

Jakobson isolated the two fundamental axes of language—selection and combination—which correspond to two types of relations among the linguistic elements: the relation of contiguity, which refers to elements linked in a context (as when we link words in a phrase); and the relation of similarity, which refers to the possibility of replacing an element or a group of elements (as when we replace a word with a synonym). From the two basic operations of contiguity and similarity Jakobson inferred that there were two fundamental poles of language: the metaphoric pole and the metonymic pole. He realized that any discourse develops along two directions: similarity, which corresponds to metaphor, and contiguity, which corresponds to metonymy. He concluded that "in verbal art the interaction of these two elements is especially pronounced" (91). The two poles alternate with and compete and prevail against each other. Jakobson went on to practice a structural analysis that consists of the study of the prevalence of one element over the other, an analysis that is not limited to literature but extends to painting and film. For example, he defined cubism as a metonymic procedure because objects are presented through their details; by contrast, he viewed surrealism as a metaphoric procedure because it transforms everyday objects. His structuralism became a theoretical approach that investigates the obscure and fundamental laws of language. He applied it in many groundbreaking essays, including "Linguistics and Poetics," in which he isolates the six functions of language that alternate or co-exist in any literary text.

French critic Roland Barthes (1915–80) was among those who appreciated structuralism for its potential to separate literature from the social production of hierarchies and oppression. He believed that literary analysis has the capacity to "explode" familiar ideas (Barthes 127). In order to value this capacity fully, he complemented Jakobson's almost exclusive emphasis on structures with a new interest in the reader and in reading as an individual process. He rejected the notion of hierarchy in the literary canon as a correlative of evil in society and conceived of literary works as unique texts cast in the "very infinity of language" (127). Consequently, for Barthes, the task of the critic is no longer to assess the meaning of a literary work but to liberate its meaningfulness (significance), its unique difference and impact on the reader. His or her task is to observe carefully and unmake the text's weave in order to understand the impact of the text. For Barthes, the critic is a lover who awaits the meaningfulness of the text as if it were the arrival of his beloved. Barthes emphasizes the specific capacity of a work of art to address a reader intimately and to invite positive effects such as love, regard, and bliss. In this way, he responds to Adorno and the paralysis of creativity after Auschwitz by resurrecting the love and pleasure of reading on condition that they are tempered by an aware-ness of (or wakefulness regarding) the potential abuses of art in the service of social evil.

Barthes's particular brand of structuralist analysis strove to liber-ate the potential of literature rather than systematize it. It is no coinci-dence, perhaps, that one of the best illustrations of his approach can be found in "The Struggle with the Angel," an essay devoted to the analy-sis of a biblical story about entitlement. This story tells of Jacob, whom God renames Israel. The renaming grants Jacob the power to ascend to supreme goodness and reflects Barthes's own desire to emancipate literature from social evil:

(22) And he rose up that night, and took his two wives, and his two women servants, and his eleven sons, and passed over the ford Jabbok. (23) And he took them, and sent them over the brook, and sent over that he had. (24) And Jacob was left alone; and there wrestled a man with him until the breaking of the day. (25) And when he saw that he prevailed not against him, he touched the hollow of his thigh; and the hollow of Jacob's thigh was out of joint as he wrestled with him. (26) And he said, Let me go, for the day breaketh. And he said, I will not let thee go, except thou bless me. (27) And he said unto him, What is thy name? And he said, Jacob. (28) And he said, Thy name shall be called no more Jacob, but Israel: for as a prince hast thou power with God and with men, and hast prevailed.

(29) And Jacob asked him, and said, Tell me, I pray thee, thy name. And he said, Wherefore is it thou dost ask after my name? And he blessed him there. (30) And Jacob called the name of the place Peniel [the face of God]: for I have seen God face to face, and my life is preserved. (31) And as he passed over Peniel the sun rose upon him, and he halted upon his thigh. (32) Therefore the children of Israel eat not of the sinew which shrank, which is upon the hollow of the thigh, unto this day: because he touched the hollow of Jacob's thigh in the sinew that shrank. (Gen. 32: 22–32, qtd. in Barthes 125)

Because of the brevity of the text, Barthes limits himself to one of the tasks of structural analysis: he inventories and classifies the actions. Accordingly, he divides the narrative into three sequences or episodes: the Crossing (v. 22–24), the Struggle (24–29), and the Namings or Mutations (27–32). In each sequence he notices factors that multiply interpretations rather than enforce one specific meaning. In the Crossing he notices a redundancy in 22 and 23: there seem to be two beginnings to the discourse. The redundancy "creates an abrasion, a grating of readability" (Barthes 129); it reveals an ambiguity as to whether Jacob has fought on the left bank of the ford, after he has crossed over, or on the right bank, where he has remained alone after sending his family and servants over. As he moves to the episode of the Struggle, Barthes notices again another "complication . . . of readability" (131), which this time is due to the interchangeability of the pronouns referring to the two opponents in the combat: "Is the 'he' of 'he prevailed not against him' (25) the same as the 'he' of 'And he said' (26)?," he asks (132). Barthes is particularly attentive to those narrative features that divert our reading. In the case of the nocturnal combat, which by definition ends at the end of the night, its function, he finds, is not to proclaim a victory but to accomplish an inversion of the combatants: at the end of the night the "weakest defeats the strongest" (134).

The sequential analysis leads Barthes to the discovery that the narrative is made up of episodes that, more than linked through cause and effect, are juxtaposed through a logic that he describes as "metonymic montage" (140). By this he means that the narrative has an abrupt character. What interests him most is not the meaning or theme derived from the chain of events but rather "the abrasive frictions, the breaks, the discontinuities of readability, the juxtaposition of narrative entities which to some extent run free from an explicit articulation" (140). The episode of the Struggle is particularly rich and dense because it touches the critic directly. In Barthes's explication, God is the founder of language, and Jacob is the word (morpheme) of a new language (135). As someone interested not only in literature but also in other sign systems such as images, photography, and film, Barthes the critic is, like Jacob, seeking entitlement and a new identity.

The third sequence, that of the Naming, deals with the theme of change through "a transgression of the rules of meaning" (136). Jacob is chosen (or marked), instead of his older brother, to be a prince akin to God. He therefore ascends toward goodness against a natural order. The narrative, Barthes concludes, is about the production of countermarks, new names that transform suddenly and without revolution the position of the protagonist and so emancipate him from a natural or established order. Jacob is given another name and, with it, the permission to affect and change many realms of experience. He becomes the counterfigure of Barthes himself; his ascension to God parallels Barthes's entitlement to change the direction of literary criticism.

At the end of his analysis Barthes explains that although Jacob's struggle fits perfectly the schema for the fairy tale already established by other scholars, his aim is not to fit literature into structural schemas. He is interested in making new discoveries about things that analysis may silence. Instead of reducing the text to one meaning (or signified), he wishes "to hold its significance fully open" (141). The dream of this openness is an eloquent correlative of the struggle between good and evil. The openness of the text as a principle of analysis strikes us as Barthes's—and criticism's—way of restoring life to Levi's man.

---

5. The One Who Asks: Jacques Derrida

Even though he was a philosopher, Jacques Derrida (1930–2004) has had a lasting influence on literary studies. He sees language itself as Barthes sees the literary text: as an open and limitless play of "signifying references." His position has been extremely influential, perhaps because it not only refuses any documentary or allegorical use of literature in support of dominant social beliefs but also calls attention to the ways in which the views that we bring to acts of understanding can themselves reproduce inherited oppressive concepts.

He demonstrates this point through a close reading of *Triste tropiques*, a pioneering study by Claude Lévi-Strauss (1908–2009), the founder of modern anthropology. Lévi-Strauss extended the structuralist approach from literature and language to the study of peoples and cultures. The resources of structuralism enabled Lévi-Strauss to found the new science of anthropology, but Derrida shows that his groundbreaking work still relies on a traditional biased view that integrates writing into evil.

Derrida begins by observing that traditionally, voice has been idealized to the detriment of writing. Spoken language has connoted not only the human spirit but also human innocence. By contrast, writing has always been secondary to the human voice. It has been considered a mere material instrument of recording and, as such, pernicious. He goes on to note that Lévi-Strauss, in his study of primitive peoples, uncritically espouses the traditional view that they lack writing. The anthropologist focuses his attention on the Nambikwara, an indigenous people of the Brazilian Amazon, and construes their incapacity to write as a "non-violence interrupted by the forced entry of the West" (Derrida 110). Considering it as if from the point of view of the beloved other, Lévi-Strauss asserts that writing, as both a system of notations and a capacity for abstract thought, symbolizes the penetration of the white man, the evil of corruption. He illustrates the association of writing and evil by recounting an episode with a chief who, although he did not know writing, could imitate it:

He asked me for one of my note pads and thus we were similarly equipped when we were working together; he did not give me his answers in words, but traced a wavy line or two on the paper and gave it to me, as if I could read what he had to say. He himself was all but deceived by his own play-acting. Each time he drew a line he examined it with great care, as if its meaning must suddenly leap to the eye; and every time a look of disappointment came over his face. But he would never give up trying, and there was an unspoken agreement between us that his scribblings had a meaning that I pretended to decipher; his own verbal commentary was so prompt in coming that I had no need to ask him to explain what he had written. (qtd. in Derrida 125)

The chief's mimicking of the white man leads up to a moment in which he puts into practice writing as he has understood it:

And now, no sooner was everyone assembled than he drew forth from a basket a piece of paper covered with scribbled lines and pretended to read from it. With a show of hesitation he looked up and down his "list" for the object to be given in exchange for his people's presents. To so and so a bow and arrows, a machete! and another a string of beads! for his neck-laces—and so on. . . . He had allied himself with the white man, and . . . he could now share in his secrets. (qtd. in Derrida 125–26)

The chief associates writing with the exertion of power over others. He uses writing without knowing how it functions nor understanding the content associated with it. As Lévi-Strauss specifies, the chief makes a "sociological" rather than an "intellectual" use of writing, a use that "merely enhance[es] the prestige and authority of one individual" (qtd. in Derrida 127).

Derrida clearly admires Lévi-Strauss's work, but he objects to his unquestioning use of writing to mark the division between societies that are capable of evil and societies that are pure. In Derrida's opinion, in drawing a distinction between a sociological and an intellectual use

---

of writing, Lévi-Strauss is also drawing a "problematic difference between intersubjective violence and knowledge" (qtd. in Derrida 127). While he agrees that "writing cannot be thought outside of the horizon of intersubjective violence," or, as Lévi-Strauss would say, outside "the exploitation of man by man" (qtd in Derrida 120), Derrida goes on to ask if there is anything "even science, that radically escapes [writing]?" (127).

It is a simple question that unveils the emotional foundations of the science of structuralism. In his desire to redress the wrongs of colonialism and ethnocentrism, Lévi-Strauss infuses his analysis with guilt and ends up producing knowledge by "remorse" (114). To Derrida, Lévi-Strauss's scientific observation appears as emotional reasoning. Derrida speaks of the anthropologist's way of reading as "empirical affect" (117).

We may wonder why emotional reasoning is wrong. If you think about it, this is what we do in the classroom when we try to understand a text through close reading. We understand precisely by observing empirically—by paying attention to the text—what affects us. Isn't close reading a form of affective empiricism also? And does this mean that it is wrong? The aim of Derrida is not to discourage close reading but rather to express his scepticism about fitting a text or a culture into a system of rules and theoretical principles. To him, Lévi-Strauss stands as an admirable example of how structuralism, as a post–World War II scientific approach, claims a role in laying bare the bleak depth of the Western soul. But in doing so, structuralism also reproduces a cycle of evil and remorse. For his part, Derrida proposes a type of reading that has been labelled "deconstructive." It is a questioning attitude, a way of reading that disengages the habit of assuming great oppositions (in Lévi-Strauss's case, evil Westerners vs. pure non-Western people) on the ground that these oppositions work to suppress "contradiction and difference" (115). The deconstructive approach advocates the capacity to exert intellectual vigilance and so turns reading into an inquiry into the categories we use in order to make sense of things.

6. Re-vision: From Feminism to Theory

It could be argued that feminism has been the best deconstructive approach. Feminism thinks of literature in a traditional way: as a mirror of human experience. It helps us to know ourselves. But it can do so if, in the words of American poet and critic Adrienne Rich, it encourages us to examine "the assumptions in which we are drenched" that prevent us from knowing ourselves (11).

Feminism refuses the self-destructiveness spread cross-nationally by World War II, which Rich calls "the self-destructiveness of male-dominated society" (11). The aim of literary analysis is to salvage what has been destroyed and counter the destructive drive with fresh ways of seeing. Rich translates Derrida's questioning attitude as the capacity for "re-vision." She defines re-vision as "the act of looking back, of seeing with fresh eyes, of entering an old text from a new critical direction." For feminism, too, the act of understanding brings to the surface contradictions previously ignored. Unlike Derrida's deconstruction, however, feminism implies a reader who documents and corrects a distorted truth. Much like a courageous diver, the feminist reader explores the wreck of civilization to salvage a suppressed world of creativity.

Feminist revision soon bore fruit in the groundbreaking volume *The Madwoman in the Attic*: *The Woman Writer and the Nineteenth-Century Literary Imagination* (1979), in which authors Sandra Gilbert (b. 1936) and Susan Gubar (b. 1944) examine women's relation of the literary tradition. The volume includes Gilbert's analysis of Mary Shelley's *Frankenstein*, which remains one of the best examples of reading as re-vision. "Horror's Twin: Mary Shelley's Monstrous Eve" first appeared in the journal *Feminist Studies* in the summer of 1978. Gilbert proposes that *Frankenstein* is its author's interpretation of a classic, John Milton's *Paradise Lost*. In her attempt "to clarify its deepest meanings for herself" (48), Shelley produced the novel. In her analysis of the novel, Gilbert describes the key feature of any genuine act of reception. We might term it extended *poiesis*, a noun related to the ancient Greek verb meaning "to make." It refers to the transformation of the receiver or reader into a producer via the experience of contact with a contagious creativity.

Gilbert sets up a comparison between Milton's Satan and Eve and Shelley's protagonists, explorer Robert Walton and scientist Victor Frankenstein, whose overachieving desire marks them out as fallen angels. Gilbert argues that Shelley's parody of the traits of Milton's sinful characters unveils the misogynistic aspect of the original. Gilbert dwells especially on the Eve-like qualities of Victor, whose appropriation of childbirth and maternity suggests the filthiness and sinfulness attached to sexuality: "in his isolated workshop of filthy creation—filthy because obscenely sexual—he collects and arranges materials furnished by 'the dissecting room and the slaughter-house'" (59). But Victor is also like Satan, "doomed and filthy," and, like the author, he gives birth by "intellectual parturition" (60) by "brooding upon the wrong books" (59). Shelley's reading, Gilbert notices, transforms the precursor's variety of characters and action into a fluid symbolic scheme whereby every character resembles all the others, as in a play of mirrors. In Gilbert's reading, Shelley's *Frankenstein* is a story about how the opposition of good and evil becomes a weapon in the service of social oppression, as the opposition creates "abhorred and solitary" creatures like the Monster. Eve- and Satan-like Victor's "intellectual similarity to his authoress" (63), Shelley, extends to all women who "have seen themselves (because they have been seen) as monstrous, vile, degraded creatures, second-comers, emblems of filthy materiality" (65).

Gilbert shows that by conjoining intellect, sexuality, and self-loathing, Shelley manifests her "anxiety of authorship." In the wake of feminist readings, Shelley's monster has become a metaphor for a long list of "minorities" that share with women the fall outside of history. Shelley's "anxiety of authorship" concerns all those whose creativity feels constrained by class, race, sexuality, and, in general, by a social identity assigned on the basis of their material condition.

In the 1980s and 1990s, feminism joined forces with psychoanalysis and cross-pollinated with the other critical movements we have reviewed. In the process, it gave rise to a new approach called "theory." Theory encourages a way of reading premised on the consciousness that evil, far from being a surface phenomenon, acts in the deepest undercurrent of the social order. To signal this deeper level, feminist theorist and psychoanalyst Julia Kristeva (b. 1941) speaks not simply of a social order but of a "socio-symbolic" order (203) to which everyone has the right to belong. Certainly, people can experience failure to belong to society on a historical level, that is, because they are members of traditionally marginalized groups. But often the same people also experience failure to belong on a deeper linguistic and psychological level (the symbolic level). For Kristeva, this fundamental exclusion results in violence:

> When a subject is too brutally excluded from this socio-symbolic stratum; when, for example, a woman feels her affective life as a woman or her condition as a social being too brutally ignored by existing discourse or power (from her family to social institutions); she may, by counterinvesting the violence she has endured, make of herself a 'possessed' agent of this violence in order to combat what was experienced as frustration— with arms which may seem disproportional, but which are not in comparison with the subjective or more precisely narcissistic suffering from which they originate. (203)

The aim of theory is to stop the cycle of brutal exclusion and retaliation described by Kristeva. Literature, as well as other forms of creative expression, becomes an opportunity to give meaning to the lives and identities that society deems unworthy so that they may become visible and be recast in a positive light.

Building on the work of Kristeva, theorists such as Judith Butler (b. 1956) initiate a new turn of thought that resists the evil of discrimination by understanding it from within, that is to say, as the product of the force of power. Power is evil, but it also binds society together. Power, Butler argues, is "prohibitive and generative" at the same time; it is based on a mechanism of repression in which we all participate (93). Butler subverts the traditional divide between victim and oppressor. She writes: "Indeed, repression may be understood to produce the object that it comes to deny. That production may well be an elaboration of the agency of repression itself" (93). Like Butler, who is especially interested in asserting the worth of queer lives, other theorists have extended the same turn of thought to the analysis of a wide variety of artistic and cultural forms. The work of Teresa de Lauretis in film studies and of Gayatri Spivak and Rey Chow in postcolonial studies is particularly representative of the achievements of theory.

7. Conclusion

This overview does not claim to be exhaustive; rather, it provides an introduction to some of the classic works of modern literary criticism and interpreters who have shaped contemporary literary analysis. This work is a fundamental background for any student who wishes to play an active role when approaching a text, of whatever nature. Hopefully, the ways in which figures such as Shklovsky, Barthes, Derrida, and Gilbert read will offer guidance in your search for your own way of reading.

As it emerges from these pages, modern literary criticism is the story of readers who, increasingly, become producers because they are free to accompany their receptive activity with reflection. But the question of good and evil has not been, properly speaking, just a perspective from which this story of emancipation could be told. In our account, literary criticism has arisen as an active response to historical evil. The question of good and evil comes forward as one that our time has asked literary criticism to hear. The transformation of literature into a wider universe that includes images and performance, among other forms of expression, results from this asking. These great changes are, in fact, an invitation for us as readers to use literature more than before. They are an invitation to use literature to refine our capacity to hear what our time is asking—to hear with our best energies and resources.

Are you ready to use literature?

Note

Special thanks to Martina and Eleonora, who make sure I stay connected to my extended literary family.

Works Cited

Adorno, Theodor W. "Cultural Criticism and Society." Trans. Samuel and Shierry Weber. *The Adorno Reader*. Ed. Brian O'Connor. Oxford: Wiley, 2010. 195–210.

Barthes, Roland. "The Struggle with the Angel: Textual Analysis of Genesis 32: 22–32." *Image, Music, Text*. Ed. and trans. Stephen Heath. London: Fontana, 1977. 125–41.

Butler, Judith. G*ender Trouble: Feminism and the Subversion of Identity*. New York: Routledge, 1990.

Derrida, Jacques. *Of Grammatology*. Trans. Gayatri Chakravorty Spivak. Baltimore: Johns Hopkins UP, 1976.

Eichenbaum, Boris M. "The Theory of the Formal Method." *Readings in Russian Poetics: Formalist and Structuralist Views*. Ed. Ladislav Matejka and Krystyna Pomorska. Ann Arbor: Michigan Slavic, 1978. 3–37.

Gilbert, Sandra M. "Horror's Twin: Mary Shelley's Monstrous Eve." *Feminist Studies* 4.2 (1978): 48–73.

Jakobson, Roman. "Two Aspects of Language and Two Types of Aphasic Disturbances." *Fundamentals of Language*. By Jakobson and Morris Halle. The Hague: Mouton, 1971. 67–96.

_____. "Linguistics and Poetics." *Modern Criticism and Theory: A Reader*. Ed. David Lodge. London: Longman, 1988. 32–57.

_____. "On Realism in Art." *Readings in Russian Poetics: Formalist and Structuralist Views*. Ed. Ladislav Matejka and Krystyna Pomorska. Ann Arbor: Michigan Slavic, 1978. 38–46.

Kristeva, Julia. "Women's Time." *The Kristeva Reader*. Ed. Toril Moi. New York: Columbia UP, 1986. 187–213.

Levi, Primo. *Survival in Auschwitz*. Trans. Stuart Woolf. New York: Touchstone, 1996.

Rich, Adrienne. "'When We Dead Awaken': Writing as Re-Vision." *Arts of the Possible: Essays and Conversations*. New York: Norton, 2001. 10–29.

Shklovsky, Victor. "Art as Technique." *Modern Criticism and Theory: A Reader*. Ed David Lodge. London: Longman, 1988. 16–30.

Virilio, Paul. *Art and Fear*. Trans. Julie Rose. London: Continuum, 2003.

Good and Evil: Inclusion and Exclusion in Life and Literature

Sherri Olson

"Why were the Christians so unpopular? The evidence points to a number of reasons, in addition to the generalized need for some one to kick which has always been an unacknowledged but influential element of human nature." (Dodds 111)

Student: "There are good Jews and bad Jews."
Sartre: "You're talking like a barbarian. Do you need a scapegoat that badly?" (qtd. in Cohen-Solal 119)

"It is the *habit* of exclusion that grows strong; the identity of those being excluded is not a major obstacle." (Paley 117)

Given the links between literature and "real" life, it is not surprising that treatment of the theme of good and evil in literature differs across time and place. Literature concerning good and evil written during the Middle Ages or the nineteenth century must speak to ideas about good and evil from those periods. What can we learn by exploring literature along these lines? How can it enrich our lives? What can it tell us about the good life? Human beings are "hardwired" to raise such questions, and history and literature belong to those "liberating studies by which men come closer to understanding their own nature" (Starr vii). This essay considers briefly a few stories and historical examples that invite us to think about good and evil in literature and life. The thread that will guide us, as indicated by the opening quotations, is the theme and reality of inclusion versus exclusion.

The Tao

In the traditions of people across time and place, there is a great deal of common ground when it comes to ideas of good and evil. Recognition

---

of these similarities is hardly new: the Roman Emperor Julian (reigned 361–63), who was raised a Christian but converted to paganism, said of the Ten Commandments that apart from the first three rules about monotheism and observing the Sabbath, the remaining seven commandments (that is, honor your parents and do not kill, commit adultery, steal, bear false witness, or covet your neighbor's wife or goods) "form part of the moral code of all peoples" (Dodds 120). Similarly, in an essay on traditional human values, which everywhere are grounded in the belief that "certain attitudes are really true, and others really false," the British writer, literary critic, and theologian C. S. Lewis provides some "Illustrations of the Tao [the way or path]," examples of common values concerning duties to parents, elders, children, and posterity and, more broadly, acts of justice, honesty, mercy, and magnanimity. These common "truths" are drawn from the teachings and literatures of the ancient Egyptians, Hebrews, Native Americans, Hindus, Greeks, Romans, Chinese, Babylonians, Christians, Australian Aborigines, Anglo-Saxons, and Norse (Lewis 95–121). For example, he cites the following as illustrations of the law of mercy:

"The poor and the sick should be regarded as lords of the atmosphere." (Hindu)

"Whoso makes intercession for the weak, well pleasing is this to Samas [god of justice]." (Babylonian)

"Has he failed to set a prisoner free?" (Babylonian list of sins)

"I have given bread to the hungry, water to the thirsty, clothes to the naked, a ferry boat to the boatless." (Ancient Egyptian)

"One should never strike a woman; not even with a flower." (Hindu)

"There, Thor, you got disgrace, when you beat women." (Old Norse)

"In the Dalebura tribe a woman, a cripple from birth, was carried about by the tribes-people in turn until her death at the age of sixty-six. . . . They never desert the sick." (Australian Aboriginal)

"You will see them take care of . . . widows, orphans, and old men, never reproaching them." (Native American)

"Nature confesses that she has given to the human race the tenderest hearts, by giving us the power to weep. This is the best part of us." (Roman)

"They said that he had been the mildest and gentlest of the kings of the world." (Praise of the hero in *Beowulf*, Anglo-Saxon)

"When thou cuttest down thine harvest . . . and hast forgot a sheaf . . . thou shalt not go again to fetch it: it shall be for the stranger, for the fatherless, and for the widow." (Ancient Hebrew) (115–16)

The *Meditations* of Marcus Aurelius

Another ancient source that helps us think about good and evil, in literature and life, is found in a kind of text that is rare in the premodern world, the autobiography or memoir. Marcus Aurelius, Stoic philosopher and emperor of Rome from 161 to 180, kept a private journal that has, miraculously, survived and come down to us as the *Meditations*. Because he was an emperor and a philosopher, his personal reflections concern reality as well as the world of ideas. For example, in commenting on the abuse of power by the elite in the Roman society of his day, Marcus observes that "patrician families tend for the most part to be lacking in the feelings of ordinary humanity" (38). Even more surprising for an emperor, he likens imperial expansion and the destruction of those who resist it to robbery: "A spider is proud of catching a fly; so is one man of trapping a hare, or another of netting a sprat, or a third of capturing boars or bears or Sarmatians [tribal peoples settled on the Danube River who threatened the Roman Empire]. If you go into the question of principles, are these anything but robbers one and all?" (155–56). A person living a good life is one "whose chief regard is for his own mind, and for the divinity within him and the service of its goodness" (58). Marcus believes that those who do evil do so because they are ignorant of what is good and evil, and as such they deserve pity. But it is clearly a person's responsibility to learn these lessons, since we can "add" to our "knowledge of the Good" through our life experiences and by deliberate reflection (47).

According to Marcus, since "living and dying, honour and dishonour, pain and pleasure, riches and poverty" happen to both "good men and bad," they "neither elevate nor degrade; and therefore they are no more good than they are evil" (48). Nothing is bad or good "if it can happen to evil men and good men alike" (72). One should keep one's soul "pure from passion, and from aimlessness, and from discontent with the works of gods or men" (49). Marcus continues, "Everything is but what your opinion makes it" (50). In any event, no matter what happens to us, we should "accept each and every dispensation as coming from the same Source as itself [that is, Nature]" (51). This is "Nature's way, and *in the ways of Nature there is no evil to be found*" (50; emphasis added). Understanding Nature seems to be the central "truth" in Marcus's worldview. If the "ways of Nature" are not evil, it becomes difficult to figure out what he regards as evil; he does accept the traditional dichotomies of soul/body, spirit/matter, good/evil, and "divinity vs corruption" (55), but otherwise evil and good seem to lack objective reality. Yet "man is born for deeds of kindness" (149), and he is living well who aspires to "the just thought, the unselfish act, the tongue that utters no falsehood" (71).

Another Face of Inclusion and Exclusion: The Problem of Bias

The textbooks used in high school and college Western civilization courses frequently incorporate an unexamined bias in favor of institutions and ideas that are seen to be the roots of modern, Western, democratic institutions, which are treated as inevitable and desirable. In a chapter on the early Middle Ages in a standard medieval history book, for example, the authors discuss the "violence and chaos" and the "decline of culture and literacy [and] other woes" that were "ushered in" by the collapse of the western Roman Empire, as well as the "cruelty of the age" (Cook and Herzman 99–100). It is true that violence and instability did plague the second half of the first millennium CE: the collapse of the western Roman Empire in the fifth century under the pressure of Germanic invasions was followed by Magyar offensives, Arab piracy, and Viking raids in the ninth and tenth centuries. Efforts at state building generated violence, as seen in the career of Clovis (d. 511), a Frankish warrior operating in the relative political vacuum of post-Roman Gaul who clawed his way to the top by murdering rivals and terrorizing everyone else. But the savagery employed to build the Roman Empire is ignored; the systematic terrorism and rapine practiced by Roman troops, century after century, are merely alluded to in the comment that we "need to remember that the Romans were hardly a gentle and peaceable folk" (100). The means of Roman imperial expansion are routinely treated as a side story (or omitted altogether) in the triumphant narrative of Roman political and legal achievements. A world-state that straddled three continents, controlled the Mediterranean, and was bounded by a ten-thousand-mile frontier (within which lived a population that was two-thirds slave—the defeated and dispossessed and their descendants—by the second century CE) was not built by peaceful expansion. It has been estimated that Julius Caesar's conquest of Gaul (roughly the area of modern France) between 58 and 50 BCE killed two million men, women, and children, to say nothing of the booty and slaves Caesar took for himself and his troops: quite a price to pay for cities, paved roads, and written law.

Similarly, while the textbook's authors choose to mention it, they do not characterize as cruel or barbarous a form of torture used by the Greeks in Sicily in the sixth century BCE in which criminals were roasted alive inside a hollow bronze bull (49). "Barbarity" and ancient

Greece are rarely paired because the overwhelming emphasis for Greek history is the story of its many "gifts" to Western civilization (democracy, the first systematic philosophy, history, and so on). Yet the revenge killings and tribal warfare of early medieval Europe define the period as a "Dark Age." Such bias may be read in part as another type of "exclusion," this time of some people and societies in the past; such exclusion helps to reaffirm the rightness of the excluder's values.

Frontier Societies

If we think of Clovis's Francia as a frontier society, we may think about how it compares with other, more recent frontiers, such as the advance of the United States' frontier into the lands of Native Americans in northern California in the second half of the nineteenth century. At issue was control over the routes to the lands of the Gold Rush after gold was discovered in Coloma, California, thirty-six miles northeast of Sacramento, in 1848. Sixth-century Francia and nineteenth-century northern California both constitute "frontier societies" in which political institutions were absent or weak, "justice" (mostly in the form of retaliation) was private, and violence was unchecked. The Lassen Trail, a famous Gold Rush route, cut through Yahi Indian country, and the conflict that began there in the 1850s drew to a close in the 1870s when the few surviving Yahi went into hiding. "Pioneer death squads" appeared, small bands of settlers who "spearheaded the extermination of the Indians" (Starn 100–1). Some of these men later wrote their memoirs—that is, they created a literature—showing that they were not "particularly concerned to hide their role" in killing the Yahi. Their exploits read like something worse than Clovis with a gun: hunters commonly "seized babies on their sorties, sometimes after killing their parents. Farm families routinely brought up the infants for laborers" (105). Indentured servitude of Native Americans was legalized in California in 1850, thus encouraging the kidnapping and sale of native children; in that same year, the state paid out more than one million dollars in reimbursements to Indian hunters. The last massacre of the Yahi came in 1871. After a group of Yahi stole a cow for food, white settlers tracked them down in retaliation and cornered them in a cave: "Norman Kingsley, the rancher for whom this cave would later be named, began to shoot down the Indians. He 'could not bear to kill these children with his 56-calibre Spencer rifle' because 'it tore them up so bad,' another pioneer later recalled: 'So he did it instead with his 38-calibre Smith and Wesson Revolver'" (112–13).

Noah's Curse: Dehumanizing the "Other"

Romans saw non-Roman peoples as barbarians and often enslaved them. In his journal entry for October 12, 1492, Christopher Columbus noted that the Taino Indians of Hispaniola were gentle and innocent people—and that they would make good servants and could be easily overpowered. Many settlers in the United States considered Native Americans to be "lower races" that "lived like swine" and looked "more like orang-outangs than human beings," prejudices that "underwrote and even justified the dispossession of Indians" (Starn 101). This story could be retold indefinitely: nearly every age, every society, has produced groups that exploit others, usually for their labor, and that justify their domination and abuse by theories of inferiority. In the ancient world, elite people believed that "civilization and culture were to be found exclusively in cities" (Fletcher 16), a prejudice that has been handed down to us in our language: words such as polite [polis], civilized [civis], and urbane [urbs] show "what a good job that elite has done in persuading posterity of its point of view. . . . Most townspeople, most of the time, looked upon the rural peasantry with mingled disgust, fear and contempt. They were dirty and smelly, unkempt, inarticulate, uncouth, misshaped by toil, living in conditions of unbelievable squalor, as brutish as the beasts they tended." Thus, the city-dwellers who were "parasitic upon the surrounding country for their essential supplies, repaid their dependence in the harsh coin of disdain," demonizing the very people upon whom they absolutely relied for their urban way of life. This same attitude is found in the literature of the elite in the Middle Ages, where we see contempt and hostility toward peasants.

The "inferiority" of these others has often been explained by turning to the Bible, specifically the story of Noah's curse as told in chapter 9 of the book of Genesis. One day Ham, Noah's youngest son, saw his father drunk and naked and told his older brothers Shem and Japheth, who did not look upon their father's nakedness but covered him with a garment. When Noah came to, he knew what Ham had done and cursed Ham's son, Canaan, saying that he should be a "servant of servants unto his brethren." The curse of Noah has been used for hundreds of years to explain the inferiority and "justify" the servitude and exploitation of various peoples: in the Middle Ages, it was thought that serfs were descended from Ham, and the same explanation was applied to Africans, Arabs, and Mongols (Freedman 86)—and in the New World, Native and African Americans.

Good and Evil (Inclusion and Exclusion) in Jane Austen

The novels of Jane Austen will help us open up another dimension of our theme of inclusion/exclusion: how the suffering that this dynamic engenders is transformed into literature. Jane Austen (1775–1817) was not only a brilliant comic author but also a deeply philosophical writer interested in good and evil, though not as simple types. "Good" and "evil" attach to the decisions, actions, or situations of her characters but not to the characters themselves; fools may abound in her novels but not villains and angels. This is one reason why Austen's work is still relevant: she is real, and nowhere more so than when she explores social exclusion, a reality with which she was very familiar.

Cleverer-than-average readers have missed this core in Austen: Charlotte Brontë thought that Austen merely "delineated the surface" of the lives of her characters and would have reacted to enthusiasm for her own novels "with a well-bred sneer" (Barker 227). Ralph Waldo Emerson read *Persuasion* and thought it was about one thing and one thing only: "marriageableness" (401–2). Sir Walter Scott, a warm and early admirer of Austen, thought *Pride and Prejudice*'s Elizabeth Bennett was serious when she told her sister Jane that she had changed her mind and decided to accept Mr. Darcy after seeing his extensive grounds at Pemberly. In fact, Austen was not a "fine lady" but a person on the margins of a society that was deeply and ruthlessly class conscious. She was educated and of gentry descent on her mother's side, and one of her brothers was "adopted" into a wealthy family and became landed gentry overnight, but she was also one of eight children of a country parson of modest means. Readers of her letters know how continually she was concerned with making ends meet, saving money on purchases, stretching resources to accommodate company, and darning and patching old clothing. She worried about the cost of repairing leaks and whether she would be able to catch a ride home after paying a visit to a friend or relation, since paying for transportation was usually beyond her means. She and her sister Cassandra were "spinsters" still living at home when their father died in 1805. As Valerie Grosvenor Myer writes in the preface to her biography of Austen, Austen was

> never secure financially and was less secure socially than many readers of her novels have assumed. She . . . spent her entire life as a poor relation. Although socializing with richer neighbors and visits to landed relatives gave her an insight into the way wealthy people lived, it was very different from her own life of genteel poverty. . . . She lived on the outside looking in. . . . As a single woman without money, she was marginal to society. Her equivocal position moulded her outlook.

When Austen writes about dependence and independence, about belonging and not belonging, especially in the case of women, she is speaking from her own experience.

Mansfield Park, Austen's most philosophical novel, is *not* a study of good versus evil (that is, of good characters versus evil characters), though readers antagonized by heroine Fanny Price often see it this way. Fanny resembles a Cinderella figure, a (slightly dull) goody-two-shoes, especially in comparison with the more vivacious siblings Henry and Mary Crawford. Others dislike Fanny for different reasons, seeing her as a judgmental monster, a "killjoy," a sort of ghoul at the table or vampire whose "lair" is the "chilly east Room" (Auerbach 106–8, 115). It is true that while the moral compass and even the awareness of everyone around her is descending into disorder, Fanny alone is clear eyed and holds true to honesty, fairness, and consideration of others. Fanny has experienced exclusion and rejection all her life, growing up as one of nine children of an alcoholic, unemployed father and a mother who cares more for her sons than her daughters. At the age of ten she is sent away to become the resident poor relation among her wealthy relatives at Mansfield Park. There her status oscillates between servant and family member, and she suffers continual abuse at the hands of Aunt Norris, who has touches of the sadist about her. The issues of dependence, servitude, and even abuse are purposefully and profoundly deepened in this novel, since Fanny's uncle, Sir Thomas Bertram, owes his fortune mostly to the slave plantations he owns in the West Indies, where the atrocities of slavery were common knowledge in the nineteenth century. In his discussion of the brutality of West Indian slavery, Olaudah Equiano, a former slave whose 1789 autobiography became a best seller, noted especially the levels of abuse on the estates of absent landowners such as Sir Thomas. Mary Prince, a West Indian slave whose autobiography was published in 1831, wondered "how English people can go out into the West Indies and act in such a beastly manner. But when they go to the West Indies, they forget God and all feeling of shame, I think. . . . They tie up slaves like hogs—moor [tie] them up like cattle, and they lick them, so as hogs, or cattle, or horses never were flogged" (Gates 214). That Austen meant her readers to consider the foundations of Sir Thomas's wealth in connection with dependence and servitude is evident from her choice of the name "Mansfield" for his lovely "plantation" in England; in 1772

Lord Mansfield, chief justice of the King's Bench, issued a famous and much-discussed judgment regarding the liberty of a single black slave, a case that was widely held to have led to slavery's abolishment in England (though not, of course, anywhere else).

In *Mansfield Park*, Austen's multifaceted exploration of good and evil also uses the frame of duty and selfishness in order to explore good versus evil *tendencies* of the sort with which everyone must struggle to a greater or lesser extent. Edmund Bertram's last words to Mary Crawford, who in spite of her shallowness, occasional heartlessness, and gold-diggerism is "almost purely governed" by "really good feelings" (120), include the fervent hope that she will not "owe the most valuable knowledge we could any of us acquire—*the knowledge of ourselves and of our duty*, to the lessons of affliction" (374; emphasis added).

Because of her wondrous subtlety, it is easy to miss what Austen is really interested in, the ideas and "truths" that drive her. Consider how, in the novel *Emma*, the character Harriet Smith is affected by her relationship with Emma after the latter has taken Harriet under her wing, "noticed" her, "given her pointers," and, in effect, taught her how to begin climbing up the social ladder by stepping on other people. The results are unpleasant, as seen in Harriet's small-minded, nasty response when Emma insists that Jane Fairfax is a better pianist than herself: "Besides, if she does play so very well, you know, it is no more than she is obliged to do, because she will have to teach" (179). We are meant to think carefully about such remarks coming from such a person as Harriet, a "natural daughter of nobody knows whom" (45) whose mind has "many vacancies" to fill (141) and who dislikes Italian songs because there is no understanding them (179). Dull-witted, practically feebleminded Harriet Smith has learned how to judge and exclude with surprising rapidity! This brief interchange between the two young women is absolutely freighted in a novel in which practically every page contains some reference to class, who is in and who is out, who matters and who doesn't, who is to be excluded and who is to be included. Every character, with the exception of the aptly named Mr. Knightley, is to a greater or lesser degree a borderline figure in terms of class: think of Mr. Elton, Mrs. Weston, Jane Fairfax, Frank Churchill, Robert Martin, and Miss Bates (who has "sunk from the comforts she was born to; and, if she live to old age, must probably sink more" [294]). Emma herself is insecure enough in her social status that she feels threatened by a dinner invitation from the lower-class Coles—will it drag her down to the level of the second- and third-rates of Highbury if she attends?—and even *she* is not safe from the proposals of Mr. Elton, who "must know that the Woodhouses had been settled for several generations at Hartfield, the younger branch of a very ancient family—and that the Eltons were nobody" (105).

Harriet Jacobs and Benjamin Simpson: The Roots of African American Literature

In contrast to Jane Austen's subtle presentation of the theme, slave and ex-slave narratives make painfully explicit the human costs of the inclusion/exclusion dynamic. According to scholar Henry Louis Gates Jr., in the "long history of human bondage, it was only the black slaves in the United States who—once secure and free in the North, and with the generous encouragement and assistance of northern abolitionists—created a genre of literature that at once testified against their captors and bore witness to the urge of every black slave to be free and literate" (ix). Between 1703 and 1944, the year in which George Washington Carver's autobiography was published, more than six thousand ex-slaves told their stories of captivity in books, essays, and interviews. "No group of slaves anywhere, at any other period in history, has left such a large repository of testimony about the horror of becoming the legal property of another human being" (ix). In other words, it is not only the elite and the beneficiaries of the status quo who tell their stories, write history, and create bodies of literature: those who are exploited, those who suffer, have always been among the creators of great art, literary and otherwise.

The links between African American literature and real life are powerfully illustrated in *Incidents in the Life of a Slave Girl* (1861), the autobiography of former slave Harriet Jacobs (1813–97). *Incidents* is remarkable not only because it was one of the first autobiographical slave narratives written by a woman but also because one part of her experience that Jacobs wished to emphasize was the sexual abuse suffered by slave women—a topic that made most nineteenth-century readers, even abolitionists, uncomfortable: "Slavery is terrible for men" she writes, "but it is far more terrible for women" (Gates 405):

> No pen can give an adequate description of the all-pervading corruption produced by slavery. The slave girl is reared in an atmosphere of licentiousness and fear. The lash and the foul talk of her master and his sons are her teachers. When she is fourteen or fifteen, her owner, or his sons, or the overseer, or perhaps all of them, begin to bribe her with presents. (382)

"Dr. Flint" (in real life, Dr. James Norcom), the father of Jacobs's young mistress and therefore her de facto master, was the father of eleven slaves. Jacobs lived in his house, and when she turned fourteen—"a sad epoch in the life of a slave girl"—Norcom began to "whisper foul words in [her] ear" (361).

> I was compelled to live under the same roof with [my master]—where I saw a man forty years my senior daily violating the most sacred commandments of nature. He told me I was his property; that I must be subject to his will in all things. . . . There is no shadow of law to protect [the slave girl] from insult, from violence, or even from death; all these are inflicted by fiends who bear the shape of men. The mistress, who ought to protect the helpless victim, has no other feelings towards her but those of jealousy and rage. The degradation, the wrongs, the vices, that grow out of slavery, are more than I can describe. . . .
>
> [The slave girl] will learn, before she is twelve years old, why it is that her mistress hates such and such a one among the slaves. . . . She listens to

violent outbreaks of jealous passion and cannot help understanding what is the cause. She will become prematurely knowing in evil things. Soon she will learn to tremble when she hears her master's footfall. She will be compelled to realize that she is no longer a child. (361)

Norcom trapped her in corners and followed her everywhere, both physically and with his "loquacious" eyes (372), sometimes beating her and sometimes holding a razor to her throat to get her to agree to submit to him. "I tried hard to preserve my self-respect; but I was struggling alone in the powerful grasp of the demon Slavery; and the monster proved too strong for me" (384–85). Alone in this terrible struggle and in despair, she responded to the overtures of a "white unmarried gentleman," "Mr. Sands" (in real life, Samuel Sawyer), a lawyer and local resident who knew Jacobs's family and had heard of her circumstances. He became "interested for" Jacobs, expressing sympathy and the wish to aid her. "He constantly sought opportunities to see me, and wrote to me frequently. I was a poor slave girl, only fifteen years old" (385). The actions of this "educated and eloquent gentleman"—"too eloquent, alas, for the poor slave girl who trusted in him" (385)—in effect mirror those of Norcom, though without the violence. When Norcom began to act on a plan he had earlier made to build a "lonely" cottage four miles outside town where he would force her to move, Jacobs, "seeing no other way of escaping the doom [she] so much dreaded . . . made a headlong plunge" (386)—that is, she became the lover of Sawyer and bore two children by him, the first when she was sixteen years old.

Many twentieth-century scholars dismissed Jacobs's book as fiction, in spite of the wealth of contemporary evidence to the contrary. One of the historians who thought Jacobs's story was merely fiction argued that it is

not credible. . . . [It is] too orderly; too many of the major characters meet providentially after years of separation. Then, too, the story is too melodramatic: miscegenation and cruelty, outraged virtue, unrequited love, and planter licentiousness appear on practically every page. The virtuous Harriet . . . refuses to bow to the lascivious demands of her master, bears two children for another white man, and then runs away and hides in a garret in her grandmother's cabin for seven years until she is able to escape to New York. In the meantime, her white lover has acknowledged his paternity of her children, purchased their freedom, and been elected to Congress. In the end, all live happily ever after. (Blassingame qtd. in Gates xvi–xvii)

Historians argued that slave narratives such as Jacobs's were really written by white abolitionists in the North and not the ex-slaves themselves; yet, white slaveholders' accounts, letters, and newspapers were regarded as valuable evidence. As one historian pointed out, scholars should not discard slave testimony

unless they are prepared to be consistent and discard most of the other sources they habitually use. Not while they still use newspapers as sources, or, for that matter, diaries and letters and politicians' speeches and the *Congressional Record* and all those neatly printed official documents and the solemnly sworn testimony of high officials. Full of paradox and evasion, contrasts and contradictions, lies and exaggerations, pure truth and complete fabrication as they are, such sources still remain the daily bread on which historians feed. The slave narratives have their peculiarities, as all types of historical sources do, but they are not all that different from the norm. (Vann Woodward qtd. in Perdue et al. xliii).

Another chapter in the genre of ex-slave narratives began in the 1930s when the United States government, prompted in part by the knowledge that time to gather this information was running out, funded the collection of the testimony of men and women who had lived under slavery. One of many individuals interviewed, Benjamin Simpson was ninety years old when workers from the Federal Writers' Project met with him in the mid-1930s. His story of suffering and trauma is his own, but it is also representative.

Simpson's parents were captured in Africa and brought to Georgia, where he and a sister, Emma, were born. They and their mother were owned by a murderer and horse thief who moved to Texas to evade the law in Georgia. In his testimony, Simpson describes how the man chained his slaves around the necks, fastened them to the horses that pulled the covered wagon, and made them walk all the way to Texas. Before leaving Georgia the owner branded the slaves: Simpson's mother was branded on her breast and between her shoulders, which "nearly kilt her" (Botkin 76). On the journey they slept at night on the ground, and when it snowed they were not allowed to wrap anything around their feet. The owner used a long rawhide whip that took skin off with it. Near the Texas border, according to Simpson, "Mother, she give out" (75)—her feet were raw and bleeding, her legs swollen out of shape. The owner took out his gun, shot her, kicked and cursed her as she lay dying, and left her there: "You know that man, he wouldn't bury Mother, just leave her laying where he shot her at."

Once they settled in Austin, the slaves were given no shelter; they slept outside at night, locked to a tree with chains around their necks. They were fed raw meat and green corn, had no clothes, and wore chains all the time, even when they worked. His sister Emma was not only "wife of all seven Negro slaves" but also "the only woman [the owner] had till he marries" (76). Emma was sold when she was nine months pregnant, at the age of fifteen, and Simpson never saw her again. The owner married a young Spanish girl named Selena whom Simpson describes as "the best thing God ever put life in, in the world." The master beat her "'cause she wants him to leave [the] slaves alone and live right." Once when he was absent Selena unchained the slaves so they could wash up in the creek and gave them cooked meat and corn. The master came back, saw what they were eating, and whipped her "till she falls. If I could have got a-loose I'd kilt him. I swore if I ever got a-loose I'd kill him." Not long after this, in 1868, Simpson's master was found hanging from a tree, killed by vigilantes for stealing horses, and "Missy turned us a-loose," five years after Lincoln issued the Emancipation Proclamation.

We do not have to go back to the nineteenth century to see slavery, of course. Globally, human trafficking is "the fastest growing means by which people are enslaved, the fastest growing international crime, and one of the largest sources of income for organised crime;" it is also the "second largest source of illegal income worldwide, exceeded only by drugs trafficking" ("Statistics"). We may take as one example the enslavement of immigrant workers in the tomato industry in southwestern Florida. According to reporter Barry Estabrook, these were not cases of

> near-slavery or slavery-like conditions. I'm talking about abject slavery. These were people who were bought and sold. These were people who were shackled in chains at night or locked in the back of produce trucks with no sanitary facilities all night. . . . [They] were forced to work whether they wanted to or not and if they didn't, they were beaten severely. If they tried to escape, they were either beaten worse or in some cases, they were killed. And they received little or no pay. It sounds like 1850. . . . The U.S. Attorney for the district in Southern Florida claims that [the twelve hundred people who have been freed to date are] a tiny, tiny tip of an iceberg because it is extraordinarily difficult to prosecute a modern-day slavery case. ("How Industrial")

The vein of inclusion and exclusion is a rich one to work in as we read history and literature; it points to historical realities and the way those realities have been understood across place and time and have found their way into literary texts of different kinds, some more famous than others. They remind us that people who are "outsiders," in life and in literature, are so because they are treated as such. Yet out of this suffering important stories and great literature can arise, literature that can indeed "liberate" us and enrich our lives by bringing us closer to understanding our own nature.

Works Cited

Auerbach, Nina. "Feeling as One Ought About Fanny Price." *Jane Austen's* Mansfield Park. Ed. Harold Bloom. New York: Chelsea House, 1987. 103–116. Mod. Critical Interpretations.

Aurelius, Marcus. *Meditations.* Trans. Maxwell Staniforth. New York: Penguin, 1964.

Austen, Jane. *Emma.* Boston: Houghton Mifflin, 1957.

_____. *Mansfield Park.* New York: Bantam, 1983.

Barker, Juliet. *The Brontës: A Life in Letters.* Woodstock: Overlook, 1998.

Botkin, B. A., ed. *Lay My Burden Down: A Folk History of Slavery.* Chicago: U of Chicago P, 1945.

Cohen-Solal, Annie. *Sartre: A Life.* New York: Pantheon, 1987.

Cook, William R., and Ronald B. Herzman. *The Medieval World View: An Introduction.* 2nd ed. New York: Oxford UP, 2004.

Dodds, E. R. *Pagan and Christian in an Age of Anxiety: Some Aspects of Religious Experience from Marcus Aurelius to Constantine.* New York: Cambridge UP, 1990.

Emerson, Ralph Waldo. *Selections from Ralph Waldo Emerson.* Ed. Stephen E. Whicher. Boston: Houghton, 1960.

Fletcher, Richard. *The Barbarian Conversion: From Paganism to Christianity.* New York: Holt, 1997.

Freedman, Paul. *Images of the Medieval Peasant.* Stanford: Stanford UP, 1999.

Gates, Henry Louis, Jr., ed. *The Classic Slave Narratives.* Harmondsworth: Penguin, 1987.

"How Industrial Farming 'Destroyed' the Tasty Tomato." *Fresh Air.* Natl. Public Radio. WHYY, Philadelphia, 28 June 2011. Radio.

Lewis, C. S. *The Abolition of Man: How Education Develops Man's Sense of Morality.* New York: Harper, 1947.

Myer, Valerie Grosvenor. *Jane Austen: Obstinate Heart; A Biography.* New York: Little, 1997.

Paley, Vivian Gussin. *You Can't Say You Can't Play.* Cambridge: Harvard UP, 1992.

Perdue, Charles L., Jr., Thomas E. Barden, and Robert K. Phillips, eds. *Weevils in the Wheat: Interviews with Virginia Ex-Slaves.* Charlottesville: UP of Virginia, 1976.

Starn, Orin. *Ishi's Brain: In Search of America's Last "Wild" Indian.* New York: Norton, 2004.

Starr, Chester G. *A History of the Ancient World.* New York: Oxford UP, 1991.

"Statistics." *Stop the Traffik.* Stop the Traffik, n.d. Web. 31 July 2011.

World without Evil? Faust's Fortunes through the Centuries _____

Robert Deam Tobin

Faust, the man who makes a deal with the devil, is—along with Don Juan, Don Quixote, Hamlet, and Robinson Crusoe—one of the great mythical figures of modernity (Watt ix–x). In the thousands of literary, musical, and artistic adaptations of the story, Faust and his deal with the devil have been used to analyze such aspects of modern life as academia, music, science, nuclear power, and the Holocaust (see Henning for an exhaustive listing of Faust treatments up until 1976). Most fundamentally, however, the Faust myth—because it features an encounter with the devil—allows readers to contemplate the status of evil in the modern world. Three of the most acclaimed literary versions of the story provide very different takes on evil: Christopher Marlowe's Renaissance play *Doctor Faustus* presents Faust as an "amiable soul" who nonetheless is damned eternally; Johann Wolfgang von Goethe's *Faust*, a play with one foot in the Enlightenment and another in romanticism, suggests that even a man who leaves a wake of tragedies behind him will go to heaven; and Thomas Mann's twentieth-century post-Holocaust novel *Doctor Faustus* rejects Goethe's optimistic humanism but holds out a glimmer of hope for the man who makes a deal with the devil. Despite all their differences, each of these literary texts has great sympathy with Faust and implies that even in the most dire situations, evil might actually lead to good and thus not be evil at all.

Christopher Marlowe's *Doctor Faustus*

Christopher Marlowe was born in 1564 and died in 1593, just a few years after the first accounts of the Faust story were published in England. It is astonishing how quickly the raw material of the Faust story became one of the great and lasting works of world literature. Marlowe's play was performed during his life but was first published after his death, appearing in several versions between 1604 and 1616.

World without Evil? Faust's Fortunes through the Centuries **59**

(This paper generally follows the so-called B1 edition of 1616—for more on the somewhat complicated textual history of the work, see *Doctor Faustus* 103–9 and Steane 261–62.) In the play, Marlowe scrupulously adheres to the religious dogma of Protestant England. It is a morality tale demonstrating that people who make deals with the devil suffer awful fates. At the same time, though, Faustus is the most sympathetic figure in the play. It is not in the least difficult to read against the grain and discover an alternative interpretation that celebrates Faustus's willingness to embrace the world that the devil offers him.

Marlowe's own worldview undercuts the strict moral message that the play might seem to give. Highly educated, the young man from a modest middle-class background embodied the social mobility that modernity offered. He led a tumultuous life that included a stint as a spy and an arrest for blasphemy. He was stabbed to death in a barroom brawl at age twenty-nine. Literary critic Ian Watt asserts that "Marlowe's personal beliefs were probably close to complete atheism" (30). One of Marlowe's contemporaries, Richard Baines, reported to the authorities in 1593 that Marlowe had claimed that "Christ was a bastard and his mother dishonest" as well as that "Saint John the Evangelist was bedfellow to Christ." In the same report, he is accused of declaring that "all they that love not tobacco and boys were fools" (Kocher 35). Scholar Paul Kocher insists that there is simply too much corroborating evidence from other sources to dismiss Baines's accusations (27). While a literary work can often transcend the opinions of the author, it does seem unlikely that Marlowe would present in his play a strictly orthodox Christian understanding of evil.

Marlowe got his information about Faust from *The History of the Damnable Life and Deserved Death of Doctor John Faustus* (commonly called the English Faust-Book), which was published in 1592. This English Faust-Book was a translation of *Die Historia von D. Johann Fausten*, a German collection of stories about Faust published in 1587 by Johann Spies, who otherwise specialized in Lutheran theological tracts. Spies's "chapbook" collected stories about a historical figure, probably actually named George or Jörg Faust, who lived from about 1480 to about 1540. This small-town charlatan and provincial mountebank traveled through Germany performing magic, predicting the future, and raising the dead. Prominent intellectuals and societal leaders, including Martin Luther, mentioned him in their letters and publications. In addition, there are court and police records detailing charges of necromancy and sodomy against the man (Ziolkowski 46–48).

Exhibiting a traditional morality, Marlowe's version of the Faust tale concludes with the death and damnation of Faustus. Despairing of his achievements, the learned scholar turns to magic and conjures up the devil, who offers Faustus twenty-four years of "voluptuousness" on earth in return for his eternal soul. After his time is up, the devil and his minions shred Faustus to bits, horrifying the scholars who find his "limbs all torn asunder by the hand of death!" (*Doctor Faustus* 5.3.6–7). The chorus declares that Faustus's primary vice is that he is "swoll'n with cunning, of a self-conceit" (prologue, line 19). According to Mephostophilis (Marlowe's spelling of the name of the devil who works with Faustus), Lucifer himself, once the most beloved of angels and now the prince of devils, falls from grace "by aspiring pride and insolence" (1.3.66). The greatest sign of this pride and conceit is simply Faustus's embrace of the devil. Mephostophilis asserts that "the shortest cut for conjuring / Is stoutly to abjure the Trinity / And pray devoutly to the prince of hell" (1.3.51–53). The sin that damns Faustus is his decision to reject God and accept the devil—regardless of the specific deeds that he undertakes with the devil's help.

In one of the play's profoundest passages, Faustus's decision to embrace the realm of evil is revealed to be a decision in favor of the here and now:

> Hell hath no limits nor is circumscribed
> In one self place, but where we are is hell,
> And where hell is there must we ever be. (2.1.126–28)

Admittedly, the source is Mephostophilis, who is not exactly trustworthy and consistently overstates the power of evil. Faustus nonetheless accepts Mephostophilis's statement at face value: "and this be hell, I'll willingly be damned" (2.1.143). If hell is the world in which Faustus lives, it is striking that Faustus's decision to renounce God is a decision to affirm the physical world. The choice for magic is actually the choice for reality. Faustus is willing to trade twenty-four years of "voluptuousness" in this world for an eternity of damnation. Rather than accept promises of salvation after death, Faust chooses this particular, finite world. Keeping strictly within the confines of traditional Christian beliefs, the play overtly condemns Faustus's decision to choose this sinful world over the heavenly one. But, especially given Marlowe's own personal convictions, it is not difficult to find support for a contrary reading that regards Faustus's deal with the devil as a very modern decision to affirm life in the here and now.

Many of Faustus's actual sinful deeds are aimed to amuse, rather than edify, the audience. When Faustus tricks a horse trader into buying a horse that turns into straw, this sin seems more an occasion for farce than anything else, especially when the horse trader returns and thinks he has literally pulled off Faustus's leg (4.5). Other deeds are more seriously antipapal and thus actually good from the perspective of Protestant England. It is hard to imagine a Protestant audience taking serious offense at Faustus gliding invisibly around a banquet in the Vatican and stealing food and wine from under the nose of the prelate (3.2). None of these tricks, which come directly from the original Faust Book, seem likely to cause an audience to believe that Faustus is a particularly sinister or wicked figure. Indeed, some of Faustus's actions lend theological support to Protestant attacks on the Pope. When, for instance, Faustus's invisible antics cause the Pope to condemn someone to eternal damnation wrongly (3.2.90), the play underscores a Protestant critique of papal arbitrariness.

At the same time, though, the play subversively challenges the entire doctrine of perpetual damnation. Watt argues persuasively that Marlowe objected to the doctrine of eternal damnation, just as John Locke and Isaac Newton would a century later (40–43). Given that even prominent intellectuals such as Locke and Newton refrained from publicly denouncing the doctrine of perpetual damnation, it makes sense that Marlowe, in a much more precarious social position, would use the ambiguous nature of literature to suggest an alternative theological reading. From this vantage point, one can imagine reading the whole play as a document in favor of embracing reality and living life to the fullest.

Many aspects of Marlowe's Faust are distinctly positive. At the end of his life, after all his adventures, he becomes a friendly, gregarious professor who has his students and colleagues over for lavish dinners. In one of the early variations of the text, Wagner, Faustus's servant, notes that his master can

> banquet, and carouse, and swill
> Amongst the students—as even now he doth—
> Who are at supper with such belly-cheer
> As Wagner ne'er beheld in all his life.
> (*Doctor Faustus with the English Faust Book* 5.1.1270–73)

The 1616 version is less poetic but conveys the same sense of a sociable professor: "He's now at supper with the scholars, where there's such belly-cheer as Wagner in his life ne'er saw the like!" (*Doctor Faustus* 5.1.5–7). Numerous friends are concerned about his fate. The scholars intercede, as does an old man, who declares, "Yet, yet, thou hast an amiable soul" (5.1.40). Faustus is convinced of the authenticity of his friends, telling them, "I know your friendship is unfeigned" (5.1.19). The very interest that his colleagues show in him suggests that Faustus is no monster. Particularly in act 5 of the play, it is difficult to reconcile Faustus's "amiable soul" with his perpetual damnation.

At times, one does not just identify and empathize with Faustus— one genuinely admires him. In his introduction to the play, Sylvan Barnet comments that "Marlowe's ability as a poet infuses in Faustus an unmistakable grandeur that is not wholly eradicated by common-sense reflection" (*Doctor Faustus* xx). Certainly Faustus hopes that the evil spirits will bring him fortune and power, but he also wants to learn new things from them: "I'll have them read me strange philosophy" (1.1.83). When Faustus considers whether he should repent of his deal with the devil, he decides against repentance because of the great poetic, musical, and artistic accomplishments that his relationship with evil has produced:

> Have not I made blind Homer sing to me
> Of Alexander's love and Oenone's death?
> And hath not he that built the walls of Thebes
> With ravishing sound of his melodious harp
> Made music with my Mephostophilis?
> Why should I die then or basely despair?
> I am resolved, Faustus shall not repent! (2.2.24–30)

Alexander in this case is another name for Paris, who falls in love with Helen and in so doing abandons his lover Oenone, who kills herself. Called upon to build a wall around Thebes, Amphion plays the lyre so beautifully that the rocks, musically entranced, move into place on their own. Defending the sale of his soul, Faustus points to cultural achievements that do not seem so evil to a secular audience—indeed, they seem good.

Marlowe's *Doctor Faustus* leaves its readers and viewers with questions about good and evil. Does a pledge of loyalty to the devil outweigh Faustus's amiable soul and the good deeds that he performs? Such a worldview certainly exists. But it is also possible to see in Marlowe's Renaissance play a hidden celebration of a man who chooses to live life to the fullest for twenty-four years. Marlowe's Faustus uses his magical abilities to learn new philosophies, hear great music, and see mythological beauty. Marlowe's play leaves open the possibility that Faustus is on the right track.

Johann Wolfgang von Goethe's *Faust*

Johann Wolfgang von Goethe (1749–1832) worked on his version of the Faust story for most of his adult life. The first drafts of the so-called "Ur-Faust" were written in the early 1770s, and the final version was published posthumously in the 1830s. More than twelve thousand lines long and divided into two parts, the play has roots in the European Enlightenment but also helped set the tone for German romanticism. Faust's seduction and subsequent abandonment of Margarete (or Gretchen, for short) is one of Goethe's contributions to the Faust tradition, as is his fantastic depiction of Walpurgisnacht, the festival of witches in the Harz Mountains. Both of these episodes, which have become some of the most beloved features of the Faust story, take place in *Faust I*, the most well-known part of Goethe's work. In *Faust II*, Faust engages in many of the more traditional aspects of the Faust story, such as conjuring forth Helen. The ending of *Faust II*, however, is not at all traditional, for Goethe explicitly redeems Faust. Indeed, Faust's very willingness to engage the devil in a deal justifies his salvation. In some ways, Goethe's *Faust* is the opposite of Marlowe's *Doctor Faustus*, which he apparently did not read until 1818: Marlowe's Faust is an amiable soul who is condemned to eternal damnation, while Goethe's Faust is man who wreaks havoc but nonetheless goes to Heaven. Goethe admired Marlowe's play tremendously, which suggests that he picked up on the subversive reading of *Doctor Faustus*; like Marlowe, Goethe sees Faust as a man whose intentions are good because he embraces life.

In an analysis of why Faust is saved, one thing becomes clear quite quickly: established religion does not have the answer to questions of morality in Goethe's play. Although the Easter bells help rescue Faust from his suicidal melancholy at the beginning of the story, it is clear that he has no intention of attending Easter mass. Pointing out that he has not gone to confession or mass in a long time, Margarete asks Faust if he believes in God; he gives an evasive answer that puts him very far indeed from any established branch of Christianity either in the time period of the historical Faust or in Goethe's own time period (lines 3415–40). In general, the established church is a negative figure throughout the play. Clergymen greedily gobble up the treasure trove that Mephistopheles leaves for Margarete (2836–40). The explicitly named "Evil Spirit" resides in the church and uses religious vocabulary to taunt the desperate, unmarried, pregnant Margarete. The final scenes of the play do employ religious imagery to describe Faust's ascent into heaven, but these scenes feature angelic and divine figures, not the leaders of human institutions. Readers must come to terms with the play's moral order without the help of organized religion.

Fortunately, God himself makes clear that striving is the absolute good in Goethe's *Faust*. Occasional errors and mistakes are of little importance: "Man errs as long as he strives," God says when Mephistopheles tries to get him to criticize Faust (317; translations of *Faust* are my own). God indicates that humanity's dimly perceived good intentions are the most important factor on the judgment day: "A good man, in his obscure urges / Knows the right way" (328–29). At the end of the play, as Faust escapes the clutches of the devil, the angels reaffirm that salvation is not so much a matter of *doing* the right thing as it is of *trying* to do the right thing: "Whoever strives and makes an effort / That's a person we can redeem" (11936–37). At first glance, one has to agree with scholar Jane K. Brown, who declares that "the amorality of the position is staggering" (47). Goethe's *Faust* puts this philosophy to a rigorous test, showing that a man whose constant striving produces great suffering—most notably for his beloved Margarete and a kindly elderly couple, Baucis and Philemon—can nonetheless achieve salvation.

God's faith in Faust is confirmed insofar as Faust converts the traditional deal with a devil (twenty-four years of magic on earth in return for an eternity of damnation) into a wager in which Faust declares that he will never give up striving:

> If I ever lie peacefully on a lazy bed,
> Then it will be over for me!

If you can flatter me into believing
That I'm satisfied with myself,
If you can fool me with pleasure,
Then that will be my last day! (1693–98)

He culminates with his famous vow never "to say to the moment / 'Tarry, thou art so beautiful'" (1699–1700). Faust's vow never to be satisfied is a curious and difficult transformation of the Faust story. Faust is not a spoiled child, throwing away his toys and spitting out his food; he fully intends to enjoy—more precisely, to experience—every moment that he gets out of his deal with the devil. Pleasure is not the primary issue for Faust, as he makes clear in one of his romantic manifestos: "You hear that I'm not talking about joy. / I'm devoted to frenzy, the most painful pleasure, / Enamored hatred, invigorating frustration" (1765–68). Instead, Faust strives to experience life to the fullest, the highest highs and the lowest lows that humanity can endure.

Just before his death, Faust insists that he has maintained his part of the bargain—he has never allowed Mephisto's offerings to sedate him, to inure him to the possibilities of future change:

I have run through the world,
Grabbing every desire by the hair.
I let go of that which didn't satisfy,
I chased after that which eluded me. (11433–39)

He completes his monologue by proudly declaring that he has been "unsatisfied every moment" (11453). Faust's dissatisfaction arises not because he dislikes the world or wishes—as Mephistopheles would put it—that the world had never been created but rather because he is constantly dreaming of new possibilities.

Evil is at least two-sided in Goethe's *Faust*. What might be thought of as traditional evil—seducing girls, partying with witches, developing fraudulent schemes to create wealth, consorting with pagans, waging illegitimate war, and displacing elderly couples in naked land grabs (all the things, in short, that Faust does)—does not seem to raise much concern in the play. Evil in this sense seems to be part of God's plan. As the Lord declares in the prologue:

> Human activity can tire all too quickly.
> People love absolute peace.
> Therefore it pleases me to give them a companion
> Who annoys and irritates and has to work like a devil.
> (340–44)

Mephisto acquiesces to the Lord's understanding of his role when he tells Faust that he "is a part of that power / That always wants evil but always creates good" (1335–36). The devil is a necessary and even positive component of human life, not an evil adversary.

Although it is part of God's plan, this kind of evil is not entirely positive, either. The Lord refers to Mephistopheles as one of "the spirits of negation" (338). Mephistopheles gives a similar self-assessment when he tells Faust that he is "the spirit who constantly negates" (1338). While this negativity can be useful, the danger of this spirit of negation lies in its logical conclusion, which is nihilism. Mephistopheles at his darkest believes that "everything that comes into being / Is worth destroying; / Which is why it would be better if nothing ever came into being" (1339–41). Mephisto's nihilism may sound similar to Faust's refusal to be satisfied, but Faust's motivation is a desire to embrace the world and experience every aspect of it, while Mephisto's motivation is ultimately to shut down the world.

If one side of evil is a critical spirit that can lead to nihilism, the more nefarious side of evil is complacency, which dulls the striving instinct that is Goethe's absolute good. While Faust claims he will never be satisfied and will continue to strive as long as he can, Mephistopheles brags to the Lord that he can make Faust "eat dust, and with pleasure" (334). Mephistopheles means that he will embroil Faust so thoroughly in the quotidian details of life that the scholar will cease to dream about future possibilities.

"Sorge"—care or anxiety—is the specific form of evil that accompanies this entrapment in day-to-day concerns, this inability to dream or envision great new possibilities. Talking with Wagner, the most pedestrian of characters, Faust explains the dangers of anxiety at the outset of the play:

> Immediately anxiety nests deep in the heart,
> Where it causes secret pains.
> Restlessly it lies there and disrupts pleasure and peace;
> It hides constantly in new masks,
> It may appear as house and court, as wife and child,
> As fire, water, dagger and poison. (644–49)

Although Faust is opposed to peace and quiet in other contexts, in this case he is targeting a special form of restlessness that has to do with worrying about preserving a comfortable existence, refusing to take risks, hiding behind home and hearth. Here perhaps more than anywhere the heterosexual masculinity of the Faustian vision becomes apparent, as this anxiety is embodied as a feminine danger to man.

Anxiety returns at Faust's death, because only she can attack Faust at this point in his life. As Anxiety clarifies, once she gets a grip on a person, that person cannot experience the world fully anymore:

> My victim hungers amidst plenty;
> Whether it's a passion or a plague,
> He puts things off for another day,
> Lives only in the future
> And therefore never finishes a thing. (11461–66)

Although Anxiety, like Faust, is a disturber of the peace, she is a hindrance to Faustian striving. Ultimately, Anxiety brings Faust's life to an end when he finally does say to the moment, "Tarry, thou art so beautiful!"

Once Faust utters these fateful words, Goethe's monumental drama can test Faust by its own standards of morality. Margarete's miserable fate might seem to weigh most heavily against Faust. The innocent girl, whom the magically rejuvenated Faust seduces and impregnates, is indirectly responsible for the death of her mother and brother, kills her child out of despair for its future, and then goes mad. As the product of unavoidable tensions between implacable imperatives, her fate is tragic. Even the strictest moralist would have to grant that it would be impossible to imagine the play ending with Faust's decision to settle down with Margarete, marry her, and raise their child, occasionally socializing with her mother and brother (Berman 57).

Before assigning too much blame to Faust, one must ask whether he is really at fault. There is a strong case to be made that Margarete's family, society, and church are really much more responsible for the terrible turn that her life takes. In the scene "At the Well," the maids in her community mock unwed mothers heartlessly (3544–76). Her own brother, the soldier Valentine, calls her a whore (3730). This is all the more disturbing when one recalls that the soldiers and maids speak quite freely of sexual acts in the scene "Before the City Gate" (see, for instance, 880–90). Clearly, rampant hypocrisy characterizes this community's attitude about sex. Most seriously, the church creates the moral world that causes Margarete to go insane. It has long been understood that the evil spirit that taunts Margarete in the cathedral (3776–833) is the representation of the Christian conscience that she has internalized (Eggert). As Brown argues, "the evil spirit is an institutional conscience, for it speaks the language of the church" (120). At the end of the play, it is revealed that Margarete has been praying for Faust all along, which suggests that she, at least, does not hold him responsible for the tragedy that befalls her.

If one recalls that the villagers and their social institutions, including the church, ultimately condemn Margarete to her fate, one can understand more easily the reason that the play seems to lend so little moral weight to the deaths of Baucis and Philemon, the kindly elderly couple who live on the hill that Faust covets at the end of the play. His responsibility for their deaths is often seen as damning in the extreme. For critic Marshall Berman, it is "Faust's first self-consciously evil act." He adds, "This is a characteristically modern style of evil: indirect, impersonal, mediated by complex organizations and institutional roles" (67). Baucis and Philemon are often compared to Margarete and considered representatives of an older traditional world that Faust's modernity sweeps away (Nemoianu 48). However, on closer analysis the elderly couple is more comparable to the community that bears responsibility for Margarete's death. Margarete transgresses the rules of her community in order to fall in love with Faust, while Baucis and Philemon uphold the rules of their community and are deeply suspicious of Faust. As sympathetically as Baucis and Philemon are portrayed and as sad as their fates are, their passing is the passing of the society that kills Margarete. Perhaps for this reason, they are not mentioned once in the discussion of Faust's salvation at the end, whereas Margarete returns to plea for him.

Goethe's *Faust* is a rich and complex work that deals subtly with difficult questions of good and evil. It seems at times paradoxical: God says Mephistopheles is on earth in order to prevent people from becoming complacent, but Mephistopheles tries to drown Faust in complacency. Faust resolves never to rest, yet he is ultimately killed by Anxiety, a spirit that also deprives people of their rest. Though it all, however, it is clear that Goethe believes that Faust will be saved by the very tendency that encouraged him to make a deal with the devil in the first place.

Thomas Mann's Doctor Faustus

After the horrors of the rise of Hitler, World War II, and the Holocaust, Thomas Mann (1875–1955) could no longer countenance Goethe's endorsement of striving as a laudable feature of the human spirit regardless of the consequences. In his novel *Doctor Faustus: The Life of the*

German Composer Adrian Leverkühn as Told by a Friend (originally published in German as *Doktor Faustus: Das Leben des deutschen Tonsetzers Adrian Leverkühn erzählt von einem Freunde* in 1947), the Faust figure is the composer Adrian Leverkühn, whose deal with the devil results in the creation of twelve-tone music, one of the most significant developments in twentieth-century art. Mann graphically emphasizes the horrific damage caused by Leverkühn's Faustian bargain, including the deaths of at least two of the people he loves. In addition, Mann spells out the parallels between Leverkühn's deal with the devil, which produces modern music, and Germany's deal with the devil, which produces fascism. Despite his rejection of Goethe's optimism, however, Mann ultimately allows for a glimmer of hope for the salvation of his Faustian figure.

By the end of the novel, Leverkühn comes to believe that he is responsible for the scandalous and shocking death of the affable and charming violinist Rudiger Schwerdtfeger (664/501; page numbers refer first to the German and then the English edition listed in the works cited). Subsequently, the universally adored child Nepomuk falls victim to a gruesome death by meningitis, again apparently because of the composer's forbidden love. Using his skill at describing disease to underscore how horrible it is to witness a child's painful death, Mann includes details such as a reference to "the typical 'hydrocephalic shriek,' against which only the physician, precisely because he knows it is typical, is tolerably armed" (630/475).

After the death of Nepomuk, Leverkühn declares "it is not to be" (634/478). Leverkühn vows to "take back" the Good, the Noble, and the Humane—specifically Beethoven's Ninth Symphony (634/478). Provoked by the cruel death of Nepomuk, Leverkühn's final piece, "The Lamentation of Dr. Faustus," features an "Ode to Sorrow," obviously contrasting with the "Ode to Joy" in Beethoven's final symphony (649/490). Beethoven's great masterpiece of 1824 stands in the novel as the high point of Western civilization, parallel to Goethe's *Faust*, which is roughly contemporaneous with the symphony. Just as

Leverkühn "takes back" Beethoven's Ninth Symphony, Thomas Mann retracts Goethe's humanistic version of the Faust story.

Serenus Zeitblom, the high school classics professor who narrates the novel as World War II draws to an end, consistently compares Leverkühn's deal with the devil with Germany's deal with the devil, which produced Adolf Hitler, National Socialism, and the Holocaust. Just a few pages after the novel describes Leverkühn's "Lamentation of Dr. Faustus," the narrator reports that a "transatlantic general has forced the population of Weimar to file past the crematories of the neighboring concentration-camp" (637/481), setting up Hitler's Buchenwald as parallel to Leverkühn's final "Lamentation." Zeitblom clearly describes National Socialism, the product of Germany's deal with the devil, as pure evil: "the outrageous contempt of reason, the vicious violation of the truth, the cheap, filthy backstairs mythology, the criminal degradation and confusion of standards; the abuse, corruption, and blackmail of all that was good, genuine, trusting, and trustworthy in our old Germany" (234/175). As in the case of Nepomuk's death, Mann makes the evil of the Faustian deal with the devil as concrete, explicit, and absolute as possible.

Arnold Schönberg, the actual inventor of twelve-tone music, was right to be disturbed by the comparison between an important form of twentieth-century art and National Socialism, which famously persecuted much modernist art as degenerate. Mann's novel suggests that the same breakdown of humanism that produced radical avant-garde art also produced a grotesque new kind of inhumane politics. As scholar Susan von Rohr Scaff argues, *Doctor Faustus* implies that "the highest human achievements, symbolized by art, are inspired in the depths of Hell" (151). This disturbing thesis is in itself a relativization of the notion of evil, for if modern fascism emerges from the same wellspring that produces great modern art, then perhaps it is not entirely evil or at least has some redeeming features.

Even though Mann tries to portray evil as starkly as possible, he keeps in play Goethe's idea that evil is part of God's plan. Fairly early on in the novel, Leverkühn and Zeitblom hear lectures by a theologian named Eberhard Schleppfuss, who "declared the vicious to be a necessary and inseparable concomitant of the holy" (134/100): "According to Schleppfuss all this—evil, the Evil One himself—was a necessary emanation and inevitable accompaniment of the Holy Existence of God, so that vice did not consist in itself but got its satisfaction from the defilement of virtue, without which it would have been rootless" (135/100). It is not clear whether Schleppfuss himself is a reliable speaker—his name refers to a limping foot, which was taken in olden times as a sign of the devil. Nonetheless, it does seem that Mann is introducing this idea as an important part of his theology of good and evil.

Leverkühn has his own version of this philosophy, according to which he regards evil as a challenge to God's love and mercifulness. In his discussions with the devil, he refers to "the most abandoned guilt and the last and most irresistible challenge to the Everlasting Goodness" (330/247). He envisions "a capacity for sin so healless that it makes its man despair from his heart of redemption—that is the true theological way to salvation" (329/247). While Zeitblom indicates that it is shockingly irresponsible to rely exclusively on God's mercy for salvation, the narrator must return to the possibility of a completely unmerited redemption, precisely because he has provided such horrendous examples of evil. In describing the last notes of Leverkühn's bleak "Lamentation of Dr. Faustus," Zeitblom finds the possibility "that out of the sheerly irremediable hope might germinate" (651/491). Movingly, he describes the "hope beyond hopelessness, the transcendence of despair . . . the miracle that passes belief":

> For listen to the end, listen with me: one group of instruments after another retires, and what remains, as the work fades on the air, is the high G of a cello, the last word, the last fainting sound, slowly dying in pianissimo-fermata. Then nothing more: silence, and night. But that tone which vibrates in the silence, which is no longer there, to which only the spirit

hearkens, and which was the voice of mourning, is so no more. It changes its meaning; it abides as a light in the night. (651/491)

The hope for forgiveness that stands at the end of the piece is incredibly tentative—reading the narrator's passage carefully, it seems that the change in meaning happens only after the high G is no longer audible. This would suggest it is impossible to prove that it really happens. It could indeed be nothing but the self-deluding fantasy of the auditors.

In 1947, when Mann published *Doctor Faustus*, it was not clear whether there would be any redemption for Germany. Zeitblom dares pray tentatively for hope in his final lines in the novel:

> Today, clung round by demons, a hand over one eye, with the other staring into horrors, down she [Germany] flings from despair to despair. . . . When, out of the uttermost hopelessness—a miracle beyond the power of belief—will the light of hope dawn? A lonely man folds his hands and speaks: "God be merciful to thy poor soul, my friend, my Fatherland." (676/510)

These final lines reinforce the interchangeability of Leverkühn and Germany. The reference to "a miracle beyond the power of belief" reminds the reader of the narrator's description of the end of Leverkühn's "Lamentation," which produces a kind of "miracle that passes belief" (in German, Mann uses the same phrase in both cases: "ein Wunder, das über den Glauben geht"). In multiple ways, the final lines of the novel emphasize the identity of Leverkühn and Germany and call for a hope beyond hopelessness that good can redeem evil. As grim as this novel is, it also leaves the reader with a wisp of hope that out of evil, good can come.

Conclusion

After reviewing the three most prominent literary versions of the Faust myth, it is useful to consider what social scientists might call the quality of the data before coming to a conclusion. Historically, these three texts cover almost the whole time period in which the Faust myth has existed. They align perfectly with what Berman outlines as the three phases of modernity: (1) the sixteenth century, when modernity sets in; (2) the revolutionary era around 1800; and (3) the triumph, but fragmentation, of modernity in the twentieth century (16–17).

On the other hand, however, these three authors in some ways reflect a narrow pool of the human experience. They are all white men—there are strikingly few versions of the Faust story in which the protagonist is a woman and not many versions written by women—from Protestant northern Europe. All three authors were privileged with high degrees of education and a certain amount of social status. Even Marlowe, who clearly had the most precarious existence of the three, enjoyed an elite education at Cambridge University and had access to powerful people in his society. It is fair to say that the Faust story frequently sees the question of good and evil from the perspective of educated elite European men. At the same time, however, the Faust story has had wide appeal among many readers in many parts of the world, so it does reflect broader societal assumptions.

Moreover, it is important to emphasize the literary nature of the material at hand. For reasons of entertainment and character development, there is a long history of making evil figures understandable and even likeable in literary texts. Even in the most overtly moralistic versions of the Faust story, the reader tends to come to appreciate Faust and often even the devil. This is an old problem with religious texts, which often find virtue, constancy, and kindness more difficult to render interestingly than sin, temptation, and evil. In addition, some literary forms make it especially difficult to find one's moral bearings. The dramatic plays of Marlowe and Goethe present only the words of the characters, which the reader or viewer must evaluate without help from a narrator. It is hard to know, for instance, whether to trust the devil when he talks about good and evil. For that matter, it is hard to know whether to trust the man who makes a deal with the devil! Mann's novel has a personal narrator who is himself a character in the story, which detracts from his ability to claim objectivity in reporting. Mann's narrator, who might have been an arbiter of truth, simply adds another layer of uncertainty to the story. Above and beyond the difficulties of these particular dramatic and narrative forms, literature itself tends toward the ambiguous and the polyvalent. A literary depiction of the Faust story is therefore unlikely ever to have a straightforward, unambiguous moral. Instead, it will present multiple sides of the question of evil and offer multiple answers.

The very multiplicity of possibilities inherent in literature, however, allows one to find a persistently positive twist to the Faust tale, even in versions that seem to condemn the principle character. In the three world-famous versions of the Faust story, the deal with the devil reveals that while evil may exist, it can at least potentially lead to good—and thus is perhaps not evil at all. Marlowe's *Doctor Faustus* ostensibly condemns the deal with the devil but suggests a certain subversive sympathy with the Faust figure. Goethe's *Faust* echoes that sympathy and implies that Mephistopheles is a fairly minor figure in an essentially benevolent cosmos where the greatest danger to salvation is complacency. Mann's *Doctor Faustus* attempts to retract that Goethean optimism but cannot leave its readership completely without hope. Despite the presence of the devil in these stories, all of these accounts allow for the possibility that good will come out of evil. If good does emerge from evil, it will be the Fausts of the world, who are willing to make a deal with the devil, who help create a world without evil.

Works Cited

Berman, Marshall. *All That Is Solid Melts into Air: The Experience of Modernity.* New York: Simon, 1982.

Brown, Jane K. *Goethe's* Faust: *The German Tragedy.* Ithaca: Cornell UP, 1986.

Eggert, C. A. "The 'Evil Spirit' in Goethe's *Faust I.*" *Modern Language Notes* 15.4 (1900): 108–11.

Goethe, Johann Wolfgang von. *Dramen I.* Ed. Erich Trunz. 13th ed. München: Beck, 1986.

Henning, Hans. *Faust Bibliographie.* 4 vols. Berlin: Aufbau, 1966–76.

Kocher, Paul H. *Christopher Marlowe: A Study of His Thought, Learning, and Character*. Chapel Hill: U of North Carolina P, 1946.

Mann, Thomas. *Doctor Faustus: The Life of the German Composer Adrian Leverkühn as Told by a Friend*. Trans. Helen T. Lowe-Porter. New York: Vintage, 1971.

_____. *Doktor Faustus: Das Leben des deutschen Tonsetzers Adrian Leverkühn erzählt von einem Freunde*. 2nd ed. Frankfurt: Fischer, 1974.

Marlowe, Christopher. *Doctor Faustus*. Ed. Sylvan Barnet. Rev. ed. New York: Signet, 2001.

_____. *Doctor Faustus with the English Faust Book*. Ed. David Wootton. Indianapolis: Hackett, 2005.

Nemoianu, Virgil. *The Triumph of Imperfection: The Silver Age of Sociocultural Moderation in Europe, 1815–1848*. Columbia: U of South Carolina P, 2006.

Scaff, Susan von Rohr. "The Duplicity of the Devil's Pact: Intimations of Redemption in Mann's *Doktor Faustus*." *Monatshefte* 87.2 (1995): 151–69.

Steane, J. B. "Doctor Faustus: The Text." *Christopher Marlowe: The Complete Plays*. Ed. Steane. New York: Penguin, 1986. 261–62.

Watt, Ian. *Myths of Modern Individualism: Faust, Don Quixote, Don Juan, Robinson Crusoe*. Cambridge: Cambridge UP, 1996.

Ziolkowski, Theodore. *The Sin of Knowledge: Ancient Themes and Modern Variations*. Princeton: Princeton UP, 2000.

Decadence and *Dorian Gray*: Who's Afraid of Oscar Wilde?

Frederick S. Roden

To study the themes of good and evil in literature, there is perhaps no better figure for consideration than the late nineteenth-century writer Oscar Wilde (1854–1900). Wilde's life and his art are blurred in both the popular and scholarly imaginations. This essay, while highlighting that relationship between art and life (the central focus of his work), will demonstrate the theory behind the author's approach to his subject. Wilde's philosophy was deeply informed by an "either-or" view of the world, similar to the opposites with which this volume is concerned: good *versus* evil, the sacred and the profane. However, the central metaphor in Wilde's thinking—and living—is that of inversion. As we will see, this term, used at the time to define the sexual "deviance" that shaped Wilde's own identity, is also a means to comprehend his thought. Wilde was associated with two important literary and artistic movements: aestheticism (literally, the focus on the "artistic") and decadence (the focus on that which is literally decaying and in the process of being lost, thus requiring a "seize-the-day" mentality, or that which is destructive or even "evil," depending on one's perspective). For Wilde, aestheticism was a means to assert the idea of the "good" that is art in contrast to the inferiority of life. The decadent movement, a late nineteenth-century outgrowth of the earlier romantic movement, which had been concerned with the exotic (and at times, even the morbid), allowed Wilde and other artists to celebrate the unusual and the strange—what others called the wicked or perverse.

There are two important works that serve as "gospels" to these two movements. Walter Pater's 1873 *The Renaissance* is a collection of critical essays that analyze art objects (stories, paintings, lives) from the Middle Ages to the eighteenth century. Pater shifts the focus from the artist or the art to the viewer of the work of art. His question is not what the art means abstractly but rather what it means to the individual who experiences it. In dramatic, lush prose, Pater calls upon the audience to seize the moment of experience—for it will soon be lost. He argues that success in life is fully experiencing the passion of the moment. *The Renaissance* was published in several editions, a number of which modify this language, as critics feared it would encourage young people to live immorally. This call to action—the suggestion that life could not be separated from art—is the cultural anxiety with which Wilde struggled in his life and works.

Joris-Karl Huysmans's 1884 novel *À rebours* (usually translated as "against nature" or "against the grain") moves beyond Pater's call to exercise one's artistic temperament in the abstract. While Pater compares the artistic sensibility to the lens of the eye through which people sense and discern intellectually everything around them, Huysmans's focus is on the art of living. The hero of his novel, Des Esseintes, explores every possible carnal pleasure—for example, he encrusts his pet tortoise's shell with precious jewels, thus killing it—and finds all to be wanting. Excess is the rule when it comes to material indulgence and physical experience; this is the try-anything-once attitude that comes to define the decadent movement. The conclusion to Huysmans's work, however, resonates with a theme found in Wilde: after having exhausted all possibilities for sensual gratification, Des Esseintes turns to mysticism and spirituality. Thus, in terms of the themes of this study, both Pater and Huysmans—theorists who might seem to place "the good" in the experiences that Victorian morality might label "the evil"—instead paradoxically locate "the good" in intellectual pleasure (abstract beauty and truth) even as they struggle with the great question of Shakespeare's *Hamlet*: which is greater, contemplation or action? In subjective, modern terms, the answer is always based on the individual's own satisfaction, not whether something is good (or evil) for society.

Oscar Wilde was born into a privileged and intellectual Irish home. His father was a prominent surgeon and his mother a poet and Irish nationalist. Wilde won a scholarship to study at Oxford University, where he came into contact with the major thought of the time—and where he first developed his own theories on art and life. Upon taking his degree, Wilde embarked on the life of the public intellectual. He published a volume of poetry, transformed himself into a celebrity, and even toured America and lectured about aestheticism. While the operetta *Patience* by W. S. Gilbert and Arthur Sullivan satirized the young "aesthete," Wilde—and the producers—took advantage of the attention each was receiving to gain greater publicity. In England, his adopted home, Wilde became an editor and essayist. He married and fathered two children. At the same time, he began exploring relationships with men, as London offered a homosexual world in which Wilde could further push the limits of sensual experience. While such behavior would label him an "invert" (the Victorian term for homosexual), it is not clear that Wilde thought of himself as such—or as gay, or even "queer," a more fluid term for sexual identity. Wilde was at the height of his artistic and commercial success—he had written several successful comedies for the London stage—when his relationship with a young aristocrat, Lord Alfred Douglas, led to a criminal trial for "gross indecency" and a sentence of two years of hard labor. During that time, he wrote an important letter to Douglas now known as *De Profundis* ("out of the depths"). Wilde died a few years after his release from prison, a broken man. His biography is often related in terms of crime and punishment; later accounts cast Wilde as the victim rather than the offender.

The late twentieth-century scholar Eve Kosofsky Sedgwick, author of *Between Men* (1985) and *Epistemology of the Closet* (1990) and a founder of queer theory, argues for the existence of the "open secret" of same-sex desire in Western literature—including the works by men such as Wilde who engaged in homosexual acts. It is thus fitting to begin a study of Wilde's views of good versus evil with his representation of deception: truth and lies. In his 1891 essay "The Decay of Lying," written as a dialogue between young men Cyril and Vivian (the names of his two sons), Wilde puts forth the gospel of art as that which is separate from life. "Lying, the telling of beautiful untrue things, is the proper aim of Art" (192). Writing during an age that glorified yet was deeply anxious about fiction, Wilde argues that truth can more easily be found there than in "non-fiction," or "Life." He implicitly takes on the puritanical suspicion of art as "against nature" because it is "false" and claims through irony and paradox—and a kind of inversion—that this is precisely why truth can be found there. Wilde's view of art is deeply suspicious of mimetic approaches, those that attempt a "realistic" imitation of life. Instead, art exists as a parallel sphere to life— and as a new religion—becoming a good in and of itself. As Wilde asserts in "The Critic as Artist" (1891), "It is through Art, and through Art only, that we can realize our perfection; through Art, and through Art only, that we can shield ourselves from the sordid perils of actual existence" (252). Art thus serves not as an incitement to vice but as a higher realm separate from the world, a Platonic space wherein acts are always inferior to ideas. Art cannot address morality; Wilde rejects Victorian views that art must serve to teach. The difficulty of Wilde's aesthetics lies in how they break down in this delicate relationship between art and life. For example, in his 1889 essay "The Portrait of Mr. W. H.," Wilde creates an entire fictional narrative about the young man to whom Shakespeare's sonnets are addressed. In the course of doing so, he makes elaborate references to the inspiration of male beauty to the male artist, a crisis that develops further in his later works. Here, as elsewhere in Wilde's writings, the author is obsessed with questions of forgery, theft, masks, and all forms of deception. These themes will dominate his society comedies, the plays that made him famous—and made the fortune he would lose after his public disgrace.

In his 1891 essay "The Soul of Man under Socialism," Wilde depicts Jesus Christ in relation to art, thus making clear his view of art's goodness. Foreshadowing the narrative he would later write in *De Profundis*, Wilde presents Christ as an artist. Wilde discusses individualism, the perfect realization of the soul achieved through self-knowledge, and he argues that this was the message of Christ, to be oneself. He concludes that Christ ultimately failed as an artist because he realized his perfection through suffering and sorrow, not through pleasure and joy.

This is a perspective Wilde would later revise, but the message is clear: art saves. Even as Victorian moralists were denouncing aestheticism and decadence as immoral or amoral—failing to instruct properly and leading the public to evil—Wilde was arguing for art and especially artistic individualism as a good. In keeping with this focus on the religion of art, he took the genres of fairy tale and comedy and remythologized them. For an artist who argued that art and morality were separate, Wilde wrote deeply moral fairy tales that serve as scathing social critiques of hypocrisy and false piety. Likewise, his plays serve as moralizing vehicles that depict liars and transgressors as valuable—and deeply humane—members of society. In *Lady Windermere's Fan* (1892) and *A Woman of No Importance* (1893), Wilde's heroines are "fallen women"—women who have had children outside of marriage or who have otherwise disregarded the Victorian ideal of mother and wife. The playwright thus inverts the ideal of good versus evil. Wilde takes on male liars in *An Ideal Husband* (1895) and *The Importance of Being Earnest* (1895). In the former play, a promising young politician is confronted with a past professional transgression, and his wife, who has put him on a pedestal, must make a compromise in her trust in him: she must accept that his life in public service is more important than disclosure of the damaging truth. *Earnest*, in contrast, is an effervescent comedy of manners in which public morality can only be parodied. The arbitrary gesture of naming, in fact being earnest, and two women's insistence on marrying men named Ernest turn every accepted belief of society upside down. This play takes its strong social argument and puts it in a domestic framework; *Earnest* suggests in the tradition of farce that lies make a happy marriage and that transgressions are best known about but not spoken of. Wilde takes the art of lying to a decidedly "life" level in this play and in so doing counters his statements about their separateness. For example, the words engraved on a silver cigarette case prove important to the plot, as they later were for Wilde in his trials, during which male prostitutes testified to having received engraved silver cigarette cases as gifts from the author. While being "bad" is "good" in the comedy of the play, at Wilde's trials, where his art was displayed as evidence for his crime, the suggestion of transgression—in the words of his accuser, "posing as a somdomite [*sic*]"—was enough to bring ruin.

On the witness stand, Wilde would be interrogated for a letter he had written to Lord Alfred Douglas. He would also be asked the meaning of the "love that dare not speak its name," an allusion to a poem written by Douglas called "Two Loves." If names matter much in *Earnest*, here the lack of naming, the lack of specificity of vice, is what matters. Speaking indirectly rather than directly about homosexual acts is the means of containing them safely in a society that forbids them. On the stand, Wilde was complicit in publicly "outing" this secrecy: moving it from the exotic, decadent, and attractive suggestion of forbidden fruit (the pleasurable good) to the criminal evil. In the process, he outed all of the same-sex desire contained in the canonical works of the Western tradition. The scandal and sacrilege—religiously and secularly—of collapsing the good and virtuous into that which is associated with evil was perhaps the most significant rhetorical gesture of Wilde's life. To associate the love of the biblical friendship between David and Jonathan, the feelings found in the poetry of Michelangelo and Shakespeare, with the evil—sin, crime, or, increasingly at this time, psychopathology—of homosexuality was Wilde's own beautiful transgression in his speech on the witness stand. While at the historic moment Wilde was castigated as a heretic and criminal, his answer to the question of "What is the 'Love that dare not speak its name'?" fundamentally challenged the prevailing notions of good and evil (Hyde 201). Wilde's naming of homosexual desire as the so-bad-it's-good temptation that had been associated with aestheticism and decadence compounded his assault on Victorian morality. It also set the stage for the modern disputation regarding the morality of homosexual acts and the place in society of the person who identifies by that same-sex desire.

Another piece of "evidence" used by the prosecution against Wilde was his popular and controversial novel, *The Picture of Dorian Gray*, first serialized in 1890 and revised for book publication in 1891. Even as Wilde advocated in his aesthetic theory for the separation of art from life, his detractors sought answers in his work. The fact that they were right to look there does not take away from the fact that Wilde saw no evil inherent in homosexual desire; the evil he experienced was society's persecution of him. Indeed, one could argue that Wilde's (and aestheticism's) advocacy for individualism and the individual can be extended to questions of diversity with respect to sexual desire. For the purpose of this analysis, we will adopt the strategies of those prosecutors and look to Wilde's novel for answers, both in terms of struggles between good and evil and strategies of representing same-sex desire.

The Picture of Dorian Gray is prefaced by a series of epigrams about art that are provocative, especially for a novel about an artist and a work of art: "To reveal art and conceal the artist is art's aim"; "There is no such thing as a moral or an immoral book"; and "All art is at once surface and symbol. Those who go beneath the surface do so at their peril. Those who read the symbol do so at their peril" (3–4; all quotes refer to the 1891 revision of the text). Wilde thus begins with the suggestion of multiple meanings and the danger of art's meaning. The novel then opens with two men looking at the full-length portrait of a young man. The painter, Basil Hallward, protests to his friend Lord Henry Wotton, "I know you will laugh at me . . . but I really can't exhibit it. I have put too much of myself into it" (6). Basil describes meeting Dorian Gray, the subject of the painting: "I knew that I had come face to face with some one whose mere personality was so fascinating that, if I allowed it to do so, it would absorb my whole nature, my whole soul, my very art itself" (9). The preface to this disclosure narrates that "Lord Henry felt as if he could hear Basil Hallward's heart beating." The intimacy of relationship between artist and art object is corporealized as Wilde reveals the artist's infatuation with his subject. But what is artistic obsession—and what is male love? Of course, Henry, after hearing Basil's description, must meet Dorian. For Dorian, the occasion of meeting the slightly older Henry "touched some secret chord that had never been touched before, but that he felt was now vibrating and throbbing to curious pulses" (19). Again, the body responds sensually. In looking at his portrait, Dorian laments the awareness that he will age while his picture will always remain young; he utters a wish that it might be otherwise. Dorian later speaks of his representation as self-love: "I am in love with it. . . . It is part of myself." Basil replies, "Well, as soon as you are dry, you shall be varnished, and framed, and sent home" (27). This crisis of representation embodies the desire for male forms whose touch is forbidden, as compared to those intangible images for which admiration is permissible. The pleasure of this encounter is echoed in the viewer, as well as the creator, of the icon. Henry later dines with Dorian. "Talking to him was like playing upon an exquisite violin. He answered to every touch and thrill of the bow. . . . There was something terribly enthralling in the exercise of influence. No other activity was like it" (33). If Basil and Dorian struggle with the ethics of representation, Henry sees influence as amoral—outside the law, as it were.

Despite the strongly homoerotic themes of the novel, its overt romance is heterosexual in nature. By chance Dorian finds his way to a cheap theater one night and becomes infatuated with a young actress, Sibyl Vane, who begins to refer to him as "Prince Charming." To his friends, Dorian calls her a "born artist" (66). Unlike Henry, Basil wishes to keep Dorian all to himself, and the news—and Dorian's determination to marry Sibyl—breaks the spell of youth and their relationship: "A strange sense of loss came over him. He felt that Dorian Gray would never again be to him all that he had been in the past. Life had come between them" (69). What was possible in art—the admiration of a perfect young man—is not possible in life. Henry can remain a promiscuous consumer in both, while Basil as a creator cannot. But when Basil and Henry join Dorian to see Sibyl onstage, she performs poorly. According to Victorian romantic rules, Sibyl is prepared to forget her art for love, anticipating marriage to Dorian. This very act makes him lose all fascination with her, as he has been seduced by Henry's theory (and Basil's practice) of art being greater than love. Whisking them out of the theater, Henry declares, "It is not good for one's morals to see bad acting" (73). Sibyl, ignorant of Dorian's devastation, proclaims to him that she will never act well again, since she has found love. When he is furious with her, she is certain that he is the one acting. Dorian leaves her, telling her he cannot see her again; his portrait, when he returns home, begins to look a bit cruel. He has fallen in love with art, the only love possible for a man such as he, and cannot be reduced to life. His actions may be cruel, but his intentions are equally so. After Sibyl dies by her own hand, Henry tells Dorian, "Mourn for Ophelia, if you like. Put ashes on your head because Cordelia was strangled. Cry out against Heaven because the daughter of Brabantio died. But don't waste your tears over Sibyl Vane. She was less real than they are" (89). Dorian overcomes his remorse; Narcissus-like, he kisses his portrait's lips, letting his representation take the tangible blame. When Basil learns of Sibyl's death and attempts to comfort Dorian, he finds the young man had already placed her in the realm of art: "She lived her finest tragedy" (93). But here it is Basil, not Dorian, who confesses a personal guilt:

> Dorian, from the moment I met you, your personality had the most extraordinary influence over me. I was dominated, soul, brain, and power by you. You became to me the visible incarnation of that unseen ideal whose memory haunts us artists like an exquisite dream. I worshipped you. I grew jealous of every one to whom you spoke. I wanted to have you all to myself. I was only happy when I was with you. When you were away from me you were still present in my art. (97–98)

Basil articulates his sins of idolatry and blasphemy even as he names the object of his obsession, the source of his art. The homoerotic theme of his confession is in its subtext, but the greater problem in the novel is this repeated crisis in which the rules of art cannot be reconciled with the realities of life. Sibyl died for it, Henry lives for it, and Basil and Dorian are both perpetrators and victims of the meeting of art and life.

For several chapters Wilde narrates Dorian's growing decadence—and familiarity with works of the decadent movement, as he paraphrases Pater's prose and alludes indirectly to Huysmans's novel: "One hardly knew at times whether one was reading the spiritual ecstasies of some mediaeval saint or the morbid confessions of a modern sinner. It was a poisonous book. The heavy odour of incense seemed to cling about its pages and to trouble the brain" (107). Wilde inserts a chapter on Dorian's flirtation with Roman Catholicism, the sensual religion that delighted so many decadents, following their fondness for all that was exotic, unusual, foreign, and ritualized. Dorian becomes a collector of beautiful objects. His growing dissipation is implied, but its nature is never made explicit. Like the best sensualists, Dorian has succeeded in splitting body and soul, materiality and spirituality. One night he happens to run into Basil and decides to take him to see the portrait hidden in his home. It has become ghastly, showing all the sins and crimes Dorian has committed. First unable to believe the transformation of his art (or the wicked transformation of his inspiration), Basil at last exclaims, "What a lesson! What an awful lesson!'" (133). The supernatural, sensational, gothic aspects of this tale meet Victorian morality, yet the latter cannot be satisfied: "There was no answer, but he could hear the young man sobbing at the window. 'Pray, Dorian, pray,' he murmured. 'What is it that one was taught to say in one's boyhood? "Lead us not into temptation. Forgive us our sins. Wash away our iniquities." Let us say that together'" (133). Basil moves from common contrition to the prayer of the priest before the sacrament of the mass. As the Catholic priest "makes" the body of Christ out of the bread and wine, so Basil has created this magical representation out of the "unnatural" influence Dorian had upon him, and Dorian in turn has allowed the power of Henry's influence to work upon himself. He has accepted freely the visible, tangible record of evil made manifest on the portrait through his own actions. As Basil continues, "The prayer of your pride has been answered. The prayer of your repentance will be answered also. I worshipped you too much. I am punished for it. You worshipped yourself too much. We are both punished" (133). The sins of self-love and nongenerative love can be forgiven. Basil's sin is that of hubris, pride; he wished to possess Dorian when he painted him. Such ownership of another is impossible, regardless of the direction of the eroticism.

Dorian was influenced by Henry, but he also allowed himself to choose how to act on that soul's influence. For Wilde, thoroughly following Plato's *Symposium*, contemplation of the beautiful is always greater than action upon the beautiful; art is always superior to life. In a second, Dorian kills Basil. Basil has reminded him of his true self, but he was also the source of all that has unfolded for Dorian. Without Basil's magical painting, the double life never could have been lived. Basil is a creator; he is godlike, having given Dorian the ultimate choice of free will and the portrait that records Dorian's sins. The love of God thus operates in that same intimacy as the influence of Dorian's beauty on the creativity of Basil the artist. In killing Basil, Dorian commits a kind of deicide in an effort to wipe away that reminder of his soiled soul: the original sin, as it were, of that moment when choice was possible. Dorian also commits the sin of despair; when reminded that he, too, could be forgiven and start over, he clearly decides it is not possible or not worth the effort.

Dorian takes Basil's life and must also destroy his body—both to be rid of the evidence and to wipe away Basil's materiality. He consults a chemist, who does the job for him. This man later becomes unable to live with his own guilt, and Dorian himself begins to be haunted as well. Here the novel turns decidedly psychological, as the title character experiences severe anxiety. How can a work of art live once it has murdered its own creator? Dorian sees doom at every turn and in fact finds what he is looking for when Sibyl's brother seems to catch a glimpse of him. Fleeing to the country, Dorian still cannot escape his pursuer, who eventually dies in a hunting accident. But Wilde's reluctant morality tale still is not over. Dorian has one more conversation with Henry, whose opinions of the world, of art and life, have not changed and who resists his own call of conscience. Dorian goes home and decides he must destroy the source of his torment once and for all. The novel ends with the servants' discovery of a painting of a beautiful young man and the body of a horrible-looking old man who has been stabbed to death. The sacrifice required to set things right is mortality; Dorian dies setting his soul free. His painting, the timeless art, can claim its own purity and perfection. The spell that bound them together—life itself, setting soul in body—has been broken. Death was necessary to release art from its shackles, from the chains of its debt to life. But would this have been the case had Dorian led an exemplary life, if he had been a man of virtue? In *The Importance of Being Earnest*, the foolish Miss Prism declares, "The good ended happily, and the bad unhappily. That is what Fiction means" (2.52–53).

In *The Picture of Dorian Gray*, Wilde succeeds in writing in several different styles, just as he does on the stage with his comedies. He writes a novel that is a morality play for the Victorian audience, with a criminal, a crime, and a punishment. Wilde writes a theology of good and evil that remythologizes the biblical Fall and Christian redemption through the lens of less mythic characters, wherein artist and art substitute for God and belief and pride and influence remain necessary (if mediated and moderated) sins for humanity. Finally, Wilde writes a thinly veiled narrative of homoerotic attraction based on Platonic suggestions of loves that are realized in body versus those that are known only in spirit. In all of these, he utilizes the backdrop of aesthetic theory and the trappings of decadence. These are themes to be found in Wilde's better decadent poems as well as, perhaps, his overtly moralizing "Ballad of Reading Gaol" (1898; written after his own imprisonment and concerning a criminal's soul) and his stylized decadent play *Salome* (1894), in which he uses biblical legend to highly sensualized effect.

Wilde's deepest articulation of a theology of good and evil comes in his prison letter, *De Profundis*, written to Douglas. In the letter, Wilde's voice is more reminiscent of Basil than Henry: "I blame myself for allowing an unintellectual friendship, a friendship whose primary aim was not the creation and contemplation of beautiful things, entirely to dominate my life" (99). Wilde maligns Douglas by saying that his interests "were in Life not in Art" (100) and calls him the "absolute ruin" of his art; Wilde allowed Douglas to stand "persistently between Art" and himself (101). The text is as much a love letter to art as it is an indictment of his relationship with Douglas. While one can imagine this argument as an assault on sexual relationships as opposed to solely intellectual or artistic ones, the document reads as a strong attack on Douglas's character. *De Profundis* is, however, more than just a critique of a lover; it is also a highly developed statement on the aesthetics of suffering. What Wilde could not accept about Christ in "The Soul of Man under Socialism" he puts forward clearly here. In having suffered for what society saw to be his sins and he saw as his failures to live by society's rules, Wilde is prepared to accept the role of martyr and by extension make Christ the suffering artist his prototype. He writes as exquisitely about pain and suffering in *De Profundis* as he writes about pleasure and beauty elsewhere. The scenes and images of human suffering and compassion become for Wilde the stylized fodder in the artist's creation; the life of Christ is the life of the artist, and its story is a beautiful poem.

Wilde makes grand statements: "I was a man who stood in symbolic relations to the art and culture of my age. . . . I made art a philosophy and philosophy an art" (151). He states his perspective from experience: "Morality does not help me. I am a born antinomian. I am one of those who are made for exceptions, not for laws. But while I see that there is nothing wrong in what one does, I see there is something wrong in what one becomes. . . . Religion does not help me. The faith that others give to what is unseen, I give to what one can touch, and look at" (154). To be sure, Wilde articulates here the philosophy embodied in the artist of *Dorian Gray*: conscience and contemplation trump public viewpoint and action. The experience of pain and sorrow—as in the sacrifice of Christ—becomes the means for bridging the gap: "What the artist is always looking for is the mode of existence in which soul and body are one and indivisible: in which the outward is expressive of the inward: in which form reveals. . . . Truth in art is the unity of a thing with itself: the outward rendered expressive of the inward: the soul made incarnate" (160–61). In *De Profundis*, Wilde writes extensively about love, which is entirely missing from *Dorian Gray*. Love is a tangible good in its ability to heal brokenness and mend the split between the beautiful soul and the broken body, between the beautiful body and the broken soul.

From here Wilde develops his aesthetic theology: "I see a far more intimate and immediate connexion between the true life of Christ and the true life of the artist. . . . There was nothing that either Plato or Christ had said that could not be transferred immediately into the sphere of Art and there find its complete fulfillment" (165). This is what has been missing, what had split art and life, soul and body: both lacked a cohesive force. Wilde describes Christ's "intense and flame-like imagination. He realized in the entire sphere of human relations that imaginative sympathy which in the sphere of Art is the sole secret of creation." Wilde places Christ with the poets and calls his life a poem. It is important to remember that in doing so, Wilde is embracing the representation of Christ in his "story"; he is taking the teachings of Christ and applying them to art. Indeed, Wilde is inserting himself into the narrative as a Christ-figure—quite literally as an "imitation" of Christ. Wilde is not endorsing or embracing an orthodox Christian theology; to the contrary, he laments how badly many Christians understand Christ. It is the beauty of Christ's story—dramatized, aestheticized, and told through Wilde's own lens—that makes it attractive to him. This is not in any way to denigrate Wilde's use of the teachings of compassion or the wisdom of growth through suffering. Indeed, Wilde's rewriting of this gospel is extremely palatable: "With a width and wonder of imagination that fills one almost with awe, [Christ] took the entire world of the inarticulate, the voiceless world of pain, as his kingdom, and made of himself its external mouthpiece" (171).

He waxes poetically on the compassion and social justice action of Christ—what was missing in Wilde's own martyrdom by Christians. Christ's theology of love is what they should have governed with: "His morality is all sympathy, just what morality should be. . . . His justice is all poetical justice, exactly what justice should be" (176).

Wilde goes on to theorize evil in terms of human action and free will. He follows a theology that requires redemption and compassion: "Christ, through some divine instinct in him, seems to have always loved the sinner as being the nearest possible approach to the perfection of man. . . . He regarded sin and suffering as being in themselves beautiful holy things and modes of perfection" (178). This is not the decadent exoticization of transgression; rather, it is its validation in the service of greater love. "The moment of repentance is the moment of initiation" (179). What "queers" this Christian theology—beside the fact that Wilde, that unlikeliest of theologians, is speaking it—is that it is written in a letter to his former lover. The love of God, the love of Christ, is deeply contrasted with Douglas's inability to love well enough. His human love fails; his art fails. Christ as artist can never fail, nor can his love. Like the portrait or the beautiful male body in *Dorian Gray*, Christ is transformative: "He is just like a work of art. He does not really teach one anything, but by being brought into his presence one becomes something" (179). Christ's influence is always good, unlike some other men's—which can be evil insofar as they are so lost in immanence that they miss transcendence.

Oscar Wilde is a peculiar figure to call a theologian of good and evil. His life and works dramatize the danger of transgression even as they celebrate the pleasure of forbidden fruit. For Wilde, art is always a good. Whether it is Christ or homoerotic influence, anything that leads from life to art will be a good, and anything that detracts from truth—and beauty—will be an evil. This essay has sought to provide a systematic overview of Wilde's thought about good and evil in relation to his artistic theory, offering just a few textual demonstrations of that vision, which could be called theological. This essay has also attempted both to indicate Wilde's significance for queer approaches to scholarly analyses of texts and to show by example what such a reading might look like. It is now up to the reader to examine Wilde's many works with these tools in mind.

Works Cited

Douglas, Alfred. "Two Loves." *Poets.org*. Academy of American Poets, n.d. Web. 2 Aug. 2011.

Gilbert, W. S., and Arthur Sullivan. *Patience; or, Bunthorne's Bride*. New York: Schirmer, 1986.

Huysmans, Joris-Karl. *Against Nature (À Rebours)*. Trans. Robert Baldick. New York: Penguin, 2003.

Hyde, H. Montgomery. *The Trials of Oscar Wilde*. New York: Dover, 1962.

Pater, Walter. *The Renaissance: Studies in Art and Poetry*. Ed. Donald L. Hill. Berkeley: U of California P, 1980.

Plato. *Symposium*. Trans. Robin Waterfield. New York: Oxford UP, 2009.

Sedgwick, Eve Kosofsky. *Between Men: English Literature and Male Homosocial Desire*. New York: Columbia UP, 1985.

_____. *Epistemology of the Closet*. Berkeley: U of California P, 1990.

Wilde, Oscar. "The Critic as Artist." *The Soul of Man under Socialism and Selected Critical Prose*. Ed. Linda Dowling. New York: Penguin, 2001. 213–79.

_____. "The Decay of Lying." *The Soul of Man under Socialism and Selected Critical Prose*. Ed. Linda Dowling. New York: Penguin, 2001. 163–92.

_____. *De Profundis and Other Writings*. Ed. Hesketh Pearson. New York: Penguin, 1986.

_____. *The Importance of Being Earnest and Other Plays*. Ed. Peter Raby. New York: Oxford UP, 2008.

_____. *The Picture of Dorian Gray*. Ed. Joseph Bristow. New York: Oxford UP, 2008.

_____. "The Portrait of Mr. W. H." *The Soul of Man under Socialism and Selected Critical Prose*. Ed. Linda Dowling. New York: Penguin, 2001. 31–102.

_____. "The Soul of Man under Socialism." *The Soul of Man under Socialism and Selected Critical Prose*. Ed. Linda Dowling. New York: Penguin, 2001. 125–60.

CRITICAL READINGS

Bonds, Needs, and Morals in *King Lear*

Gregory Kneidel

In a 1999 essay published in the *New York Times Magazine*, the controversial Australian philosopher Peter Singer outlines what he calls the "Singer Solution to World Poverty." He begins the essay by posing the following ethical dilemma.[1] Bob invests all of his net worth in a fancy but uninsurable Italian sports car, a Bugatti. One day he parks the Bugatti in a train yard and goes out for a stroll. After a time he is horrified to see a runaway train barreling toward a small child playing on the tracks in the distance. As luck would have it, Bob is immediately able to locate a railway switch: he can divert the train from the child's path, but in doing so he would put the train on a track leading directly toward his Bugatti. Bob's choice: save the car or the child?

Now, even the most callous of us would not allow a child to be killed in order to save a car, even a Bugatti. But Singer goes on to argue that that is, in effect, what we do every time we spend money on luxuries beyond life's most basic necessities—when, for example, we eat at expensive restaurants instead of more frugally at home or when we hit the mall for the latest fashions instead of making do with what is already in our closets. Any money we spend beyond basic necessities (which Singer estimated at the time to cost approximately $30,000 per household per year) could and should instead be donated to charity in order to save the lives of malnourished children around the world. "The formula," Singer explains, "is simple: whatever money you're spending on luxuries, not necessities, should be given away." He concludes:

> Evolutionary psychologists tell us that human nature just isn't sufficiently altruistic to make it plausible that many people will sacrifice so much for strangers. . . . If it is the case that we ought to do things that, predictably, most of us won't do, then let's face that fact head-on. Then, if we value the life of a child more than going to fancy restaurants, the next time we

---

dine out we will know that we could have done something better with our money. If that makes living a morally decent life extremely arduous, well, then that is the way things are.

There are numerous possible objections to the Singer Solution: employees at fancy restaurants and expensive clothing stores might, for example, begin to wonder where *their* next meals are supposed to come from. But it neatly encapsulates two interrelated moral problems that will be the subjects of this essay: How do we measure our obligations to others? And how then do we value their lives over our luxuries? These questions are posed by William Shakespeare's great study of just how arduous it is to live a morally decent life, how hard it is to do what is good and avoid what is evil—*King Lear*.

"According to my bond, no more nor less."

To approach the two problems posed by the Singer Solution, I will focus on two word groups in *King Lear*: the language of bonds and the language of needs. Singer stipulates that the child on the train track is a stranger because Bob's decision might be prejudiced by any kind of prior connection he has had with the child. It would make a difference, for example, if the child was a relative, a member of his church, or even someone who had done him a small kindness (maybe Bob was lost and the child gave him directions to the train yard). In *King Lear*, this connection would be called a bond. This term comes to the fore early in the play with Cordelia's famous answer to the question posed by Lear as he, intent on transferring "all cares and business" from himself to "younger strengths" (1.1.38–39), divides his kingdom between his three daughters. "What," Lear asks, "can you [Cordelia] say to draw / A third more opulent than your sisters?" (1.1.85–86). After twice answering bluntly "nothing" (1.1.87, 89), Cordelia is commanded to speak once again, and so she explains:

Unhappy that I am, I cannot heave
My heart into my mouth. I love your majesty
According to my bond, no more nor less. (1.1.91–93)

Traditional readings of the play praise Cordelia's response as honest, heartfelt, and virtuous, and so it may seem when compared to (what seems to be) the overblown flattery of her two older sisters, Goneril and Regan, whose viciousness then animates much of the rest of play. But it is also not difficult to see something legalistic, something a little overprecise about Cordelia's "According to my bond, no more nor less." The inappropriateness or perhaps even calculated offensiveness of Cordelia's response is especially evident if we understand the first scene as a ritual with a predetermined outcome (the map of the divided kingdom seems to have already been drawn [1.1.3–7]) rather than a contest or trial of true love with the end result really in doubt.

At the very least, we should wonder what exactly is this "bond" that she should value so precisely. This important term and its various synonyms recur throughout the play; the magnificent first scene alone gives us "business," "charge," "duty," "care," and "allegiance." These terms describe the quality, origin, and durability of the ties that bind us together as a society and that subsequently shape our conduct toward others. In *King Lear* such bonds vary according to the several different kinds of relationships the characters share either within families (parent and child, siblings, spouses, relatives), within social or political units (subject and king, servant and master, guest and host, recipient and donor, countrymen, citizens, friends), or, in the play's harrowing storm scenes, in a state of nature seemingly outside of or beyond any of these. These different kinds of bonds imply different kinds of obligations, and, because more than one bond can exist between two individuals, it is sometimes necessary to distinguish between them. Like Goneril and Regan, Cordelia vacillates throughout the play between treating her bond to Lear as a familial one (father and daughter) and a political one (king and subject, as suggested by her use of the term "majesty").

Crucially, these different types of bonds and their different origins were, in Shakespeare's time more so than our own, assumed to form concentric circles radiating outward from the smallest basic social unit, the family, to include ultimately the whole human race. In between the smallest but strongest circle (the family) and the largest but weakest circle (the human race) were any number of intermediary kinds of affiliations (extended family, city, country, church, etc.). This theory of concentric bonds is articulated most influentially in Cicero's *De officiis* (On duties), which scholar Stephen Greenblatt has called the "treatise on the ethics of authority that was most esteemed in Shakespeare's time" (24). In it, Cicero catalogs and ranks the various kinds of bonds that hold human society together (Cicero uses the terms *vinculum*, a chain, rope, or fetter, and *obligatio*, from the root verb *ligo*, to tie or bind, like a ligament). These bonds or degrees of association range in Cicero's analysis from the most general—the ties of reason and speech that link humans together as a species—to the bonds of nationhood, citizenship, and various degrees of extended and biological family relations (Cicero 1.53–60). Cicero downplays biology and heredity (i.e., blood ties) because of the importance of adoption among the Roman elite. But blood ties within families and the natural bond between parents and children were emphasized by (to name only a few sources linked by scholars to *King Lear*) Plutarch's essay "On Affection for Offspring" and Michel de Montaigne's essay "Of the Affection of Parents to Their Children," legal principles and customary practices that prescribed the mutual duties of parents to children, and innumerable sermons, catechisms, and other religious works expounding the biblical commandments to honor, love, and obey parents. Indeed, as critic Judy Kronenfeld has convincingly demonstrated, the common Christian tradition in which *King Lear* was written and first performed served primarily to intensify Cicero's essentially ethical scheme. That is, this Christian tradition took Cicero's exposition of the ties that bind society together and enhanced it with Christian concepts (e.g., charity, church community) but left it structurally unaltered, effectively sanctifying the concentric spheres in which Christians found themselves bound to their families, friends, neighbors, masters, and countrymen.[2]

King Lear also examines the origins and limits of these various sorts of bonds: are they natural (instinctive and universal), legal (human-made and culturally specific), or divine (sacred and unbreakable)? The importance of these categories is made evident in the play's second scene. The scene begins with Edmund's scintillating "stand up for bastards!" soliloquy, which opens with a vow: "Thou, Nature, art my goddess; to thy law / My services are bound" (1.2.1–2). Here Edmund brazenly combines the three categories—the natural, the legal, and the divine—into one, personified by the law-issuing goddess Nature, whom he vows to serve in a boundlessly self-interested and appetitive way ("I grow, I prosper" [1.2.21]). Edmund then deceives his father, Gloucester, into thinking that Edgar, his half-brother and Gloucester's legitimate heir, has begun "to find an idle and fond bondage in the oppression of aged tyranny" (1.2.49–50). The implicit threat of patricide, phrased pointedly in the intensified language of "bondage," is made all the more troubling because it combines (conventionally) the familial with the political, so that the elderly father becomes the figure of the cruel tyrant and the murdering son becomes the figure of the justified rebel. (Emphasizing divine rather than legal authority, Edmund will later insist that the "revenging gods" themselves protect the "manifold and strong . . . bond" with which "the child [is] bound to the father" [2.1.45–48].) For his part, Gloucester is perfectly content to view the bonds that hold together human society as nested in each other, derived from similar sources, and consequently threatened by the same forces:

> These late eclipses in the sun and moon
> portend no good to us. Though the wisdom of Nature
> can reason it thus and thus, yet nature finds itself
> scourged by the sequent effects. Love cools, friendship

falls off, brothers divide: in cities, mutinies; in
countries, discord; in palaces, treason; and the *bond*
cracked 'twixt son and father. . . .
We have seen the best of our time.
(1.2.103–12; emphasis added)

Conservative readings of *King Lear* echo Gloucester's view of the in-
terconnectedness of these different bonds: the good friend is the good
brother is the good citizen is the good countryman is the good servant
is the good son. And such a well-bound person is compelled to ob-
servant dutifulness not just by natural instinct or legal obligation but
by divine influence as well (according to Gloucester's astrological notions, the eclipse is evidence of the lapse of all three). Tragedy ensues
when what Lear calls "the offices of nature, bond of childhood, / Effects of courtesy, dues of gratitude" (2.2.367–68) are not just violated
or broken but separated or distinguished from one another. To separate or distinguish between these bonds—to assert, for example, that
a rebellious daughter can still be a loyal citizen or that an upstanding
Christian can disobey his household master—is to invite social chaos.
Radical readings of the play, however, argue the contrary: *King Lear*
demonstrates the moral hazards of insisting that the various bonds
holding together human society are always mutually reinforcing and
so very nearly self-identical. In doing so, the play stands at the cusp of
the Western modern liberal tradition, where the bonds enumerated by
Cicero and Gloucester are still powerfully felt but no longer felt to be
concentric and mutually reinforcing.

Such a radical possibility—not only the possibility of breaking the
bonds that hold society together but also the possibility of unbundling
those different types of bonds—is best illustrated in the gruesome
scene in which Gloucester is blinded. Shakespeare often dramatizes
his play's key thematic terms in unexpectedly provocative scenes
(consider, for example, the mad-made-maid-madam language in and
around the imprisoning of the "mad" Malvolio in *Twelfth Night* or the

plots-plotting language and the wedding masque of *The Tempest*). The blinding of Gloucester might be considered such a scene in the context of the play's language of bonds. Indeed, although it is usually linked to *King Lear*'s thematic language of physical sight and moral insight, the scene might even be labeled the binding of Gloucester. Before brutally gouging out both of Gloucester's eyes ("Out, vile jelly, / Where is thy luster now?" [3.7.82–83]), the sadistic Cornwall first bids his servants three times to bind Gloucester to a chair: "Bind fast his corky arms" (3.7.29); "Bind him, I say" (31); and "To this chair bind him" (34). The fact that Cornwall must issue the command three times suggests that his own servants are already, at the scene's very onset, reluctant to follow his orders. To put it another way, their bond of obedient service to Cornwall conflicts with a stronger bond (never explicitly classified) to the helpless Gloucester. Scholar Richard Strier has rightly put this scene—with its juxtaposition of bonds that might be called political (Gloucester is charged with treason), familial (Gloucester learns of Edmund's treachery), legal (the servants must by law obey their master, Cornwall), and social (Cornwall is technically Gloucester's guest)—at the epicenter of the play's study of "the kinds of situation in which resistance to legally constituted authority becomes a moral necessity, and in which neutrality is not a viable possibility" (104). The heroic and active resistance of Cornwall's own unnamed servant—

> Hold your hand, my lord.
> I have served you ever since I was a child,
> But better service have I never done you
> Than now to bid you hold. (Shakespeare 3.7.71–74)

—ironically rephrases the language of bondedness to emphasize restraint instead of aggression ("hold . . . hold"). This moment can count as politically radical precisely because the servant separates one bond, his legal bond to obey his master, from another, his moral duty to protect Gloucester from Cornwall's cruelty even though Gloucester's innocence at this point is far from clear (as Strier observes, the scene would have a much different effect if Gloucester's own servant, and not Cornwall's, had intervened). In short, the servant privileges one kind of bond over the other. As such, the scene dramatizes the unbundling of the various natural, legal, and religious bonds that hold together the world of *King Lear*.

"O, reason not the need"

A common critical approach to *King Lear* is to place the story of Gloucester and his sons next to that of Lear and his daughters. One way of doing that—to see how Lear ends up just where Gloucester does after his binding and blinding—is to return briefly to Cicero's *De officiis*. In an essay on Cicero's problematic influence on the Western human rights tradition, philosopher Martha C. Nussbaum explains that *De officiis* distinguishes between duties of justice (*justitia*) and duties of material aid (*benivolentia*, or what in a Christian context has come to be called charity [see Nussbaum 181–87]). Cicero has a strong sense of *justitia*. Duties of justice require our honorable conduct with others regardless of the strength of the bonds between us: we are, for example, required to keep promises to our enemies even in times of war. To return briefly to Singer's dilemma, it may seem, as a duty of justice, that we should choose to save the child whether or not he or she is a relative, a fellow citizen, or a coreligionist. But Cicero stands prominently in a long tradition that maintains that duties of material aid—duties that may require us to surrender or sacrifice something that is ours, such as Bob's Bugatti, to our own potential detriment—are different because they *are* potentially limited. As Nussbaum puts it, "Cicero proposes a flexible account that recognizes many criteria as pertinent to duties of aid: gratitude, need and dependency, thick association—but which also preserves a role for flexible judgment in adjudicating the claims when they might conflict" (187). Such criteria must "be taken into consideration in every act of moral duty" (Cicero 1.59), and so Cicero insists that we must "become good calculators of duty [*boni ratiocinatores officiorum*], able by adding and subtracting [*addendo deducendoque*] to strike a balance correctly and find out just how much is due to each individual." In this regard, Cordelia seems to have read (or misread) her Cicero. She might say that we should offer material aid to others according to our duty, "no more nor less."

Nussbaum condemns Cicero for establishing what she takes to be a false distinction between duties of justice and duties of material aid (justice, she notes, costs money too), and her critique helps us see the connection between bonds and needs in *King Lear*. The terms are nearly synonymous: to say "I am bound to" is *just about* the same as saying "I need to." Both verbs convey a sense of compulsion to act, one from duty, the other from necessity. In *King Lear*, "necessity" sometimes comes close to meaning fate, as when Edmund mocks his father's astrological habit and tendency to blame his failings on the movement of the stars: "This is the excellent foppery of the world, that when we are sick in fortune, often the surfeits of our own behavior, we make guilty of our disasters the sun, the moon and the stars, as if we were villains on necessity" (1.2.118–22). To claim to be a villain "on necessity" is to deny having had any choice about or any responsibility for doing something evil. But *King Lear* is a play filled with the language of all and nothing, of more and less, and in this sense "need" and "necessity" can be best thought of as antonyms of excess, surplus, and luxury, concepts designating *more* than the bare minimum, *more* than the basic necessities.

The opposition between need and luxury in *King Lear* begins with a burst of legal fast-talk that Lear interjects, much to the surprise of Goneril, Regan, and their respective husbands, at just the moment he seems to divest himself of his royal authority:

> I do invest you jointly with my power,
> Pre-eminence and all the large effects
> That troop with majesty. Ourself by monthly course,
> With reservation of an hundred knights
> By you to be sustained, shall our abode

> Make with you by due turn; only we shall retain
>
> The name, and all th'addition to a king: the sway,
>
> Revenue, execution of the rest,
>
> Beloved sons, be yours . . . (1.1.131–39)

Lear separates the "power," "pre-eminence," and "large effects" of "majesty," which he gives away here, from his retinue of one hundred knights and the "name, and all th'addition to a king," which he expects to retain at his daughters' shared expense. The term "addition" is usually glossed as honors, distinctions, or titles (cf. *OED* s.v. "addition" 4–5; see also 2.2.23 and 5.3.69). Though he no longer wields his royal power, Lear still wants some royal pomp. But, although Lear initially distinguished his "addition" from his knights, those knights come effectively to symbolize his "addition" as the play proceeds.

It is the loss of his knights, of his "addition," that prompts Lear's great "O, reason not the need" speech in a scene that, like the blinding of Gloucester and the language of bonds, dramatizes the play's focus on the language of needing. Leading up to this scene, Lear and his knights wear out their welcome in Goneril's castle because of their riotous behavior; she asks Lear to "disquantity" his "train" a little (1.4.240). Rather than do that, Lear takes the knights to Regan's castle. Regan too balks at the obligation to sustain Lear and his hundred knights. Lear starts to play one daughter's best offer off of the other's, but when Goneril appears on the scene, she and Regan collude together, and Lear's bargaining power vanishes. Desperate, Lear decides to accept Goneril's initial offer to house fifty knights, as that is "double" Regan's twenty-five (and so Goneril's love must be "twice" Regan's). But Goneril insists that the offer no longer stands. She interjects,

> Hear me, my lord:
>
> What need you five and twenty? Ten? Or five?
>
> To follow in a house where twice so many
>
> Have a command to tend you?" (2.2.449–52)

When Regan chimes in with "What need one?" (452), Lear bursts out in anger:

> O, reason not the need! Our basest beggars
> Are in the poorest things superfluous;
> Allow not nature more than nature needs,
> Man's life is cheap as beast's. Thou art a lady;
> If only to go warm were gorgeous,
> Why, nature needs not what thou gorgeous wear'st,
> Which scarcely keeps thee warm. But for true need—
> You heavens, give me that patience, patience I need!
> (453–60)

The crux of Lear's argument initially is that his knights are analogous to Goneril's and Regan's "gorgeous" clothing: just as their "gorgeous" clothing is, strictly speaking, unnecessary (because it "scarcely" does what clothing is supposed to do, keep them warm), Lear's knights are unnecessary. And yet Goneril and Regan are apparently no more eager to give up their gorgeous clothing than Lear is to give up his knights. Shakespeare does not give any clear indications that Goneril and Regan are particularly interested in clothing; this motif seems to have been left over from one of Shakespeare's immediate sources, *The True Chronicle History of King Leir and His Three Daughters, Gonorill, Ragan, and Cordella*, a play published anonymously in 1605. In this play, it is Gonorill who voices sentiments closest to those of Lear's "O, reason not the need" speech. Speaking to her steward Skalliger (a sort of Oswald figure), she complains that her grumpy father criticizes her spending habits. This King Leir especially condemns the amount of money she wastes on clothing and food:

> I cannot make me a new fashioned gowne,
> And set it forth with more then common cost;
> But his old doting doltish withered wit,

Is sure to giue a sencelesse check for it.
I cannot make a banquet extraordinary,
To grace my selfe, and spread my name abroad,
But he, old foole, is captious by and by,
And sayth, the cost would well suffice for twice.
(1.9.782–89)

Here it is Gonorill who is the apologist for excess, for gowns of "more then common cost" and "extraordinary" banquets. She is angry at her father for complaining about her spending and at her sister for not sharing the expense of maintaining him and his knights. For his part, Leir thinks she is spending too much and not getting enough for her money.

Shakespeare seems to have chosen to transfer this apology for excess from Gonorill to Lear. But to what effect? In *King Leir*, Gonorill's speech seems designed to characterize her, in a traditionally sexist way, as given over to the vices of vanity and pride. She is an ungrateful brat. In *King Lear*, by contrast, Lear's speech seems designed, by him at least, to articulate something essential about human nature and human ethics. Lear, in other words, represents himself as a representative of humankind. His needs are human needs, never mind that the "basest beggars" might balk at the notion that Lear, who up until quite recently has been the richest person in the kingdom and still lives well, should speak for them. This is a key interpretive question for the play. Are we to agree with Lear that if the standard for our moral decision making is mere necessity (basic food, clothing, shelter—the things that Singer says cost about $30,000 per household per year), then "Man's life is [as] cheap as [a] beast's" and we are, in effect, no better than the animals? If so, Lear's point is that what makes a human life more valuable, more excellent than a beast's, is that we demand something extra, some strictly unnecessary "addition" in our lives (the occasional dinner out, a new sweater, perhaps even a Bugatti). Or are we to think that Lear's perspective is unrepresentive, that an old and angry king cannot be our best guide to good and evil, that the fact that Lear so confidently speaks for "Man" in general may, in fact, be evidence of mental infirmity? If so, then Lear's prayer—"You heavens, give me that patience, patience I need!"—ironically redefines necessity (first he needed knights, now he needs patience) and also signals not heroic suffering but indulgent self-delusion, perhaps even madness.

"And each man have enough"

After refusing to reason his need, Lear abandons his daughters and ventures out onto the heath at the height of a storm. Gloucester, unbound and likewise expelled from the security of human society, makes his way toward Dover. Again, their journeys track each other, and at the height of their misery, they are, curiously, made to voice their concerns for the suffering of the weak and powerless. At one point during the storm, exposed to the elements and temporarily declining the aid offered to him by Kent and the Fool and the protection offered by the hovel, Lear kneels down and prays:

> Poor naked wretches, wheresoe'er you are,
> That bide the pelting of this pitiless storm,
> How shall your houseless heads and unfed sides,
> Your looped and windowed raggedness, defend you
> From seasons such as these? O, I have ta'en
> Too little care of this. Take physic, pomp,
> Expose thyself to feel what wretches feel,
> That thou mayst shake the superflux to them
> And show the heavens more just. (3.4.28–36)

This is Lear's version of the Singer Solution. He recognizes the suffering of "poor naked wretches" who endure the storm without shelter, food, or clothing. Still feeling a bit kingly, perhaps, he regrets that he has "ta'en / Too little care" of them. "Take physic" means submit to medical treatment, usually some kind of harsh purging; "pomp" means something like luxury, indulgence, or "addition." This "pomp" or "superflux" (a noun related to our adjective "superfluous," meaning extra or additional) should be treated and "shake[n]" to the "wretches" so that the heavens appear "more just." Soon after this Lear lends his clothing (he even calls them "lendings") to a beggar, Poor Tom. A few scenes later, we find Poor Tom (who is, of course, really Edgar in disguise) with his father, Gloucester, on the road to Dover. Like Lear, Gloucester will offer Poor Tom material aid (a valuable jewel [4.6.27–29]), an offer that seems to be explained in a way that anticipates the Singer Solution:

> Let the superfluous and lust-dieted man
> That slaves your ordinance, that will not see
> Because he does not feel, feel your power quickly:
> So distribution should undo excess
> And each man have enough. (4.1.70–74)

After their downfalls, then, both Lear and Gloucester condemn excess as evil. It is evil specifically because "each man [should] have enough," even if that means a fundamental redistribution of society's wealth.

For both Lear and Gloucester, the new concept in their moral thinking is not to see good and evil but to feel them instead: "Expose thyself to feel what wretches feel"; "Because he does not feel, feel you power quickly." Lear, one might say, has learned not to reason need but to feel it instead. In Cicero, by contrast, feeling is discounted. In *De officiis*, for example, Cicero argues that "when things turn out for our own good or ill, we realize it more fully and feel [*sentimus*] it more deeply than when the same things happen to others and we see them only, as it were, in the far distance; and for this reason we judge their case differently from our own" (1.30). For Cicero, this feeling of personal involvement in a choice leads to uncertainty, and the best rule when faced with uncertainty is not to act. Consequently, Shakespeare critics have argued that the new morality voiced here by Lear and

Gloucester is an infusion of Christian ethics into a pagan play (the issue is very thorny: the historical Lear lived before Christianity came to what is now England and the Christian god is not mentioned in the play, but *King Lear*, of course, was written by a Christian playwright for a Christian audience). In fact, against critics who see these calls for wealth redistribution rooted in more socially radical or heterorthodox versions of post-Reformation Christianity, critic Debora Shuger has argued that the phrasing of Lear's and Gloucester's speeches is borrowed from traditional medieval church law concerning the "basic obligations of the rich towards the poor," at least in times of "extreme necessity" (note that word "necessity" again). Thus, according to Shuger, Lear and Gloucester both are made to feel momentarily "the nature of Christian *caritas* [charity]" (53).

Still, whether it is based in radical or traditional Christian values, does *King Lear* offer something approximating the "Shakespeare Solution to World Poverty"? We have seen that as part of his examination of the language of bonds and needs, Shakespeare at least makes two of his protagonists articulate something similar to Singer's proposal during their direst moments of crisis. But it is hard to say that this is the solution that Shakespeare proposes. In the play's final act, things do not get better for Lear or Gloucester or for those around them; most of the characters die. Rather than witness the systematic redistribution of wealth throughout Lear's kingdom, we watch Albany and Edgar (the lawful heir who ironically receives most of the offered charity) contemplate the future government on a stage strewn with corpses. Unlike traditional Christian productions of the play, which stress (or invent) Lear's and Gloucester's spiritual rebirths just prior to their physical deaths, more recent and decidedly more pessimistic versions of the play emphasize the meaninglessness of their suffering and, by implication at least, the impossibility of realizing their newly formed understanding of good and evil. Thus, perhaps the best that can be said about the play is that Shakespeare's point is what Singer notes when he reluctantly admits that most people will both agree with his moral standards and disregard his proposed solution: "If we don't [embrace his solution], then we should at least know that we are failing to live a morally decent life—not because it is good to wallow in guilt but because knowing where we should be going is the first step toward heading in that direction."

Notes

1. I have simplified Singer's example, which is itself a simplified version of a case presented in Unger, 135–39.
2. This essay is in some ways a distillation and in others an expansion of Kronenfeld's fine book.

Works Cited

Cicero. *De officiis.* Trans. Walter Miller. Cambridge: Harvard UP, 1913.

Greenblatt, Stephen. "Images of Power in Shakespeare." *Bulletin of the American Academy of Arts and Sciences* 58.4 (2005): 22–25.

Kronenfeld, Judy. King Lear *and the Naked Truth: Rethinking the Language of Religion and Resistance.* Durham: Duke UP, 1998.

Nussbaum, Martha C. "Duties of Justice, Duties of Material Aid: Cicero's Problematic Legacy." *Journal of Political Philosophy* 8.2 (2000): 176–206.

Shakespeare, William. *King Lear.* Ed. R. A. Foakes. London: Thomson, 2005.

Shuger, Debora K. "Subversive Fathers and Suffering Subjects: Shakespeare and Christianity." *Religion, Literature, and Politics in Post-Reformation England, 1540–1688.* Ed. Donna B. Hamilton and Richard Strier. Cambridge: Cambridge UP, 1996. 46–69.

Singer, Peter. "The Singer Solution to World Poverty." *New York Times Magazine* 5 Sept. 1999. Web. 21 June 2011.

Strier, Richard. "Faithful Servants: Shakespeare's Praise of Disobedience." *The Historical Renaissance: New Essays on Tudor and Stuart Literature and Culture.* Ed. Heather Dubrow and Strier. Chicago: U of Chicago P, 1988. 104–33.

The True Chronicle History of King Leir and His Three Daughters, Gonorill, Ragan, and Cordella. London, 1605.

Unger, Peter. *Living High and Letting Die.* Oxford: Oxford UP, 1996.

John Milton's *Paradise Lost* and the Problem of Evil _____

Mitchell M. Harris

John Milton's poem *Paradise Lost* (1667) begins with the common epic convention of the invocation of the Muse. Attempting to distinguish his epic from the great epics of classical literature (such as those by Homer and Virgil), Milton invokes a specific "heav'nly Muse" to aid his

> advent'rous song,
> That with no middle flight intends to soar
> Above th' Aonian mount, while it pursues
> Things unattempted in prose or rhyme. (1.6, 13–16)

These lines display a certain boastfulness on Milton's behalf. The reference to "th' Aonian mount" slights Homer and Virgil of their accomplishments; the *Iliad*, *Odyssey*, and *Aeneid* are relics of a pagan past and thus, in Milton's opinion, the products of misguided and false religious beliefs. Pursuing "things unattempted in prose or rhyme," Milton intends to recount a Christian explanation for humankind's loss of its Edenic roots:

> Of man's first disobedience, and the fruit
> Of that forbidden tree, whose mortal taste
> Brought death into the world, and all our woe,
> With loss of Eden. (1.1–4)

Thus, within his first sentence, a full twenty-six lines of verse, Milton marks his epic as a clearly religious and specifically Christian enterprise. What is particularly compelling about Milton's invocation, then, is its distinct Christian posture: by its end, there is no mistaking that Milton envisions it as a prayer.

And chiefly thou, O Spirit, that dost prefer
Before all temples th' upright heart and pure,
Instruct me, for thou know'st; thou from the first
Wast present, and with mighty wings outspread
Dove-like sat'st brooding on the vast abyss
And mad'st it pregnant: what in me is dark
Illumine, what is low raise and support,
That to the highth of this great argument
I may assert eternal providence,
And justify the ways of God to men. (1.17–26)

The last line of this invocation/prayer has been a repeated site of critical interest for Milton scholars, as the suggestion that Milton intends to "justify the ways of God to men" establishes the poem as an exercise in what theologians term the "theodicy." A theodicy, in the Western Christian tradition, is a philosophical and theological study that asks how, if God is omnipotent (all-powerful), omniscient (all-knowing), and omnibenevolent (all-good), one can make sense of the existence of evil. Milton's *Paradise Lost* engages the fundamental questions of the theodicy by turning to the Genesis account of Adam and Eve and the creation and fall of humankind as its motivating source of epic imagining. By retelling the Edenic myth from a poetic perspective, however, Milton's *Paradise Lost* is free to grapple uniquely with the question of God's goodness—and hence the problem of evil—in ways both unfamiliar and untraditional to theologians and philosophers. This essay will examine how previous scholarship has attempted to make sense of Milton's *Paradise Lost* as a theodicy—as a poem that encounters the problem of evil.

Paradise Lost and the Theodicy

While the term "theodicy," deriving from the Greek *theos* (god) and *dike* (justice), entered the English language through philosopher Gottfried Wilhelm Leibniz's *Theodicée* (1710) a number of years after Milton's death, literary critic Dennis Danielson suggests that the concept of the theodicy "is virtually synonymous" with Milton's phrase "to justify the ways of God" (2). Indeed, in his lengthy study of *Paradise Lost* as an exercise in theodicy, *Milton's Good God*, Danielson argues summarily that "Milton believed that such elemental questions about genesis and meaning could not be answered without reference to the God from whom, in whom, and to whom are all things. And they could not be answered in a way supportive of faith, hope, or love unless that God were believed to be a good God" (228–29). Thus, the theodicy itself seems to operate via circular logic—that is, the theodicy begins from a point of affirming God's goodness and returns to that very same point after asking its three key questions; "the goodness of God is a foundation, and in this sense theodicy's conclusion is also its starting point" (229). Nonetheless, Danielson also is quick to point out that despite its circular reasoning, Milton's account of God's goodness does not lead "nowhere." Rather, "it led Milton through profound depths of thought and meaning to incomparable spiritual and poetic heights" (229).

Such "spiritual and poetic heights" are recognized with regard to Milton's God in book 3 of *Paradise Lost*, in which he appears as a literary character—an epic protagonist. Milton, however, mostly avoids direct physical descriptions of God, instead focusing on his attributes, and it is by focusing on his attributes that Milton is able to speak theologically through his poem. For example, Milton almost immediately notes that God is omniscient, thus defending one of his fundamental attributes in the project of theodicy. Milton defends the notion of God's omniscience by focusing mostly upon his ability to see the future (God's ability to *foreknow*). Milton asserts this position while God sits enthroned in heaven, surrounded by the angels and his "Son": "Him [Satan] God beholding from his prospect high, / Wherein *past, present, future he beholds*, / Thus to his only Son *foreseeing* spake" (3.77–79; emphasis added). In this scene, God witnesses Satan wandering the earth, and he realizes that Satan will ultimately lead Adam and Eve to fall from obedience. God *knows* that they will eat the forbidden fruit of the Tree of Knowledge. "For man will hearken to his glozing lies," he tells the Son (93).

As a result, God's omniscience (or "foreknowledge") seems as if it could implicate him in the creation of evil, raising some very important questions: if God foreknows that Adam and Eve will "hearken" to Satan's "glozing lies," why doesn't he simply stop Satan in his tracks and return him to hell? By allowing them to attend to those lies, isn't God complicit in the creation of evil on earth? Milton anticipates these very questions, so he poetically renders an answer by asserting the existence and action of human free will. As God tells the Son,

> so will fall
> He [Adam] and his faithless progeny: whose fault?
> Whose but his own? Ingrate, he had of me
> All he could have; I made him just and right,
> Sufficient to stood, though *free to fall*.
> (95–99; emphasis added)

While the concept of free will may seem quite conventional today, it was a point of theological controversy dating as far back as Saint Augustine's interactions with the Pelagians, a group of fifth-century Christians (ultimately declared heretics) who followed their leader, Pelagius, in believing that original sin did not infect humankind (Adam was merely a bad example to humankind) and that the human will alone could desire and attain the highest forms of virtue (God's grace through Christ's Atonement of the Cross was thus unnecessary). The issue of free will returned to the fore at the onset of the Reformation when Martin Luther famously accused the Roman Catholic Church of maintaining the Pelagian heresy by defending the freedom of the human will. His opponent in his theological debates was none other than Desiderius Erasmus, the famous humanist philosopher, theologian, and author. Luther's anti-Pelagian (or, more appropriately, "necessitarian" position) was ultimately upheld by John Calvin, the French Reformer. Calvin argues in book 3 of the *Institutes of the Christian Religion* (1536) that "God not only foresaw the fall of the first man, and in him the ruin of his posterity; but also at his own pleasure arranged it" (3.23.7). Calvin believed that one could not assert that God's arrangement of the fall was evil because humankind does not have the ability to see such acts from God's perspective. Thus, according to Calvin, humans do not possess the fundamental ability to declare what is just or unjust in God's eyes.

Calvin's position on God's role in the fall of humankind is quite different from Milton's in that Calvin does not flinch at the idea of God predestining the fall. Thus, while Milton traditionally was linked to Puritanism (and its Calvinist theology), his discussion of free will aligns him more closely to Arminianism, a continental Reform movement named after its founder, Jacobus Arminius. Arminius studied in Geneva under the tutelage of Theodore Beza, Calvin's immediate successor (Danielson 70). As Danielson argues, "Arminius's ideas seem to have developed in the first place primarily out of an attempt to bring Reformed theology into line with the requirements of theodicy" (71). Instead of suggesting that some individuals were predestined to hell, as Calvin did, Arminius believed that God provided a regenerative grace to *all* human beings that allowed them to incline their wills to God's ultimate grace. Thus, in Arminius's view, even those who ultimately reject God's grace, the "non-Elect," receive a form of grace. The poetic expression of this Arminian position occurs when Milton's God tells the Son that the fallen

> trespass, authors to themselves in all
> Both what they judge and what they choose; for so
> I formed them free, and free they must remain,
> Till they enthrall themselves: I else must change
> Their nature, and revoke the high decree
> Unchangeable, eternal, which ordained
> Their freedom; they themselves ordained their fall. (3.122–28)

For Milton, God provides the grace necessary to resist all temptation, including the first transgression that leads to Adam and Eve's demise. So while God foresees their fall, he does not cause them to fall. Rather, they fall of their own accord. Thus, God remains omnibenevolent because he neither desires for humankind to fall nor takes pleasure in such a fall.

If free will justifies God's omniscience and omnibenevolence, at least in Milton's eyes, then what does it say about God's power? Augustine, Luther, and Calvin were suspicious of the concept of free will because it seemed to place limits on God's power. The argument might be put this way: if a person can act according to his or her own volition, then God cannot be all-powerful because human actions (as free actions) are outside of his control; hence, God's power is limited. Such a line of reasoning was one that Milton took as a serious threat to the theodicy. In fact, in his theological treatise *De doctrina christiana* (On Christian doctrine; first published 1825), Milton rebukes such logic by pointing out that God is "supremely kind" (1152) and that God's kindness is made manifest when he shows "the glory of his mercy, grace and wisdom" (1162). In other words, Milton argues that God's power is entirely directed to his mercy and grace, which is to say his omnibenevolence: "He made the salvation of man the goal and end, as it were, of his purpose" (1162). Thus, what might look like a loss of power (permitting humans to have and express free will) is simply God's own willful expression of his power; God directs his power to his ends, mercy and grace. For Milton, God's ultimate expression of his power is his ultimate expression of his benevolence. By being omnibenevolent, God *is* being omnipotent. Omnibenevolence and omnipotency are two sides of the same coin, so to speak.

Where, however, is this position expressed in *Paradise Lost*? In book 11, God commands the archangel Michael to descend to earth in order to reveal to Adam just how powerful God is. In order to understand the extent of God's power, Adam first must witness the future destruction, suffering, pain, and hubris of humankind—all stemming from his own sinful act. Michael slowly shows Adam visions from biblical history. These visions are horrifying confessions of human suffering (a powerful form of evil in the world), and Adam is required to witness all of them—from the murder of his son Abel by his other son, Cain, to the usurping power of Nimrod. Yet, as this history becomes increasingly unbearable for Adam to witness, Michael begins to hint at God's special provision of mercy and grace, which rests in faith. "So law appears imperfect," Michael tells Adam,

> and but giv'n
> With purpose to resign them in full time
> Up to a better cov'nant, disciplined
> From shadowy types to truth, from flesh to spirit,
> From imposition of strict laws to free
> Acceptance of large grace, from servile fear
> To filial, works of law to works of faith. (11.300–6)

Michael's phrase "a better cov'nant" directly refers to what is termed the "New Covenant." In the Western Christian tradition, the New Covenant takes precedence over all previous covenants that God made with the Israelites. The previous covenants relied upon human obedience to laws; by being obedient to these laws, God's people would become (at least theoretically) pleasing in his eyes and reconciled to him. However, as Michael points out to Adam, because of their broken condition in the fallen (or postlapsarian) world, humans are unable to uphold such a covenant. God's ultimate purpose behind the fall, then, is to lift human beings to the "free / Acceptance of large grace." For Milton, this "large grace" is the New Covenant, grace that human beings receive through the Atonement of the Cross:

> The law of God exact he [the Son] shall fulfill
> Both by obedience and by love, though love
> Alone fulfill the law; thy [humankind's] punishment

He shall endure by coming in the flesh
To a reproachful life and cursèd death,
Proclaiming life to all who shall believe
In his redemption, and that his obedience
Imputèd becomes theirs by faith, his merits
To save them, not their own, though legal works. (12.402–10)

Mercy and grace, then, are God's ultimate expressions of his omnibenevolence; his kindness and goodness are so extensive that he is willing to send the Son to be sacrificed so that humankind is not bound to laws that they cannot fulfill. As Michael puts it,

But to the cross he nails thy enemies,
The law that is against thee, and the sins
Of all mankind, with him there crucified. (415–17)

Of course, as we have seen, God's omnibenevolence in the expression of his grace and mercy is the ultimate expression of how far-reaching his power is: omnibenevolence is omnipotence and vice versa. Milton allows God to express this position directly to his readers:

So Heav'nly love shall outdo Hellish hate,
Giving to death, and dying to redeem,
So dearly to redeem what Hellish hate
So easily destroyed, and still destroys
In those who, when they may, accept not grace. (3.298–302)

Learning of the ultimate purpose behind the fall, Adam turns to Michael and openly praises the goodness of God's actions. The following passage spoken by Adam is what scholars often refer to as Adam's expression of the *felix culpa* ("happy fault" or "happy fall"). The theological tenet behind the *felix culpa* is that God permits evil insofar as he can create a greater good from it, or, as Adam says:

O goodness infinite, goodness immense!

That all this good of evil shall produce,

And evil turn to good; more wonderful

Than that which by creation first brought forth

Light out of darkness! Full of doubt I stand,

Whether I should repent me now of sin

By me done and occasioned, or rejoice

Much more, that much more good thereof shall spring,

To God more glory, more good will to men

From God, and over wrath grace shall abound. (12.469–78)

By the time he and Eve are called to leave Eden, Adam is convinced of the justness of his punishment. More importantly, he is convinced of God's goodness. Though he and Eve have created evil in the world, God, because of his powerful attributes (omniscience, omnipotence, and omnibenevolence), will make good of all evil, and thus, for Adam, God is good.

But Is God *Truly* Good?

While this essay has summarized briefly the nature of Milton's theodicy, how he attempts to "justify the ways of God to men" and thus make sense of how evil exists apart from God's will, this discussion of God has been limited to books 3, 11, and 12 of *Paradise Lost*. While God certainly appears in other books of the epic, he is absent from the first two. These books are largely controlled by Satan and the narrative he asserts regarding dissension and rebellion in heaven. In fact, as an epic poem, *Paradise Lost* begins in medias res with Satan struggling to re-move himself from the Lake of Fire. Once upon solid ground, he calls the other fallen angels to him and asserts that God is not the benevolent character Christians would believe him to be. Rather, he is seen as a "potent victor" and tyrant (1.95). "Sole reigning," God "holds the tyr-anny of Heav'n" (124). There can be no doubt that Satan is a compelling character. He is rhetorically sophisticated and often convincing in the arguments he makes against God. From a purely aesthetic point of view, compared to Milton's God, Satan is more energetic and dynamic. This might be to say that he is more *human* than God and thus a better object of our sympathy, and a long critical history supports such a belief.

Since the romantic movement, many readers have argued that Satan, not God, the Son, or even Adam and Eve, is the epic protagonist of the poem. William Blake notoriously claimed that "the reason Milton wrote in fetters when he wrote of Angels & God, and at liberty when of Devils & Hell, is because he was a true Poet and of the Devil's party without knowing it" (88). Another romantic writer, Percy Bysshe Shelley, was even more adamant in defending the notion that Satan was Milton's most compelling character. "Nothing can exceed the energy and magnificence of the character of Satan as expressed in *Paradise Lost*," Shelley writes in *A Defence of Poetry*. "It is a mistake to suppose that he could ever have been intended for the popular personification of evil" (498). Moreover, Shelley believed that "Milton's Devil as a moral being is as far superior to his God as one who perseveres in some purpose which he has conceived to be excellent in spite of adversity and torture. . . . Milton has so far violated the popular creed (if this shall be judged to be a violation) as to have alleged no superiority of moral virtue to his God over his Devil" (498).

While this view of Milton's Satan diminished during the Victorian and Edwardian periods, it returned with a vengeance in the early 1960s. Shortly after World War II, William Empson, an already established literary scholar, traveled to China to teach English at the university level. Empson's time in China challenged him to think of traditional English works, such as Milton's *Paradise Lost*, outside of their normative cultural contexts. Thus, Empson, an ardent critic of what he termed the "neo-Christian" bias in literary studies, willfully sought to read *Paradise Lost* from a non-Christian point of view, a move that he credited, in part, to his work with Chinese students. In 1961, he published his groundbreaking *Milton's God*, to which Danielson's *Milton's*

Good God is, in part, a response. Empson essentially reopened the question of Milton's theodicy and whether it was a successful venture. According to Empson, Milton struggles "to make his God appear less wicked . . . and does succeed in making him noticeably less wicked than the traditional Christian one; though, after all his efforts, owing to his loyalty to the sacred text and the penetration with which he makes its story real to us, his modern critics still feel, in a puzzled way, that there is something badly wrong about it all" (11). Of course, one will note an atheistic bias in such a line of reasoning. To Empson's credit, however, he confesses this very bias: "I think the traditional God of Christianity very wicked, and have done since I was at school" (10).

Once one moves beyond attempting to assess Empson's personal biases, however, one encounters a compelling reading of *Paradise Lost* in which Empson capably demonstrates just how complex the plot of the poem is. A major point of contention is that God is not good. Rather, he is a capricious figure in Empson's mind. "I am not denying, what Milton regularly asserts, that Satan fell out of pride and envy," he writes, "but as Satan believes God to be a usurper he genuinely does believe him to be envious" (40). Empson asks his readers to "waive" their "metaphysical presumptions" in order to come to this conclusion (40); in other words, he asks that his readers suspend their Western, Judeo-Christian presumptions with regard to the heaven-hell and God-Satan dynamic. Moreover, Empson declares that Satan has very good reasons to believe that God is not all-powerful: "If they [the fallen angels] can fight against him [God] for three days, that is enough to prove that he has not got absolute or metaphysical power . . . therefore he has been cheating them, and, however powerful he may be, to submit to him would be dishonourable" (41). This seems a fair point to raise. If God is omnipotent, then why does he permit the war in heaven to last for three days? But Empson's questions do not end here. Take the following passage from *Paradise Lost*, for example, which highlights Satan's position on the Lake of Fire after he falls from heaven:

So stretched out huge in length the Arch-Fiend lay
Chained on the burning lake, nor ever thence
Had ris'n or heaved his head, but that the will
And high permission of all-ruling Heaven
Left him at large to his own dark designs,
That with reiterated crimes he might
Heap on himself damnation, while he sought
Evil to others, and enraged might see
How all his malice served but to bring forth
Infinite goodness, grace and mercy shown
On man by him seduced, but on himself
Treble confusion, wrath and vengeance poured. (1.209–20)

After citing this very passage, Empson points out that "here we are specifically told that God's actions towards Satan were intended to lead him into greater evil" (42). Indeed, it is hard to imagine another way to interpret the passage. However, Empson uses God's logic in this instance to probe further how he may have intentionally led Satan astray regarding his power: "thus we have no reason to doubt that God had previously intended to give Satan a wrong metaphysical argument when he made the War in Heaven last three days" (42–43).

While many scholars have disagreed with Empson's conclusions and even his methodology (for example, he does not consider Milton's discussion of why God chooses to harden certain hearts and how the hardening of hearts does not violate free will in *De doctrina christiana*), many scholars have defended them. In *The Satanic Epic*, Neil Forsyth also argues against the perceived neo-Christian bias in Milton studies, suggesting that there "has been what looks like a largely unconscious drive to protect vulnerable young readers, and perhaps the critic himself, from the Satanic power" of *Paradise Lost* (4). Tobias Gregory flatly states that "Empson is actually right about *Paradise Lost*" (74). The Empsonian trajectory also has been taken up by Michael Bryson, who contends that *Paradise Lost* "has, almost from the day of its publication, troubled many Christian readers who, to their dismay (and often outrage) see in his Father a character who is as far from the 'good' god they believe in as Satan himself" (11). Where Bryson largely differs from Empson, however, is in his historicist approach to Milton. Whereas Empson avoids an account of *Paradise Lost* that fully investigates the specific theological, political, and social contingencies that undergird Milton's thinking, Bryson looks at Milton's contemporary political milieu and treats Milton's God and Satan as entities that must exist outside the course of tyranny into which kings inevitably seem to fall. Thus, he suggests that "the Father is not Milton's illustration of how God *is*, but Milton's scathing critique of how, all too often, God is *imagined*" (12). In Bryson's view, then, Milton "writes to re-imagine God" (12). His treatment of Milton's Satan is equally nuanced. Satan "seems heroic because he *is* heroic" (83). According to Bryson, Satan's initial rejection of God's tyranny is not without warrant and deserving of admiration. However, Satan, like the tyrant God, ultimately succumbs to the power that comes along with monarchical rule; "Satan becomes a tyrant because in establishing his infernal monarchy, he appeals to the very system of power that he once rejected" (109).

One final note should be made about Empson and Empsonian approaches to the issue of Milton's God. Recent criticism is, if not wholly, at least in part indebted to Empson, as an increasing number of scholars have begun to investigate the unorthodox nature of much of Milton's theology, from his treatment of divorce to his rejection of belief in the Trinity. Though many of such scholars divest themselves of having a direct interest in securing the goodness (or badness) of Milton's God, they are interested in securing the freedom to explore the unorthodox side of Milton without apology, and it seems unlikely that this could have happened were it not for Empson.

Am I Evil?

The issue of evil is central to Milton's *Paradise Lost*. From one perspective, it seems as if Milton successfully demonstrates to his readers that God is omnipotent, omniscient, and omnibenevolent. Evil, then, is Satan's creation, and it wreaks havoc upon the earth not because God wills it, creates it, or even desires it but because humans succumb to it of their own free will. From another perspective, however, Milton's God is not good, and Milton has just cause for showing us why this is so. As a result, evil is of God's own doing, and Satan puts up a heroic struggle against an unjust deity.

When we read Milton's *Paradise Lost*, then, we are left with some challenging questions: is God good or is God bad? Where does evil originate? If anything, this essay has shown that the answers are not simple. While the critical positions examined to this point diverge over a number of issues, they do hold one thing in common: both positions believe that the ultimate answer to such questions rests within the text of *Paradise Lost*. In other words, whether one believes in Danielson's thesis or Empson's thesis, by believing in either, one is conceding that the answer to the question lies in the text. But what if we were to stop thinking this way? What if we were to consider the possibility that the answers to such questions lie not in the text but in our own reading experience? Is it not possible to suggest that *how* each person reads *Paradise Lost* may color his or her interpretation of the text and thus his or her beliefs regarding the origins of evil? After all, Danielson confesses that the theodicy is tautological—arriving where it began in the first place—and Empson confesses his own atheistic biases. In other words, someone who sets out to demonstrate that God is good already believes that he is good, and someone who sets out to prove that God is not good already believes that he is not good. Does *Paradise Lost* reveal more about its readers than it does about the metaphysical origins of evil? Does the poem reveal our own relationship with evil?

In one of the most important works of criticism with regard to Milton scholarship, *Surprised by Sin*, author Stanley Fish answers such questions in the affirmative. Yes, our reading of *Paradise Lost* says something important about us as readers, and yes, our reading of the poem even says something important about our relationship with evil.

As Fish argues, "Milton consciously wants to worry his reader, to force him to doubt the correctness of his responses, and to bring him to the realization that his inability to read the poem with any confidence in his own perception is its focus" (4). In a strange way, then, he agrees with both Danielson and Empson: Milton's God is good, but Satan also is mighty tempting to follow—that is, Satan is aesthetically good in his own right. In Fish's interpretation, Milton intentionally writes the text in such a way so that its readers will follow the same path as their human counterparts in the poem: "Milton's method is to re-create in the mind of the reader (which is, finally, the poem's scene) the drama of the Fall, to make him fall again exactly as Adam did and with Adam's troubled clarity" (1). While Fish's argument has been a site of contention within the community of Milton scholars, it remains one of the most provocative and formative readings of *Paradise Lost* to date. Though he may not have anticipated its ultimate reach, it is safe to say that his argument raises important issues about the ethics of reading. Do we create meaning or moral and ethical values as we read? Does our act of reading reveal something about our own hearts and souls? Does our act of reading reveal whether we are good or evil? These very questions, Fish argues, seem to be behind Milton's construction of *Paradise Lost*. If Fish is correct, then this essay cannot truly answer the questions it raises. Rather, this essay can merely remind readers of *Paradise Lost* that the poem is asking them such questions all along. It is up to us as readers to decide whether we are willing to entertain those questions and, more importantly, whether we are prepared to answer those questions and be accountable to our answers. Perhaps this is why *Paradise Lost* remains a poem of great interest and provocation, even three hundred years after its initial publication.

Works Cited

Blake, William. *Blake's Poetry and Designs*. Ed. Mary Lynn Johnson and John E. Grant. New York: Norton, 1979.

Bryson, Michael. *The Tyranny of Heaven: Milton's Rejection of God as King*. Newark: U of Delaware P, 2004.

Calvin, John. *Institutes of the Christian Religion*. Trans. Henry Beveridge. 2 vols. Grand Rapids: Eerdmans, 1975.

Danielson, Dennis Richard. *Milton's Good God: A Study in Literary Theodicy*. Cambridge: Cambridge UP, 1982.

Empson, William. *Milton's God*. London: Chatto, 1961.

Fish, Stanley. *Surprised by Sin: The Reader in* Paradise Lost. 2nd ed. Cambridge: Harvard UP, 1997.

Forsyth, Neil. *The Satanic Epic*. Princeton: Princeton UP, 2003.

Gregory, Tobias. "In Defense of Empson: A Reassessment of *Milton's God*." *Fault Lines and Controversies in the Study of Seventeenth-Century English Literature*. Ed. Claude J. Summers and Ted-Larry Pebworth. Columbia: U of Missouri P, 2002. 73–87.

Milton, John. *The Complete Poetry and Essential Prose of John Milton*. Ed. William Kerrigan, John Rumrich, and Stephen M. Fallon. New York: Modern Library, 2007.

Shelley, Percy Bysshe. *Shelley's Poetry and Prose*. Ed. Donald H. Reiman and Sharon B. Powers. New York: Norton, 1977.

Driven by Demons: "The Rime of the Ancient Mariner"

Mark Kipperman

1.

In an increasingly secular and modernizing world, the question of whether our destinies are controlled by vast cosmic moral laws haunted thinkers and artists of the romantic era with ever mounting urgency. This was a time in which massive historical forces such as the French Revolution, the antislavery movement in England, and the slowly growing power of industrial capitalists challenged traditional authority and its theological and moral orderings. The period was marked by a growing interest in tales of deep psychological conflict and gothic scenes of disorientation and horror. But even in those gothic tales and the increasingly popular vampire literature, evil is a palpable presence and supernatural malevolence is real, even if its ways and designs on us are inscrutable. In contrast, Samuel Taylor Coleridge's 1798 poem "The Rime of the Ancient Mariner" is one of literature's most haunting narratives of moral terror in the face of a universe that may be neither good nor evil but blankly indifferent.

Indeed, one of the most disturbing questions the poem raises is why the narrator's moral lesson is so uncannily disconnected from the narrative he relates: the "dear God who loveth us" (line 616) cannot free the Mariner from a life of compulsive repetition of a horror that leaves his listener "sadder and . . . wiser" (624). Has the sailor learned a lesson of love for all living things, or is he desperately self-deceived? If that is the case, we may be uncertain whether the demons who drive him on are real or projections of his fears. And we don't know if the Mariner unleashed those demons by his unmotivated killing of the albatross or if the killing is as random an act as the punishments meted out to him and the crew. The universe he has sailed through may be filled with evil powers or just empty of any meaning at all, an even more horrific possibility. The more the author tries to explain the moral of the tale, the less certain we as readers are that any explaining will encompass the true nature of the albatross or the motive for its murder.

Coleridge's tale was first published in a collection of poems by Coleridge and William Wordsworth, *Lyrical Ballads*, in 1798. The goal of the collection was to explore the ways in which nature and super-nature intertwine in our experience and lead us to a faith in the good-ness and rightness of our place in the cosmos without any appeal to a traditionally transcendent God. In other words, our own experience is our teacher about good and evil, and nature will lead us to a sense of the workings of the ultimate justice of existence. In Wordsworth's poems in the volume, the lives of rural folk allow the more sophisti-cated reader a more direct experience of human emotion, often under the pressure of enormous pain and loss. These folk sometimes offer supernatural explanations for events outside their control. Yet in their directness and simplicity of feeling and speech, they display a deep bond to a world that does respond in unexpected ways to their need for justice and meaning.

Coleridge's poem is a rather different kind of work, oddly out of place in the volume. Wordsworth did not like it; he felt its uncanni-ness disturbed the ultimate faith he believed the volume advanced (though his own poems are often themselves more disturbing than they superficially seem). In his apologia for his own career as a writer, *Bio-graphia literaria* (1817), Coleridge attempts to explain what he and Wordsworth had planned to do:

> It was agreed, that my endeavours should be directed to persons and char-acters supernatural, or at least romantic; yet so as to transfer from our in-ward nature a human interest and a substance of truth sufficient to procure for these shadows of imagination that willing suspension of disbelief for the moment, which constitutes poetic faith. Mr. Wordsworth, on the other hand, was to propose to himself, as his object, to give the charm of novelty to things of every day, and to excite a feeling analogous to the supernatu-

ral, by awakening the mind's attention from the lethargy of custom, and directing it to the loveliness and the wonders of the world before us. . . . With this view I wrote the "Ancient Mariner." (2.6–7)

Coleridge suggests that his main interest was not with the reality of good or evil in the Mariner's world but rather with a certain state of mind. This helps us address one of the most common questions that readers ask: how much of what the Mariner tells is "real"? Are we to take some parts of his story, such as the reanimation of the dead crew, as a hallucination? Are the demons that he hears damn him all in his mind?

These are reasonable questions, and readers in Coleridge's day certainly puzzled over them. But Coleridge's very point might have been to explore just what "all in the mind" really means, what becomes real to a mind driven by guilt and haunted by a need to undo an evil act. In *Biographia literaria*, Coleridge suggests that the interest of the supernatural events "was to consist in the interesting of the affections [of the reader] by the dramatic truth of such emotions, as would naturally accompany such situations, supposing them real" (2.6). We are being directed not to question what is real in the tale but rather to focus on a mind tormented by apparently malevolent forces and trying desperately to understand its own thoughts and experiences. To what degree and in what sense did the Mariner bring these punishments upon himself? And if his "guilt" is both his act *and* the guilty feeling he is doomed to carry with him, how can he undo what he has done or free himself from its emotional consequences?

The narrative itself does not really help us answer these questions. The Mariner says that the first time he told the tale "this frame of mine was wrenched / With a woeful agony, / Which forced me to begin my tale" (578–80). He is compelled by outside forces and given "strange power of speech" (587), and until his tale is told yet again, "this heart within [him] burns" (585). Yet he also implies he has reached a certain peace and worships a loving God:

'Tis sweeter far to me
To walk together to the kirk [church].

. . . and all together pray,
While each to his great Father bends,
Old men, and babes, and loving friends. (601–2; 606–8)

We see little of this loving God in the poem. Indeed, we may even wonder if the Mariner understands his own tale. At the end of the poem, he tells the Wedding Guest that "the dear God who loveth us, / He made and loveth all" (616–17). But did this God love the crew, whose deaths seem arbitrary and cruel? Did he doom the Mariner to eternal living death, or was the Mariner's fate dictated by the roll of dice by demons on the ghost ship (195–98)? The horrific possibility of a random or malevolent universe makes the concluding moral lesson to love "all things both great and small" (615) seem confusing and ambiguous. Coleridge himself insisted the poem had no moral and that it is futile to seek one, and perhaps it intrudes too much on the poem's effect: "the fault of 'The Ancient Mariner' consists in making the moral sentiment too apparent and bringing it in too much as a principle or cause in a work of such pure Imagination" (*Coleridge's Poetry and Prose* 98).

2.

The "pure" imaginative feeling of "The Rime of the Ancient Mariner" is evident from the beginning. The poem is presented as a "literary" ballad, set in an obscure, remote time and written in an often artificially archaic style. This only enforces our sense of being transported to a place and time of folktale, superstition, and magic. The poem we usually read is Coleridge's 1817 version (as reprinted, slightly revised, in 1834). But in 1798, Coleridge published a rather different poem, featuring more medieval-sounding language, titled "The Rime of the Ancyent Marinere." This earlier version includes no marginal gloss, and there are fewer variations from traditional ballad stanza form—four lines rhyming *abcb*, the stresses alternating 4-3-4-3 (see Coffin). By setting the poem in the distant past and using archaic language, Coleridge evokes a world of medieval Catholicism, of saints and demons, a world in which ballads tell of wonders and fearsome punishments.

Lyrical Ballads was published at a time in which translations of German "ballad" tales of supernatural events, murders, ghosts, and vengeance were popular with British readers, and Coleridge certainly meant to tap into this form (Jordan 172–86). But even by these standards, the tale was perplexing, haunting. In 1800, for the second edition, Coleridge modernized the spelling, and in 1817 he added the gloss in the margin, apparently to explain the action and even to impose some sense of moral judgment on the acts of Mariner and crew. But for most critics, the "glosser" only adds another voice (not necessarily Coleridge's) to the many possible perspectives on the events.[1]

Even the poem's opening is disorienting. The Mariner enters as a disruptive force, an "it" that violates the "merry din" of a wedding:

> It is an ancient Mariner
> And he stoppeth one of three.
> "By thy long grey beard and glittering eye,
> Now wherefore stopp'st thou me?" (1–4)

The strange man does not answer this question and instead abruptly says, "There was a ship" (10). We do not know why the Mariner chooses this man to talk to, but we come to see that he is compelled to speak. At the same time, the Wedding Guest is compelled to listen, as if mesmerized, caught in a spell:

> He holds him with his glittering eye—
> The wedding-guest stood still,
> And listens like a three years' child,
> The Mariner hath his will. (13–16)

The glosser says that "the wedding guest is spell-bound by the eye of the old sea-faring man, and constrained to hear his tale" (gloss to 13). The two men seem bound in a relationship of narrator and listener that they cannot control. We do not initially know with whom we, as readers, should identify or whom we should trust, as there are multiple levels of storytelling: poet to reader, Mariner to Guest, glosser to us (Davies 261–5). Above all these perspectives, some force of compulsion seems to hover. This image of the eye, haunted and haunting, will recur as the site of a powerful "curse in a dead man's eye" ("Rime" 252), one of many signs of guilt and punishment that dog the Mariner.

Repetition is one of the key motifs of the poem. These feelings of repetition and compulsion—both in the telling of the tale and within the tale itself—are also reflected in the obsessive rhyming that both carries the reader along and also makes him or her feel trapped in a hall of mirrors:

> With sloping masts and dipping prow,
> As who pursued with yell and blow
> Still treads the shadow of his foe,
> And forward bends his head,
> The ship drove fast, loud roared the blast,
> And southward aye we fled. (45–50)

The rhymes here are piled on, *aaabcb*, with an internal rhyme (*c/c*) in the fifth line. The sounds here reproduce the sense of wild pursuit, of running in terror, as well as the sense of being carried forward. The rhymes trap us in repetitions throughout the poem, but at times they yoke together opposites:

> Nor dim nor red, like God's own head,
> The glorious Sun uprist:
> Then all averred, I had killed the bird
> That brought the fog and mist.

> 'Twas right, said they, such birds to slay,
>
> That bring the fog and mist. (97–102)

As critic Arden Reed points out, the rising sun here is, ironically, linked by rhyme to spreading fog and mist, and we can never tell in the poem if the sun is truly glorious or only an ominous, punishing light (178–82).

When the Mariner sees the skeleton ship, the setting sun peers through the ship's ribs, and the imagery is of death and imprisonment: indeed, it may be the Mariner who is in the metaphorical dungeon, as the "grace" of Mary is paired with the rhyme "burning face":

> And straight the Sun was flecked with bars,
>
> (Heaven's Mother send us grace!)
>
> As if through a dungeon-grate he peered
>
> With a broad and burning face. ("Rime" 177–180)

The sense that there is no escape from an evil deed, only eternal penance, drives the poem onward. But how do we know that killing the Albatross really was evil in the first place?

The plot of the poem at first seems basically simple. A seaman shoots a harmless bird in an impulsive and unmotivated act of violence, violating the harmony of nature and of all living things—what Coleridge calls "the one Life, within us and abroad" in his 1817 revision of "The Eolian Harp" (26). For this, he and the crew who initially approved his act are punished by the bird's friend, the Polar Spirit, and the Mariner is sentenced to Life-in-Death by phantoms in a ghost ship. The crew has condemned him to wear the dead bird around his neck. But near the middle of the poem, he blesses the creepy water snakes, a "spring of love" gushes from his heart ("Rime" 284), and he learns to worship the one Life and inspire others to do so. As we have seen, though, the strangeness of the poem and its haunted narrator make this reading hard to believe. In fact, this reading makes the poem much less interesting and challenging than it is.

It is difficult to believe in the moral about simple faith in a loving God. The punishment, of both Mariner and crew, seems wildly disproportionate to the crime. Certainly it is good to be kind to helpless animals. But in what sense is killing one an act of almost unforgivable evil? The fact is, because the Mariner never tells the Wedding Guest *why* he shot the bird, we cannot say for certain that his motives were evil. If his act was motiveless and arbitrary, that would be a bad thing, a thoughtless thing, but would it merit the punishment? The Polar Spirit who demands eternal penance is presented only as an angered friend of the bird, not as an agent of good or justice. Moreover, the Mariner is punished by strange apparitions on a skeleton ship, who choose *his* fate randomly by a dice throw and hardly seem to be representatives of either benign nature or a loving God. For critic Edward Bostetter, this dice game is crucial to undercutting any notion of cosmic justice: "it knocks out any attempt to impose a systematic philosophical or religious interpretation, be it necessitarian, Christian, or Platonic, upon the poem. . . . It throws into question the moral and intellectual responsibility of the rulers of the universe" (244).

Bostetter finds the death of the crew particularly hard to justify: "the men are guilty of no more than the usual human frailty. . . . [The rulers of the universe] are revealed as holding the same contempt for human life that the Mariner held for the bird's life" (245). Only the glosser seems to make sense of this, but again, he may only be one voice trying to impose reason and clear cause and effect on the story. When the crew sees the bird they greet it hospitably but superstitiously believe it "caused" the south wind to help them leave the frozen wastes of the South Pole. The glosser, too, believes that "the ancient Mariner inhospitably killed the pious bird of good omen" (gloss to 79). The ship is then eerily becalmed by the "bloody Sun" near the equator (112). But when a fair breeze sends them north again, the members of the crew change their minds, believe the bird becalmed them, and so "make themselves accomplices to the crime" (gloss to 97). "Then all averred, I had killed the bird / That brought the fog and mist" (99). From the Mariner's point of view at the time, why should the crew be right the first time but not the second?

In other words, we, the Mariner, and the crew are always reasoning "backward," from effects to causes, as we attempt to interpret events. This is one reason why both the plot and the moral of the poem are so hard to understand: the Mariner only later understands his act was evil (by some standard he could not guess at the time), and even the "spring of love" that "gushe[s]" from his heart takes him by surprise. For critic Frances Ferguson, this problem explains much of the interpretive confusion: "the criticism of 'The Rime of the Ancient Mariner' reflects a craving for causes. . . . For the poem is as thorough a work of backwardness . . . as we have" (617, 620). The psychological critic David Miall agrees with Ferguson. He sees the poem's "dream logic" originating in "regressive childhood fear" of severe punishment from adult authority as well as an adult's fear of entrapment and death (645, 644).

This imagery of stasis and movement is central to the poem and is one clue to the Mariner's spiritual journey and emotional turmoil. These images are present at almost every key moment, another one of the poem's obsessive patterns. One such moment occurs when the "bloody Sun at noon / Right up above the mast did stand" (111–12), seeming to pin the ship down in revenge for the killing:

> Day after day, day after day
> We stuck, nor breath nor motion
> As idle as a painted ship
> Upon a painted ocean.
>
> Water, water, every where,
> And all the boards did shrink;
> Water, water every where,
> Nor any drop to drink. (115–22)

The horror here is emphasized by the repeated broad, empty-sounding vowel in the repeated words "day" and "water." These become the limits and the whole extent of the Mariner's world. The feeling of frustration mounts as we see time passing but the man fixed in place, unable to escape or find spiritual cleansing.

Of course, the Mariner's doom is that he is always stuck, even when he is moving. He travels the word but never escapes his fate, never completes his mission. But there is one moment when he seems to have moved onward spiritually, arrived at a vision of universal love. This takes place right after he feels his curse the most, feels most trapped and alone:

> Alone, alone, all all alone,
> Alone on a wide wide sea!
> And never a saint took pity on
> My soul in agony. (232–35)

Once again, the open vowels echo his loneliness and the cruel, vast emptiness of his world.

The Mariner feels responsible not only for his own misery but also for the death of the crew:

> The many men so beautiful!
> And they all dead did lie:
> And a thousand thousand slimy things
> Lived on; and so did I. (236–39)

He feels the "curse" of the dead men's eyes always staring at him: "Seven days, seven nights, I saw that curse, / And yet I could not die" (261–62). The Mariner feels what we now call "survivor guilt," and he hates himself and wishes that he, a wretch no better than those slimy sea snakes, could just die (see Miall 645–47).

Suddenly, from this position of absolute fixity the Mariner looks up at the moon:

> The moving Moon went up the sky,
> And nowhere did abide:
> Softly she was going up,
> And a star or two beside. ("Rime" 263–66)

Though the narrating voice does not tell us what he feels, the glosser offers us a glimpse into his heart: "In his loneliness and fixedness he yearneth towards the journeying Moon, and the stars that still sojourn, yet still move onward; and every where the blue sky belongs to them, and is their appointed rest, and their native country and their natural homes, which they enter unannounced, as lords that are certainly expected and yet there is a silent joy at their arrival" (gloss to 263). The yearning here is a desire to move onward and yet be at peace, at home. The moon and stars are always "journeying" and yet "still [always] sojourn [stay and rest]." The Mariner will always wander and never be at rest, but in nature, nothing moves outside some vast harmony, and every movement is a kind of homecoming.

At this point, the Mariner sees the phosphorescent water-snakes that he had once found so hideous: "Blue, glossy green, and velvet black, / They coiled and swam" (279–81). Again, there is that powerful yearning for harmony, the eternal "at-homeness" of natural beings he once despised. Here is the poem's crucial moment of hope, when, as the glosser says, "he blesseth them in his heart" (gloss to 285):

> O happy living things! no tongue
> Their beauty might declare:
> A spring of love gushed from my heart,
> And I blessed them unaware:
> Sure my kind saint took pity on me,
> And I blessed them unaware. (282–87)

In this moment of joy, "the Albatross fell off, and sank / Like lead into the sea" (290–91). The glosser says, "The spell begins to break." Unfortunately, this is not true. The Mariner is still and (as we know) will always remain under a spell, a curse. If we read this passage of blessing closely and carefully, we see that it is an odd moment and difficult even for the Mariner to explain. The love "gushe[s]" from him as if unwilled, not from a process of growing awareness or conscious repentance. In fact, he says he "blessed them *unaware*." He even repeats the sentence, as if he hardly understands it himself. How does he know he blessed them? He was overcome by a positive emotion, yes. But he seems, once again, to be reaching backward for an explanation. "*Sure* my kind saint took pity on me," he says, but he does not know this, and his explanation seems to originate from a desperate *need* to believe that some guardian saint reached into his heart. In this sense, he seems to be a man driven by a will that he does not himself control or comprehend. This now appears as true of his blessing as it does of his impulsive killing.

Then, too, the consequences of his actions, in this case the blessing, are not something he can know or understand. His change of heart does not seem to count for much with the Polar Spirit. That spirit, "from the land of mist and snow," compels the ship wildly onward without wind (378). He "still requireth vengeance" (gloss to 377). The Mariner, in a trance, as if hearing from the depths of his "soul," hears a demon say, "The man hath penance done; / And penance more will do" (396, 408–9). Indeed, he is in for more rough sailing. The dead crew is mysteriously reanimated as zombies:

> All fixed on me their stony eyes,
> That in the Moon did glitter.
>
> The pang, the curse, with which they died,
> Had never passed away:
> I could not draw my eyes from theirs,

>   Nor turn them up to pray. (436–41)

"And now," he tells the Wedding Guest, "this spell was snapt" (442). But though the glosser says "the curse is finally expiated," there is no reason—given the Mariner's ultimate fate—to think this is so.

3.

It is rare today for a critic to argue that "The Rime of the Ancient Mariner" depicts a universe of beauty that the Mariner arrogantly offends and demonstrates that by learning kindness to living creatures we can be redeemed. The poem would then be a parable of Christian love and salvation. But we do not know that the Wedding Guest has been turned to such love, nor do we know that either he or the Mariner is in any sense redeemed. We only know that the Wedding Guest leaves the scene "stunned . . . of sense forlorn" and is a "sadder and a wiser man" (622–25).

It is tempting to agree with critic A. M. Buchan, for whom the Mariner "is caught up in a chaos of unwilled movement, and he himself is an alien speck of human purpose tossed meaninglessly about in the roaring winds of fate" (679). Are we, then, to leave this remarkable poem with only a sense of terror at the indifference or even random malevolence of the universe?

Not necessarily. This is not in itself an unreasonable conclusion and is one dimension of our reading experience of the tale. Yet there is another level on which the poem, taken as a whole, is more complex than this. Coleridge also wrote other poems (such as "The Eolian Harp" and "Frost at Midnight") of naturalistic and spiritual faith—or at least of the struggle to believe in these. Bostetter has summarized this conflict well: "What [Coleridge] wanted to believe in and increasingly devoted his intellectual energies to asserting was a universe in which man possessed freedom of will and action to mold his own destiny; what he feared was a universe in which he was at the mercy of arbitrary and unpredictable forces. "The Rime" envisions such a universe" (251).

It is a strange state, this wanting or needing or hoping to believe. Without active belief, this is a state that cannot deny belief either, that needs to see and feel that loving a beautiful world will somehow *count*. The need here is both the Mariner's and Coleridge's. In the 1800 edition of the poem, Coleridge oddly subtitled it "A Poet's Reverie." This draws our attention to the poem as not only the hero's but also the poet's imaginative emotional vision. Of course, a "reverie," a daydream, comes with as little conscious will as the Mariner's tale, so we might take Coleridge at his word that in this poem he is developing an imagined world of powerful emotions, of feeling torn between horror and hope.

Coleridge's poem may not be a statement about how the universe *is* so much as about the emotional experience of how we feel and need it to be. The best way to think of "The Rime of the Ancient Mariner" is not as a moral fable or even as an amoral horror tale of a random universe. Rather, it is an exploration of powerful conflicting emotional states of hope and fear and of a universe that reflects the eye that sees it.

What Coleridge really fears most is that his Mariner has so little control over his inner life and his own will. Evil, then, is not just the random cruelty of the universe. It is also the possibility that our own wills are not clear to us and can force us to move in directions we cannot understand and repeat errors we can never escape. Perhaps this whole nightmare comes from a fear that forces inside us might unleash demons outside us—not external forces but projections of our fears of helplessness.

"The Rime of the Ancient Mariner" may not instill a moral after all. It does, however, record a wild conflict between two powerful emotions. The first is the fear of our own helplessness to our inner compulsions in a world in which we cannot understand all the forces that determine the meaning and value of our acts. But the second feeling is the *hope* that our minds have some power to see the natural good even in what appears evil. Perhaps this power or faith can rob the demons of their power over our minds. Coleridge's great poem does not show us *how* a corrupt will can turn to faith and love, but it conjures a fearsome vision of what happens when we fail.

Note

1. For a helpful summary of the differences between the 1798, 1800, and 1817 editions, see the headnote to the poem in *Coleridge's Poetry and Prose* 56–57. This edition prints both early and late versions on facing pages. On the role of the glosser, see Dyck 595–600 and Lipking 613–21.

Works Cited

Bostetter, Edward. "The Nightmare World of 'The Ancient Mariner.'" *Studies in Romanticism* 1.4 (1962): 241–54.

Buchan, A. M. "The Sad Wisdom of the Mariner." *Studies in Philology* 61.4 (1964): 669–88.

Coffin, Tristram. "Coleridge's Use of the Ballad Stanza in 'The Rime of the Ancient Mariner.'" *Modern Language Quarterly* 12.4 (1951): 437–45. *MLA International Bibliography*. Web. 11 June 2011.

Coleridge, Samuel Taylor. *Biographia literaria*. Ed. James Engell and W. Jackson Bate. Princeton: Princeton UP, 1984.

_____. *Coleridge's Poetry and Prose*. Ed. Nicolas Halmi, Paul Magnuson, and Raimonda Modiano. New York: Norton, 2004.

_____. "The Rime of the Ancient Mariner." Halmi, Magnuson, and Modiano 58–99.

Davies, Lindsay. "The Poem, the Gloss and the Critic: Discourse and Subjectivity in 'The Rime of the Ancient Mariner.'" *Forum for Modern Language Studies*. 26.3 (1990): 259–71. *MLA International Bibliography*. Web. 11 June 2011.

Dyck, Sarah. "Perspective in 'The Rime of the Ancient Mariner.'" *Studies in English Literature* 13.4 (1973): 591–604. *JSTOR*. Web. 11 June 2011.

Ferguson, Frances. "Coleridge and the Deluded Reader: 'The Rime of the Ancient Mariner.'" *Georgia Review* 31 (1977): 617–35.

Jordan, John. *Why the* Lyrical Ballads? *The Background, Writing, and Character of Wordsworth's 1798* Lyrical Ballads. Berkeley: U California P, 1976.

Lipking, Lawrence. "The Marginal Gloss." *Critical Inquiry* 3.4 (1977): 609–55. *JSTOR*. Web. 11 June 2011.

Miall, David S. "Guilt and Death: The Predicament of 'The Ancient Mariner.'" *Studies in English Literature* 24.4 (1984): 633–53.

Reed, Arden. "The Mariner Rimed." *Romanticism and Language*. Ed. Arden Reed. Ithaca: Cornell UP, 1984. 168–201.

The Inadequacy of Closure in Charlotte Brontë's *Jane Eyre*; or, Why "Reader, I Married Him" Is One of the Most Disappointing Sentences in Victorian Literature _____

Katie R. Peel

Scholars, particularly those performing feminist and postcolonial readings, have uncovered numerous evils in Charlotte Brontë's *Jane Eyre* (1847). These evils tend to be gender related as well as consequences of an imperialist ideology. *Jane Eyre* scholarship has been greatly influenced by Sandra Gilbert and Susan Gubar's groundbreaking feminist study *The Madwoman in the Attic* (1979), which draws its title from *Jane Eyre*. In reading nineteenth-century texts in terms of the effects of gender oppression on women's writing processes, Gilbert and Gubar find "a common, female impulse to struggle free from social and literary confinement through strategic redefinitions of self, art, and society" (xii). They emphasize Jane Eyre's relationship with Antoinetta Bertha Mason Rochester, whom they refer to as "Jane's truest and darkest double . . . the angry aspect of the orphan child, the ferocious secret self Jane has been trying to repress ever since her days at Gateshead," and the character who does everything that Jane only wishes she could do (359–60).

Beginning with Gayatri Chakravorty Spivak in a 1985 essay, numerous scholars have offered postcolonial readings of *Jane Eyre* that examine the roles of imperialist ideology (the theory governing empire building in the form of colonization). Patrick Hogan, author of *Colonialism and Cultural Identity*, writes that a postcolonial approach is to look at

> literature emerging from the historical encounter between culturally distinct and geographically separated societies, where for some extended period one society controls the other politically and economically; moreover, during this period, the dominated society remains numerically and

culturally prevalent in its own geographical location, and the dominant society justifies its control through the denigration of the dominated culture and through the ideological insistence that the dominated people are an inferior race. (1–2)

Edward Said, whose 1978 text *Orientalism* is one of the foundational texts of postcolonial theory, writes that the colonial relationship is based on a specific power dynamic between the colonizer and the colonized, one that relies on domination and employs various forms of violence. This power dynamic, according to Said, is governed by an ideology of entitlement and implemented via a "systematic discipline by which European culture was able to manage—and even produce—the Orient politically, sociologically, militarily, ideologically, scientifically, and imaginatively" (3). For Said, "Europe" and "Orient" are specific examples of "colonizer" and "colonized." The Orient is not a place but a Western ideal (1). Drawing upon the work of Said, Spivak argues that imperialist ideology informs *Jane Eyre* and that the novel accordingly perpetuates this ideology. Spivak writes, "Imperialism, understood as England's social mission, was a crucial part of the cultural representation of England to the English. The role of literature in the production of cultural representation should not be ignored" (243). Novels such as *Jane Eyre*, then, according to both Spivak and Said, are complicit in empire building. Spivak argues that Jane's success depends upon this relatively unexamined imperialist ideology. This essay draws upon both feminist and postcolonial readings of *Jane Eyre* and argues that the evils in the novel are located in the colonial dominant/subordinate power dynamic. When examining the narrative structure of the novel, one finds that the "good" resolution of the text, namely Jane's marriage to Rochester, is not enough to counter or compensate for the numerous evils that create the book's conflicts. *Jane Eyre* places readers, who for most of the novel are encouraged to privilege Jane's industry and independence over heterosexual marriage, in the ideologically awkward if not impossible situation of needing to reverse their value systems in order to celebrate her marriage to Rochester.

Generally, postcolonial readings of *Jane Eyre* focus on Rochester's involvement in the plantation economy of Jamaica and his marriage to the Creole woman Bertha as well as on St. John Rivers's missionary work in India. The kinds of activities in which both men are engaged are historically part of England's empire-building strategy and are damaging to the colonized. Brontë demonstrates that they are damaging to the colonizers as well: Rochester must fight off listlessness and depression in the arms of various European women, and St. John ultimately dies due to both his overzealous exertion and local conditions. The men's actions are most egregious with respect to Bertha, who might be understood to combine aspects of both the colonizer and the colonized. Rochester marries Bertha, who was born and raised in Jamaica, because she is a financially desirable match. When she demonstrates symptoms of mental illness, Rochester, unable to divorce her due to her medical diagnosis, takes her to England and confines her to an attic room. (Writer Jean Rhys examines these events from Bertha's point of view in the 1966 novel *Wide Sargasso Sea*.) Spivak reads Bertha as emblematic of the effects of imperialism's violence and as a stereotypical representation of a colonial subject who self-destructs "for the glorification of the social mission of the colonizer" (251). Laura E. Donaldson, who takes Spivak's argument and applies it even more specifically to Gilbert and Gubar's work on *Jane Eyre*, adds that Bertha's "insistence upon the violent physical destruction of both Thornfield and herself constitutes an act of resistance not only to her status as a woman in a patriarchal culture but also as a colonized object" (76). Feminist and postcolonial scholars now read Bertha as a sympathetic object of the colonial power dynamic.

Jane's own goodness, while the moral center of the narrative, is entwined with and predicated upon these various evils. The money she earns from Rochester, for example, is tainted in that it comes from his Jamaican earnings. Furthermore, as Spivak writes, "it is the active ideology of imperialism" that facilitates and ensures Jane's success in obtaining both financial stability and kin (247). Jane profits from imperialism and specifically from the removal of Bertha.

The evils perpetuated by Rochester in the West Indies and by St. John in India are not the only abuses of power in the novel. The evils of a patriarchal, imperialist culture extend to the home front and, in particular, to women/female authors and women/female characters. The residue of imperial enterprise is located not only abroad but also in British domestic spaces. Interpersonal relationships such as those between adult and child, master and servant, and Rochester and Jane can be read as working similarly to more global dynamics of power and appropriation. Some of the most intimate relationships call to mind Great Britain's practices with regard to territorial, cultural, and physical domination. Jane, who functions at various times as child, servant, and Rochester's partner, becomes a more local "other," and, like Bertha, the object of a power dynamic at work not only overseas but also at home.

The dominant/subordinate power dynamic is evident in the relationships between adults and children in *Jane Eyre* as well as in the empire's relationships with its colonies. Children's literature scholar Perry Nodelman uses a passage from *Orientalism* to demonstrate the ways in which this power dynamic works between adults and children. He substitutes words related to constructs of childhood so that the passage reads as follows:

> Child psychology and children's literature can be discussed and analyzed as the corporate institution for dealing with childhood—dealing with it by making statements about it, authorizing views of it, describing it, by teaching it, settling it, ruling over it; in short, child psychology and children's literature as an adult style for dominating, restructuring, and having authority over childhood. (29)

Adults create and reproduce an idea of childhood and use it to justify their own authority and perpetuate their power over children. In

Jane Eyre, Jane is reminded by Aunt Reed, Mr. Brocklehurst, and even Aunt Reed's servants that, as both a child and a dependent, she is in a subordinate position to adults. Both Aunt Reed and Mr. Brocklehurst exercise their dominance over Jane by prejudicing others with respect to her character: both tell other authority figures that Jane is a liar. Aunt Reed uses physical force against Jane, privileges her own children, sends Jane away, and later denies her kin and inheritance. When a servant refers to John Reed as Jane's master, she asks, "How is he my master? Am I a servant?" "No," the servant responds, "you are less than a servant, for you do nothing for your keep" (9). For his part, Mr. Brocklehurst, who is an adult in the position of both religious authority and school authority, orders that cheap materials and inadequate clothing be given to the schoolgirls and starves them in order to render them "hardy, patient, [and] self-denying" (53). "Semi-starvation and neglected colds had predisposed most of the pupils to receive infection," and consequently Lowood is decimated by an epidemic of typhus (65). In these instances, significant ones in Jane's early life, adults' power over children is manipulative and destructive. It constitutes the "denigration of the dominated culture" and the "insistence that the dominated people are an inferior race" that Hogan states is part of the colonial practice.

Although servants in the nineteenth century were paid, their relationships with their employers very often took on a form of the colonizer/colonized power dynamic. Middle- and upper-class English often considered members of the working class to belong to another, inferior race and treated them accordingly. Brontë's repeated use of the rhetoric of master and slave, as noted by Mark Stein in his essay on discourses of empire in *Jane Eyre*, makes this power dynamic especially visible, particularly when Aunt Reed and Rochester bark orders at their servants. M. Jeanne Peterson has studied the liminal status of nineteenth-century governesses and noted that they were often considered upper servants due to the fact that although genteel, they were still women paid for labor. This status is underscored by the conversation that

Rochester's guests have about governesses, the "anathematized race" (150–51). When proposing to Jane, Rochester tells her, "You will give up your *governessing slavery* at once" (230, emphasis added). Similarly, Diana and Mary Rivers are to be governesses, "regarded only as humble dependents," and when she inherits, Jane liberates them from this work, regarding this act as her triumph (300). Service work is literal servitude, replicating the colonial relationship, and the colonized, if not the colonizers, in *Jane Eyre* are painfully aware of this.

Jane's relationship with Rochester, like her later relationship with St. John, employs this same power dynamic. Rochester tests Jane in conversation, allows her to misread Grace Poole's identity, hides Bertha from her, approaches her in disguise as a Gypsy, and lures her into a bigamous relationship. Much as he participates in imperialist enterprise, Rochester rules his home. He attempts to manipulate Jane from the start. When first meeting her in the lane outside of Thornfield, Rochester asks, "Whose house is it? . . . Do you know Mr. Rochester? . . . He is not resident, then? . . . Can you tell me where he is?" (97). Coupling this examination with physical manipulation, he orders her to stand so that he can lean on her in order to get back onto his horse (96). Later disguised as a Gypsy, Rochester tells Jane that he is to be married to Blanche Ingram and is especially cruel in saying that when he marries Blanche, Jane will have to leave to take a new situation in Ireland (170–71, 213–15). He does this, of course, to test what kind of response Jane will have when she learns that they will be apart, and he elicits just the reply that he hopes to hear: when asked from what the sea will bar her, Jane replies, "From *you*, sir" (214).

While at Thornfield, Rochester orders Jane to the fireside in a manner less polite than the one in which he requested tea from his servant (103). He says, "Excuse my tone of command; I am used to say 'Do this,' and it is done: I cannot alter my customary habits for one new inmate" (106). While "inmate" was more commonly used in the nineteenth century to refer to an inhabitant, the early nineteenth century saw an increase in the word's usage when referring specifically to an inhabitant of a prison or asylum ("Inmate"). The latter is the more common usage today, and again the word's appearance in the novel underscores the oppressive power relationship in Rochester's home. After interviewing Jane, requiring her to play the piano, and examining her artwork (102–8), Rochester explains, "I put my request in an absurd, almost insolent form. Miss Eyre, I beg your pardon. The fact is, once for all, I don't wish to treat you like an inferior: that is . . . I claim only such superiority as must result from twenty years' difference in age and a century's advance in experience" (114). Then he asks Jane, "Do you agree with me that I have a right to be a little masterful, abrupt?" Jane replies in the negative: "I don't think, sir, you have a right to command me, merely because you are older than I, or because you have seen more of the world than I have; your claim to superiority depends on the use you have made of your time and experience." When Rochester tells her that "leaving superiority out of the question, then, [she] must still agree to receive [his] orders now and then, without being piqued or hurt by the tone of command," Jane reminds him that she is his paid subordinate and therefore receives monetary compensation to suffer their relationship (114–15). Rochester is well aware of his colonizer's authority and feels it justified. Jane's status as a paid laborer, while offering her some compensation for her treatment by Rochester, keeps her in an inferior status.

Jane, however, resists. She does not cower under Rochester's attempts to manipulate her but instead thrives. When Rochester is brash with her, Jane considers this her advantage: "A reception of finished politeness would probably have confused me: I could not have returned or repaid it by answering grace and elegance on my part; but harsh caprice laid me under no obligation; on the contrary, a decent quiescence, under the freak of manner, gave me advantage" (102). When Rochester orders her to speak, Jane smiles, "and not a very complacent or submissive smile either" (113). Despite Rochester's attempt at manipulation and domination, Jane maintains a sense of autonomy, and this is what intrigues him. Jane recounts, "Retaining every minute form of respect, every propriety of my station, I could still meet him in argument without fear or uneasy restraint: this suited both him and me" (134). Her responses in this banter impress Rochester, who "mentally shake[s] hands" with her (115). It is because she is paid that Jane feels at liberty to banter with Rochester; she would have had to express more reverence and deference had she not a defined professional relationship with him. Later, when they are openly in love, Jane goes so far as to tease Rochester in a manner similar to the ways he has teased her. She is cagey and delays disclosing details to him about Bertha's visit to her bedroom at night and St. John's marriage proposal. Ultimately, however, Jane's early impression holds true: "I felt at times as if he were my relation, rather than my master: yet he was imperious sometimes still; but *I did not mind that; I saw it was his way*" (125, emphasis added). Jane *accepts* Rochester's imperiousness as "his way." She does not reject his efforts to manipulate her, nor does her resistance change his dominance. Furthermore, Jane's acceptance indicates that Rochester's behavior, like imperialism, has had the hoped-for effect: the colonized, as a result of the "naturalization" of the imperial practices, begin to believe in their own inferiority. This particular power dynamic is evident in Jane and Rochester's relationship and is maintained even after their marriage. In the novel's conclusion, Jane bends to Rochester's will, and the only change he must endure is physically imposed from without, as he has been blinded and disfigured by the Thornfield fire.

Readers expect narrative closure to right the wrongs of the novel, to offer a corrective resolution, to offer a "good" to counter the "evil." Peter Brooks writes that readers look to the closure of a narrative to impose meaning and coherence upon the narrative as a whole, so much so that we read with an "anticipation of retrospection" (23). For female characters, however, there are only a few options for resolution in nineteenth-century narrative. Rachel Blau DuPlessis writes that in the nineteenth century, "the rightful end, of women in novels was social— successful courtship, marriage—or judgmental of her sexual and social failure—death. These are both resolutions of romance" (1). DuPlessis notes that for female characters in nineteenth-century novels, narratives cannot satisfy readers' expectations for a heroine's romance *and* education/development; narratives usually present "an ending in which one part of that contradiction, usually quest or *Bildung* [educational, social, or moral development], is set aside or repressed, whether by marriage or by death" (3–4). This either/or situation helps to explain the mis-fit of the closure of *Jane Eyre*.

The good established by *Jane Eyre*'s narrative closure is not enough to compensate for the aforementioned evils. While the means whereby the narrative resolves conflict and rights itself include Bertha's death and Rochester's maiming and partial recovery, all of these have to do with facilitating Jane's marriage to Rochester. This marriage, although the fulfillment of Jane's romantic desire, is inadequate and does not offer enough good to counter the imperial evils of the text. Furthermore, this marriage requires Jane to relinquish her work and independence, which readers have been guided by the text to value. In fact, what readers have learned to recognize as good in Jane must be devalued in order to privilege marriage, which, until the end of the novel, has been depicted as evil.

The good of the narrative throughout most of the novel lies not in heterosexual union, which is most often portrayed as destructive, but rather in Jane's own industriousness and self-sufficiency. Largely because of these qualities, readers are, from the beginning of the novel, guided by the narrative to empathize with Jane. Victimized from the start by her cousins and aunt and forced to grow up with minimal affection and harsh conditions, Jane learns to fend for herself. Her coping methods in the face of these conditions are to work hard and become self-reliant. Readers first encounter Jane when, sitting in the window seat and reading, she hides from the torment of her cousins (5). This is an early example of how she learns to protect and contain herself. Once at Lowood, where the physical conditions are dangerous, Jane resolves to succeed:

I from that hour set to work afresh, resolved to pioneer my way through every difficulty: I toiled hard, and my success was proportionate to my efforts; my memory, not naturally tenacious, improved with practice: exercise sharpened my wits; in a few weeks I was promoted to a higher class; in less than two months I was allowed to commence French and drawing. (63)

Jane is not naturally gifted at studies but works hard at them, and doing so enables her to thrive as a student and, later, as a teacher: "During these eight years my life was uniform: but not unhappy, because it was not inactive. . . . I *availed myself fully* of the advantages offered me. In time I *rose* to be the first girl of the first class; then I was *invested* with the office of teacher; which I *discharged with zeal* for two years" (71, emphasis added). The energy and dedication with which Jane commits herself to overcoming her obstacles makes her especially appealing to readers. She claims that her happiness is located in her activity, which is where readers now expect to find her fulfillment. Furthermore, Jane's qualifications, which are the result of her hard work, are validated by the board of the school where she has been working; her new position at Thornfield requires that the Lowood board submit a testimonial on her behalf (76). When Jane decides that "a new servitude" is what she needs, she actively seeks one out, advertising for a position and moving to Thornfield (73). Such daring makes Jane an unusual heroine; in the mid-nineteenth century, the ideal middle-class woman was a stay-at-home wife and mother who had probably traveled very little. Jane's behavior is also quite risky. She admits, "In thus acting for myself, and by my own guidance, I ran the risk of getting into some scrape! And, above all things, I wished the result of my endeavors to be respectable, proper, *en règle*" (75). She acts for herself, and her self-sufficiency makes her useful. Readers learn to like these qualities in Jane and even to cheer her on.

Readers also empathize with Jane because of her recurring experience of hardship. Repeatedly, she is left destitute and humbled. Even when she has steady work, she suffers at times. At Thornfield, she must sit in a room with Rochester's guests while they say offensive things about governesses (150–51). Upon leaving Thornfield, Jane struggles to find shelter and is turned away when she looks for honest work (277–87). It is through her labor that she proves her worth to those who take her in (290–91). She tells the Rivers family, "Show me how *to work*, or how *to seek work*: that is all I now ask; then let me go, if it be but to *the meanest cottage*" and assures them that she will do any kind of labor offered (297, emphasis added). Of course, this is after Jane has been nearly duped by Rochester into engaging in a bigamous relationship and pressured by him to become his mistress. Jane draws upon her own resources, her willingness and ability to work, in order to get out of this particular "scrape." She uses her own industry in order to overcome Rochester's attempts to colonize her, and readers are encouraged to value and celebrate this.

When she discovers on her wedding day that Rochester already has a wife, Jane becomes "a cold, solitary girl again: her life was pale; her prospects were desolate" (252). For her, this marriage proves to be incompatible both legally and morally. Even worse is Rochester's proposal to live together as husband and wife without marriage (269–70). Jane is strong in her resolve to resist the entreaties of this man, who begs her to be his and who has just proven to her that he has another. Jane informs him, "I care for myself. The more solitary, the more friendless, the more unsustained I am, the more I will respect myself," and this is how readers are encouraged to value Jane (270). Jane rejects her colonizer and the attempts to corrupt her that are directly linked to his imperial wrongs, especially his marriage to Bertha. This moment, like the one in which Jane rejects St. John's equally problematic marriage proposal, is an instance for readers to celebrate.

Jane's goodness contrasts with the evil evident in the marriages she encounters. Marriage, referred to by Jane as a "catastrophe" (169), is a central concern of the novel; it is the determining event of a nineteenth-century middle-class woman's life. In *Jane Eyre*, however, nearly all of the marriages depicted result in negative consequences. The answer to the charade in which Rochester and Blanche act as bridegroom and bride is Bridewell, the name of an English prison (157). The marriage of Jane's parents as well as those of Uncle and Aunt Reed and Rochester and Bertha are depicted as damaging, as are the potential unions between Rochester and Blanche, St. John and Rosamond Oliver, St. John and Jane, and Rochester and Jane. Until the final chapter, only Miss Temple and Bessie are afforded ostensibly happy marriages, and these go largely undepicted in the novel. Regarding Miss Temple, Jane notes, "At this period she married, removed with her husband (a clergyman, an excellent man, almost worthy of such a wife) to a distant county, and consequently was lost to me" (71). Similarly, readers get only a slight glimpse of Bessie's relationship with Robert Leaven when she welcomes him home (188–89). Brontë spends far more time and space detailing the problems of marriage than its joys.

Bertha and Rochester's marriage, explicitly integrated into England's colonial venture, is the most problematic of the damaging unions and has been detailed as such by many scholars. Even Rochester's own story of his marriage to Bertha is one of damage. Rochester's father and brother devised the scheme to garner a fortune for him via marriage into a Jamaican plantation family. Rochester claims that he was duped into marrying Bertha and then found it too late to extricate himself due to divorce laws and her diagnosis of madness (261).

In *Jane Eyre*, the act of proposing marriage itself leaves much to be desired. Rochester refers to marriage as his "intention to put [his] old bachelor's neck into the sacred noose, to enter into the holy estate of matrimony" (213). He proposes to Jane using the language of possession: "You, Jane. I must have you for my own—entirely my own. Will you be mine? Say yes, quickly" (217). When Rochester pushes her to remain with him out of wedlock, he uses the language of possession (269), as does St. John when he proposes to Jane: "I claim you" (343). Furthermore, Rochester literally hurries Jane to the church. He nearly forces her (245) and then, when leading the wedding party to discover

Bertha, literally drags her back to Thornfield (249). Jane's first attempt at marriage is halted abruptly in a manner that can only be traumatic for her (247). From the moment of proposal through the fulfillment of the marriage arrangement, marriage is largely determined by the men and depicted as replicating the colonial power dynamic; it is traumatic for both Jane and Bertha.

Marriage, though the ostensible practical life-goal for women, was anything but an equal partnership in nineteenth-century England. It is no coincidence that in both England and the United States, developments in the movements for women's rights and for the abolition of slavery overlapped with each other. Following their exclusion from the World Anti-Slavery conference held in London in 1840, seven years before the publication of *Jane Eyre*, American and English women resolved to agitate for women's rights. As scholars including Stein have noted, Brontë draws on the language of abolitionism, using the rhetoric of master and slave to describe several relationships, including that between husband and wife. The nineteenth century did see developments in women's power within marriage. The Custody of Infants Act of 1839, for example, made it possible for a married woman to be given custody of her children under the age of seven. At the time of the publication of *Jane Eyre*, though, England was still ten years away from passing the Matrimonial Causes Act of 1857, which overhauled divorce law and legislated that women could retain their own earnings when separated from their husbands, and twenty-three years away from the Married Woman's Property Act of 1870, which legislated that women could retain their property as well as inherit when married. In other words, in 1847, Brontë's use of the slavery metaphor in her treatment of marriage in *Jane Eyre* made both emotional and legal sense.

Given the efficacy of the slavery metaphor, the novel's ending is especially troubling. Despite the fact that readers are encouraged to privilege Jane's work and independence over marriage, the final chapters of the narrative require readers to change their values. Jane's marriage to Rochester suddenly asks the reader to accept marriage as a fit reward for her, even though until this moment in the text, marriage has largely been portrayed as evil. Marriage as a "good" is problematic. It is certainly not good for Bertha and many of the others in the text. The "good" marriage of Jane and Rochester and those of Diana and Mary to their respective husbands occur only in the final chapter of the book, and, like Miss Temple's and Bessie's marriages, exist largely outside of the novel's narrative gaze. Jane trades teaching for marriage, and though her new domestic work fulfills her continued desire for a "new servitude" (73), it also makes Jane a woman who "confine[s herself] to making puddings and knitting stockings, to playing on the piano and embroidering bags" (93). She becomes just the kind of woman that she has positioned herself against throughout the entire novel. Moreover, she marries the imperial agent himself. In so doing she becomes the eyes and hand for her maimed husband: symbolically, she sustains his colonial vision and reach.

For Jane's story to end in a conventional marriage plot is jarring. Ironically, Jane's reward for all of her hard work and independence is to surrender them both. She forsakes them in order to serve her husband. Her doing so is a disappointment, especially because Jane develops value through her work. Yet, because genteel women were not supposed to work in nineteenth-century England, narrative convention requires that Jane be conquered by marriage. Jane's marriage to Rochester adheres to the master-servant, colonizer-colonized power dynamic and thus cannot counter the evils produced by it. Jane's marriage to Rochester does not avenge Bertha, nor does Rochester become any less manipulative.

Biographer Lyndall Gordon suggests that Brontë struggled in negotiating issues of women's independence upon marriage in her personal life, as indicated by the advice she sought from friends such as Ellen Nussey and Elizabeth Gaskell (293). Both *Jane Eyre* and Brontë's later novel *Villette* (1853) take up the complicated relationship between women's work, independence, and marriage. In her narrative cageyness, Lucy Snowe, *Villette*'s protagonist, offers a counter to Jane's

"Reader, I married him" by denying readers absolute romantic closure. Ultimately, *Jane Eyre*'s conclusion does not facilitate narrative coherence; it does not reconcile good and evil. Particularly when readers have valued Jane's industry and self-reliance, her "good" marriage to Rochester cannot be expected to compensate for various evils committed at home and abroad. Jane's willingness to become Rochester's wife, the colonized subject in a narrative rife with colonial evils, makes "Reader, I married him" a disappointment rather than a cause for celebration.

Works Cited

Brontë, Charlotte. *Jane Eyre*. Ed. Richard J. Dunn. New York: Norton, 2001.

Brooks, Peter. *Reading for the Plot: Design and Intention in Narrative*. Cambridge: Harvard UP, 1984.

Donaldson, Laura E. "The Miranda Complex: Colonialism and the Question of Feminist Reading." *Diacritics* 18.3 (1988): 65–77.

DuPlessis, Rachel Blau. *Writing beyond the Ending*. Bloomington: Indiana UP, 1985.

Gilbert, Sandra M. and Susan Gubar. *The Madwoman in the Attic: The Woman Writer and the Nineteenth-Century Literary Imagination*. New Haven: Yale UP, 2000.

Gordon, Lyndall. *Charlotte Brontë: A Passionate Life*. New York: Norton, 1994.

"Inmate." *Oxford English Dictionary Online*. Oxford UP, n.d. Web. 30 Jul 2011.

Nodelman, Perry. "The Other: Orientalism, Colonialism, and Children's Literature." *Children's Literature Association Quarterly* 17.1 (1992): 29–35.

Peterson, M. Jeanne. "The Victorian Governess: Status Incongruence in Family and Society." *Suffer and Be Still: Women in the Victorian Age*. Ed. Martha Vicinus. Bloomington: Indiana UP, 1972. 3–19.

Spivak, Gayatri Chakravorty. "Three Women's Texts and a Critique of Imperialism." *Critical Inquiry* 12.1 (1985): 243–61.

Stein, Mark. "Discourses of Empire: Complicity and Disjunction in *Jane Eyre*." *Crabtracks: Progress and Process in Teaching the New Literatures in English*. Ed. Gordon Collier. Amsterdam: Rodopi, 2002. 199–223.

Hawthorne's Pearl: The Origins of Good and Evil in *The Scarlet Letter*

Karen J. Renner

One need read only a handful of Nathaniel Hawthorne's most famous works—"Young Goodman Brown" (1835), "The Minister's Black Veil" (1836), "The Birth-mark" (1843), and, of course, *The Scarlet Letter* (1850)—to realize that the author was profoundly interested in matters of good and evil. Time and time again, Hawthorne reminds us that all humans are guilty of some sort of evil: symbolically, we all wear a black veil or scarlet letter or are marred by a birthmark of some kind. This is not to say, however, that Hawthorne has a purely bleak view of humankind. As we will see, "good" and "evil" are more psychological than metaphysical concepts in Hawthorne's world, qualities that arise from the choices we make and actions we take. The most evil characters in Hawthorne's universe are those who either deny their own moral shortcomings or obsess about the sins of others without accepting that humankind is universally imperfect. It is our responses to our own evil and the evil we see in others that ultimately determine the moral state of our souls. These ideas are central to Hawthorne's most famous work, *The Scarlet Letter*.

The genre and setting that Hawthorne selected for *The Scarlet Letter* profoundly shape its conceptions of good and evil. His choice to construct the book as a romance, as the subtitle of *The Scarlet Letter* declares it to be, allows his themes to exist as metaphysical truths in addition to psychological ones. A narrative in which a tinge of the mystical elevates its events above the everyday, a romance implies that forces beyond the ordinary are at play and thus that the "truths" it contains have a universal application. *The Scarlet Letter* is more specifically a historical romance, as the story takes place in a time period that predates Hawthorne's own era by two hundred years. This historical setting affords Hawthorne an opportunity to define his ideas of good and evil in opposition to those of the Puritan leaders of early New England, whose beliefs he shows to be often harmful. Whereas the Puritans understood evil as a natural product of humankind's imperfect nature that therefore warranted little study, Hawthorne suggests that evil results from a choice to act in ways we know to be wrong. Understanding how and why some go astray could promote sympathy and a sense of community and might even prevent others from making similar mistakes. It would appear, though, that Hawthorne deviates from his psychological understanding of evil in his characterization of Pearl, the child of Hester Prynne and Arthur Dimmesdale, for throughout the text she seems very much an impish creature made so simply by her origins in adultery. As this essay will show, Hawthorne ultimately traces Pearl's strange and sometimes disconcerting behavior back to her treatment by both the community that estranges her and the mother for whom, like the scarlet letter itself, she is a constant reminder of shame. As Pearl demonstrates, evil, for Hawthorne, is not an inherited quality but a psychological response.

While today we think of a romance as a narrative in which romantic love dominates, for Hawthorne and his readers, the word had a very different meaning, defined largely in contrast to the novel. Hawthorne makes the distinction between the two clear in "The Custom-House," the preface to *The Scarlet Letter*, in which he describes a novel as being concerned first and foremost with veracity; he likens a novel to seeing a familiar room at "a morning or noontide visibility" (29). The writer of romances, on the other hand, is more interested in the same room viewed in moonlight so that "whatever . . . has been used or played with, during the day, is now invested with a quality of strangeness and remoteness." Hawthorne expands on the distinction between novel and romance in the preface to his next novel, *The House of the Seven Gables* (1851), in which he writes,

When a writer calls his work a Romance, . . . he wishes to claim a certain latitude, both as to its fashion and material, which he would not have felt himself entitled to assume, had he professed to be writing a Novel. The latter form of composition is presumed to aim at a very minute fidelity, not merely to the possible, but to the probable and ordinary course of man's experience. The former . . . has fairly a right to present that truth under circumstances, to a great extent, of the writer's own choosing or creation. (351)

According to Hawthorne, in a romance, material is handled with a more imaginative hand so that the writer can explore themes in more symbolically suggestive ways.

This potential of the romance is called upon within the very first pages of *The Scarlet Letter* when the narrator imagines plucking a flower from a rosebush and offering it to the reader as a symbol of "some sweet moral blossom" (37). We do not usually think of everyday life as organizing itself around lessons, but at the end of *The Scarlet Letter*, Hawthorne makes it clear that the events of the tale do offer just this kind of "moral blossom," specifically to "be true! Be true! Be true! Show freely to the world, if not your worst, yet some trait whereby the worst may be inferred" (163). Hawthorne's decision to write *The Scarlet Letter* as a romance suggests that he was less interested in providing a historical record than he was in creating a tale that would emblematize a psychological truth. For this reason, it is probably most accurate to term *The Scarlet Letter* a "psychological romance" (Duyckinck 237), as one of Hawthorne's contemporaries did.

That Hawthorne believed that the central message of the tale was to "be true" tells us a great deal about his conception of good and evil. After all, *The Scarlet Letter* is not a condemnation of adultery or even a critique of the type of revenge that Chillingworth undertakes. The sin on which Hawthorne focuses is Dimmesdale's: an unwillingness to confess his own sin, which leaves him wracked with guilt and alienated from his community, a fate that all humans who present a false front to the world will share, according to Hawthorne. To Hawthorne, hypocrisy is "evil" not simply because a moral law has labeled it so but because of its dire mental and emotional consequences for both the individual and the larger community.

Why would Hawthorne choose to explore this theme within a temporal setting that preceded his own by two hundred years instead of simply composing a tale set in his own present time? Perhaps one reason is that *The Scarlet Letter* emerged during a time of remarkable literary output for the nation as a whole. In fact, American authors during the mid-nineteenth century appeared so prolific in retrospect that in 1941 literary critic F. O. Matthiessen dubbed the era the "American Renaissance." Critics since then have used Matthiessen's term to refer roughly to the years between 1830 and the Civil War, during which a great number of classic works of American literature were published, among them Frederick Douglass's *Narrative of the Life of Frederick Douglass* (1845), Herman Melville's *Moby-Dick* (1851), Harriet Beecher Stowe's *Uncle Tom's Cabin* (1852), Henry David Thoreau's *Walden* (1854), and Walt Whitman's *Leaves of Grass* (1855). These texts focus on American topics, perhaps responding to a general feeling at the time that the country needed to develop a cultural heritage distinct from European subjects and traditions. As Ralph Waldo Emerson makes clear in his essay "The American Scholar," the sense was that while America had achieved political independence, its artistic and intellectual output was still overly dependent upon the works of the Old World; "We have listened too long to the courtly muses of Europe," Emerson declares (70). In "Self-Reliance," he similarly laments the fact that "our Religion, our Education, [and] our Art look abroad" for inspiration (279). Public intellectuals such as Emerson urged American writers to embrace distinctly American topics, to capture the rich variety of the country's landscape and culture, perhaps, or to preserve the nation's unique history, as Hawthorne does in *The Scarlet Letter*.

The historical setting of *The Scarlet Letter* affords Hawthorne a unique opportunity to examine his ideas about good and evil, redemption and sin, by contrasting them with the past Puritan attitudes that differed so sharply from his. In *The Scarlet Letter*, Hawthorne probes the psychological consequences of Puritan beliefs, many of which he considers debilitating and harmful. For one, he repeatedly condemns the Puritans for their cruel treatment of outsiders to their community, a criticism delivered with particular piquancy when Hawthorne describes Puritan children as "the most intolerant brood that ever lived" and imagines them "disporting themselves in such grim fashion as the Puritanic nurture would permit; playing at going to church, perchance; or at scourging Quakers; or taking scalps in a sham-fight with the Indians" (64). In addition, Puritans held to the idea of natural depravity: the belief that humans are born sinful. By the time Hawthorne was composing *The Scarlet Letter*, dominant religious beliefs had changed considerably such that sin was viewed as a chosen action or sentiment rather than an innate condition. William Ellery Channing, a close acquaintance of Hawthorne, clearly captures this shift in thought in "The Evils of Sin" (1832), in which he explains that sin is not "some mysterious thing wrought into our souls at birth" (11); rather, "to sin is to resist our sense of right, to oppose known obligation, to cherish feelings, or commit deeds, which we know to be wrong" (214).

That Hawthorne held a similar view is evident in his depiction of Chillingworth. Although Chillingworth is the most evil character in the text, he is not malevolent by nature. He first becomes associated with Satan when he learns of his wife's affair: "writhing horror twisted itself across his features, like a snake gliding swiftly over them" (45). Chillingworth's demonic characteristics are further emphasized when he discovers for certain that Dimmesdale is Hester's silent partner in sin: "Had a man seen old Roger Chillingworth, at that moment of his ecstasy, he would have had no need to ask how Satan comports himself, when a precious human soul is lost to heaven, and won into his kingdom" (92). Chillingworth becomes evil because he chooses to perpetuate Dimmesdale's suffering rather than ease it. The narrator tells us, for example, that when Chillingworth first arrived in town "his expression had been calm, meditative, scholar-like," but after years of tormenting Dimmesdale, "there was something ugly and evil in his face" (85–86). Chillingworth is guilty of what Hawthorne describes in an 1844 entry in his *American Notebooks* as an "Unpardonable Sin," committed when a person "prie[s] into" the "dark depths" of the human soul, "not with a hope or purpose of making it better, but from a cold philosophical curiosity,—content that it should be wicked in whatever kind or degree, and only desiring to study it out" (215).

It might seem, then, that Dimmesdale should also be an evil character, since for years he has chosen to present himself daily to the community as a thoroughly virtuous man. Although cowardice is surely one reason for Dimmesdale's behavior, he also believes that in remaining silent about his adultery, he is trying to maintain "a zeal for God's glory and man's welfare" (88). In Dimmesdale's view, some men hide their true selves because "no good [could] be achieved by them" (88) if they did not. Dimmesdale believes that the community would be severely disrupted by the revelation that their minister is an abominable sinner, and thus he feels compelled to keep his secret. His desire to flee the town with Hester and live as lovers elsewhere is a greater sin than his silence because it is entirely selfish; no longer would he be serving the larger community. After he makes this decision, he is possessed by the urge to commit other wicked deeds. He feels a desire to make "certain blasphemous suggestions" to an "excellent and hoary-bearded deacon" (139) and to deposit into the soul of a young and virtuous girl "a germ of evil that would be sure to blossom darkly soon" (140). Shocked by his own behavior, Dimmesdale wonders, "Am I given over utterly to the fiend? Did I make a contract with him in the forest, and sign it with my blood?" (140). The narrator confirms his suspicion: "He had made a bargain very like it! Tempted by a dream of happiness, he had yielded himself, with deliberate choice, as he had never done before, to what he knew was deadly sin. And the infectious poison of that sin had been thus rapidly diffused throughout his moral system" (141). One becomes evil, Hawthorne implies, by willfully engaging in a wrongful act, behavior that he suggests will lead to further wickedness.

Hawthorne's treatment of Chillingworth and Dimmesdale indicates that he viewed evil as a condition that arises from a willingness to commit sinful acts. The character of Pearl would, however, seem to call that very claim into question, for Pearl's impish behavior seems to be an outcropping of her very nature rather than the result of purposeful action. Pearl is from birth a tempestuous and somewhat wayward child, and the suggestion is that she is like this because she is the product of a sinful act. She thus would seem to refute the assertion that Hawthorne viewed evil as the result of choice and suggest that he believed that evil could be innate or inherited. Certainly, Hester believes the sinfulness of Pearl's origins will influence Pearl's character: "[Hester] knew that her deed had been evil; she could have no faith, therefore, that its result would be for good. Day after day, she looked fearfully into the child's expanding nature; ever dreading to detect some dark and wild peculiarity" (61). As she watches Pearl mature, Hester believes that she can see within her daughter the "wild, desperate, defiant mood, the flightiness of her temper, and even some of the very cloud-shapes of gloom and despondency that had brooded in her [own] heart" (61) while Pearl was growing inside her.

These passages suggest that Pearl could somehow absorb both the passion Hester experienced at the time of Pearl's conception and the anguish she later suffered throughout her pregnancy. To a modern reader, such assertions would suggest supernatural mechanisms at play, but during Hawthorne's time, as critics such as Barbara Garlitz and Franny Nudelman have demonstrated, the inheritance of moral, emotional, and psychological material from one's mother was considered both feasible and biologically likely. In fact, the influence of a pregnant mother's emotional and mental state upon the physical and psychological characteristics of her child was a salient idea due partly to the prominence of P. T. Barnum's American Museum in Hawthorne's milieu. Estimated by historian A. H. Saxon to have been more popular in its years of operation than Disneyland (107–8), Barnum's American Museum frequently exhibited a variety of "freaks," including Bearded Lady Madame Clofullia, the so-called Siamese twins Chang and Eng, and General Tom Thumb. Quite often, the deformities of these "freaks" were accounted for by calling upon the premise of maternal impression. A theory dating back to antiquity, maternal impression held that a pregnant mother's mental state could be passed onto her unborn child in the form of mental or physical abnormalities. Thus, the deformity of Ann E. Leak, the "Armless Wonder," was attributed to her mother having seen her husband coming home with "his overcoat thrown over his shoulders without his arms in the sleeves" (qtd. in Bogdan 219), and General Tom Thumb's diminutive size was explained as having been caused by his mother's deep grief over the drowning of a puppy (151).

To a certain extent, Hawthorne does ascribe Pearl's personality to some version of maternal impression. At one point, for example, he characterizes Pearl as much happier than her Puritan counterparts because "she had not the disease of sadness, which almost all children, in these latter days, inherit . . . from the troubles of their ancestors" (119). There is a spiteful lawlessness to many of Pearl's actions that mirrors her mother's own former rebellion against the community's laws. Pearl is uninhibited by rules of propriety: she dances where she pleases, even on the graves of Puritan patriarchs (89). She also expresses a bitter hatred of those who treat her as an outcast, a sentiment that her mother must have felt during her pregnancy. The narrator tells us, "If the children gathered about her, as they sometimes did, Pearl would grow positively terrible in her puny wrath, snatching up stones to fling at them, with shrill, incoherent exclamations that made her mother tremble, because they had so much the sound of a witch's anathemas in some unknown tongue" (64). Pearl's desire to wreak revenge on the community that reviles her is evidenced further in the games she plays: "The unlikeliest materials . . . were the puppets of Pearl's witchcraft. . . . The pine-trees, aged, black, and solemn . . . needed little transformation to figure as Puritan elders; the ugliest weeds of the garden were their children, whom Pearl smote down and uprooted, most unmercifully" (65).

Nevertheless, Pearl's behavior can also be explained psychologically, and, in fact, the narrator pushes us toward understanding Pearl in this way. At one point, for example, Pearl is described as rushing after a group of Puritan children. The narrator tells us that in that moment "she resembled . . . an infant pestilence,—the scarlet fever, or some half-fledged angel of judgment" (69). But what prompts Pearl's behavior is the children's voiced desire to "fling mud" at Pearl and her mother. Pearl's response to this type of cruel treatment from those around her, the cause of which she does not understand, seems understandable in light of the narrator's sympathetic explanation: the children "scorned [Pearl and Hester] in their hearts, and not infrequently reviled them with their tongues. Pearl felt the sentiment, and requited it with the bitterest hatred that can be supposed to rankle in a childish bosom" (64). While we might be tempted to see Pearl as a symbolic manifestation of her mother's deep resentment of the Puritan community, Pearl's behavior also has a clear psychological impetus.

The other aspect of Pearl's behavior that makes her seem if not supernaturally demonic then at least preternaturally cruel is her kinship with the scarlet letter. On the one hand, it is no surprise that Pearl should be linked to her mother's token of shame; after all, like the letter, Pearl is a marker of Hester's past sin. On the other hand, her relationship to the scarlet letter goes beyond a shared origin in Hester's adultery, for Pearl's mission seems to be to chastise her mother for her past crime. At times, Pearl seems to function as some sort of conscience for Hester, a reminder that the scarlet letter and all it represents can never be discarded. The narrator notes that even as a baby, Pearl is captivated by the scarlet letter: "But that first object of which Pearl seemed to become aware was—shall we say it?—the scarlet letter on Hester's bosom! One day, as her mother stooped over the cradle, the infant's eyes had been caught by the glimmering of the gold embroidery about the letter, and putting up her little hand, she grasped at it, smiling, not doubtfully, but with a decided gleam" (66). As she grows up, she constantly draws attention to the letter: at one point, she flings wildflowers "at her mother's bosom; dancing up and down . . . whenever she hit the scarlet letter," even though, all the while, her mother "look[s] sadly into little Pearl's wild eyes" (66). At another point, she simply decorates the letter with burrs (89). Pearl seems intent on keeping Hester forever aware of her shame.

Pearl performs a similar function for Dimmesdale. She shows him an unusual affection that suggests she instinctively recognizes him as her father, but at the same time, her behavior subtly points out his hypocritical existence. Even as an infant, Pearl is drawn to the voice of her unacknowledged father: "the poor baby . . . directed its hitherto vacant gaze towards Mr. Dimmesdale, and held up its little arms with a half pleased, half plaintive murmur" (49). Furthermore, Pearl's continual requests for him to stand at the scaffold "with mother and me, to-morrow noontide" (101) seem like demands that he publicly confess his part in her creation. Dimmesdale's unwillingness to appease Pearl causes her to withdraw her affection by pulling her hand away or washing off his kiss. Perhaps most unsettling is that Pearl seems cognizant of a connection between the two objects of her interest: when her mother asks her if she knows "wherefore [her] mother wears this letter," Pearl responds, "It is for the same reason that the minister keeps his hand over his heart!" (116). Pearl seems a messenger of retribution, ever delivering a fresh round of punishment for her parents.

Much of Pearl's enigmatic behavior can, however, be accounted for without calling on supernatural explanations. Take, for example, Pearl's fascination with the scarlet letter as an infant. If we examine the passage carefully, it becomes clear that the narrator suggests it is the "glimmering of the gold embroidery about the letter" (66), not the letter itself, that draws the baby's attention. As critics such as Lois Cuddy, Douglas Powers, and Daniel Hoffman have noted, it is really not very surprising that baby Pearl is captivated by the scarlet letter, a piece of bright red fabric "surrounded with an elaborate embroidery and fantastic flourishes of gold thread" (40). Surely Hester's drab dresses, which are "of the coarsest materials and the most sombre hue" (58), only serve to highlight the "fertility and gorgeous luxuriance of fancy" (40) that characterize the scarlet letter, which must seem to blaze upon dresses "of the plainest and most ascetic description" (58). In fact, the scarlet letter and Pearl's clothing are the only spots of color among the "sable simplicity that generally characterized the Puritan modes of dress" (57), the only contrasts to the Puritans' "sad-colored garments" (36).

The continued attention that Pearl gives the letter as she matures makes sense as well. After all, the residents of the town pay a great deal of attention to the scarlet letter, and Pearl has noticed their behavior. She tells Hester, for example, that she overheard an "old dame" say that the "scarlet letter was the Black Man's mark" (120) on Hester. With Pearl aware that the symbol on her mother's chest is an object of great interest to everyone in the town, it is no surprise that her attention would be drawn to it as well. Hester and Dimmesdale are prone to exaggerate the significance of Pearl's behavior toward objects associated with high emotions and unresolved tensions, such as the scarlet letter or Dimmesdale himself. In turn, because Hawthorne focuses our awareness on Pearl's actions toward these emotionally charged objects and characters, we also are apt to see Pearl as something more than just an intuitive little girl, and because her behavior causes both of her parents such distress, she seems like a vengeful sprite who refuses to allow them to transcend their painful past.

The scarlet letter is a painful reminder of Hester's traumatic past and lonely present; thus, the mere sight of Pearl must surely evoke distress for Hester, for we are told that it is "a remarkable attribute of [Pearl's] garb, and, indeed, of the child's whole appearance, that it irresistibly and inevitably reminded the beholder of the token which Hester was doomed to wear upon her bosom" (69). And yet Hester herself has cultivated this resemblance by fashioning Pearl's clothing so that she is very much a visual reflection of the scarlet letter, ensuring that her daughter is linked in her mind with the detestable symbol. The narrator several times mentions the attire Hester has made for Pearl, and with each mention, his disapproval becomes more apparent. He initially claims, rather mysteriously, that "the child's attire . . . was distinguished by a fanciful, or, we might rather say, a fantastic ingenuity, which served, indeed, to heighten the airy charm that early began to develop itself in the little girl, but which appeared to have also a deeper meaning. We may speak further of it hereafter" (58). He mentions Hester's fashioning of Pearl's garb in more negative terms a few pages later but still refuses to discuss it in detail: "Her mother, with a morbid purpose that may be better understood hereafter, had bought the richest tissues that could be procured and allowed her imaginative faculty its full play in the arrangement and decoration of the dresses which the child wore" (62). When the narrator finally delineates the correspondence between Pearl's attire and the scarlet letter, he describes Hester's desire to fashion such a similarity as the result of a morbid preoccupation on Hester's part: "The mother herself—as if the red ignominy were so deeply scorched into her brain, that all her conceptions assumed its form—had carefully wrought out the similitude; lavishing many hours of morbid ingenuity, to create an analogy between the object of her affection, and the emblem of her guilt and torture" (69).

By purposely clothing Pearl in this distressing outfit, Hester ensures that Pearl's appearance will always cause her anguish. Even her choice of Pearl's name—"she named the infant 'Pearl,' as being of great price,—purchased with all she had" (61)—emphasizes that the child is as much a burden as a treasure. Can much of Pearl's seemingly evil behavior be explained by the fact that in many ways, Hester is a bad mother? Her maternal shortcomings are certainly understandable considering her great plight; however, the narrator, at the very least, emphasizes that Hester's perception and treatment of Pearl is problematic.

First of all, it is apparent that Hester's love for Pearl does not immediately blossom at her birth. Hester's actions toward Pearl at the beginning of the novel appear on the outside to be those of a caring mother, but the narrator shows us otherwise by allowing us a peek inside Hester's heart. As Hester emerges from prison, "her first impulse [is] to clasp the infant closely to her bosom; *not so much by an impulse of motherly affection, as that she might thereby conceal a certain token,* which [is] wrought or fastened into her dress" (40, emphasis added). Moments later, Hester again clutches her child "so fiercely . . . that it [sends] forth a cry" (44). This gesture is repeated a third time, again without any sort of maternal care: "she pressed her infant to her bosom, with so convulsive a force that the poor babe uttered another cry of pain. But the mother did not seem to hear it." On the scaffold, Hester remains oblivious to Pearl's pain: "The infant . . . pierced the air with its wailings and screams; she strove to hush it, mechanically, but seemed scarcely to sympathize with its trouble" (50). Were we to view Hester's actions only from the outside, we would think her behavior that of any mother protectively clasping her child, but the narrator repeatedly emphasizes that Hester's feelings toward Pearl are far more complicated.

So conflicted are Hester's feelings, in fact, that she contemplates killing Pearl several times. When Hester is returned to the prison after her distressing time on the scaffold, she is given "constant watchfulness, lest she should perpetrate violence on herself, or do some half-frenzied mischief to the poor babe" (50). While we might accept that the torment of Hester's public shaming might cause her to act more erratically than usual, we find seven years later that Hester still at times questions whether the child's birth is a positive occurrence. Believing that "the child's own nature had something wrong in it, which continually betokened that she had been born amiss," Hester is often "impelled . . . to ask, in bitterness of heart, whether it were for ill or good that the poor little creature had been born at all" (108). As much as we may pity Hester, many readers would find it difficult to sympathize with her sentiments here. (In fact, the previous owner of one of my copies of the novel left a note in the margin alongside this passage: "I think it was good that she was born.")

Thus, although at times Pearl may seem somewhat fiendish, it is important to recognize that many of the more sinister descriptions of her are actually Hester's perceptions, not the narrator's. In fact, the narrator is often very careful to distinguish his perceptions of Pearl from Hester's. When describing Hester's tendency to see a disturbing creature in Pearl's eyes, the narrator even implies that sometimes Hester's perceptions are just plain wrong:

> Once, this freakish, elvish cast came into the child's eyes, while Hester was looking at her own image in them . . . and suddenly,—*for women in solitude, and with troubled hearts, are pestered with unaccountable delusions,*—she *fancied* that she beheld, not her own miniature portrait, but another face in the small black mirror of Pearl's eye. It was a face, fiend-like, full of smiling malice. . . . It was *as if* an evil spirit possessed the child and had just then peeped forth in mockery. Many a time afterwards had Hester been tortured, though less vividly, by the same *illusion.* (66, emphasis added)

The italicized phrases in this passage clearly show the gap between Hester's beliefs and the narrator's, a gap the narrator wishes to emphasize. Hester's perceptions, the narrator suggests, cannot always be trusted. Consider, too, that what Hester really sees when gazing into Pearl's eyes is simply a reflection of herself: in other words, any evil she sees in Pearl is possibly merely a projection of the evil that she senses within herself.

Perhaps the most telling moment occurs when Hester and Pearl visit Governor Bellingham's mansion. Pearl delights in seeing her reflection in a suit of armor and calls her mother over. What Hester observes in the polished breastplate is emblematic of the distorted way in which she views her own daughter. She first sees the token of shame on her breast, but "owing to the peculiar effect of this convex mirror, the scarlet letter was represented in exaggerated and gigantic proportions, so as to be greatly the most prominent feature of her appearance" (72). At the same time, Hester also sees an image of Pearl smiling "with the elfish intelligence that was so familiar an expression. . . . That look of naughty merriment was likewise reflected in the mirror with so much breadth and intensity of effect, that it made Hester Prynne feel as if it could not be the image of her own child, but of an imp who was seeking to mould itself into Pearl's shape" (72). To Hester, the scarlet letter looms unnaturally large, and the image of her daughter next to it seems unnatural and menacing. This passage seems a fitting emblem for the ways in which Hester's trauma has warped her view of her daughter. Since Hester is our point-of-view character for the majority of the book, our perception of Pearl is distorted as well.

In short, then, even Pearl, the character whose mischievous personality most seems to affirm a nature-over-nurture argument, can be explained in psychological terms. She, like Chillingworth, shows that Hawthorne understood good and evil—though he was far more interested in evil—as states of being that result from action and choice. Thus, Hawthorne assigned to all individuals not only the power but also the responsibility to determine their own moral outcomes. In addition, he gave his work an important purpose: by investigating the psychological interiors of tragic and wayward characters, Hawthorne could offer "moral blossoms" that might prevent his readers from erring and encourage them to treat those who do with compassion and understanding.

Works Cited

Bogdan, Robert. *Freak Show: Presenting Human Oddities for Amusement and Profit.* Chicago: U of Chicago P, 1988.

Channing, William Ellery. "The Evils of Sin." *Discourses.* Boston: Bowen, 1832. 213–30.

Cuddy, Lois A. "Mother-Daughter Identification in The Scarlet Letter." *Mosaic: A Journal for the Interdisciplinary Study of Literature* 19.2 (1986): 101–15.

Duyckinck, Evert A. Rev. of *The Scarlet Letter,* by Nathaniel Hawthorne. *Literary World* 30 Mar. 1850: 323–25. Rpt. in Hawthorne, Nathaniel. *The Scarlet Letter and Other Writings.* Ed. Leland S. Person. New York: Norton, 2005. 237–39.

Emerson, Ralph Waldo. "The American Scholar." *Emerson: Essays and Lectures.* Ed. Joel Porte. New York: Literary Classics, 1983. 51–72.

_____. "Self-Reliance." *Emerson: Essays and Lectures.* Ed. Joel Porte. New York: Literary Classics, 1983. 257–82.

Garlitz, Barbara. "Pearl: 1850–1955." *PMLA* 72.4 (1957): 689–99.

Hawthorne, Nathaniel. "From American Notebooks." *The Scarlet Letter and Other Writings.* Ed. Leland S. Person. New York: Norton, 2005. 215–19.

_____. *The House of the Seven Gables. Hawthorne: Collected Novels.* Ed. Millicent Bell. New York: Literary Classics, 1983. 347–628.

_____. *The Scarlet Letter*. *The Scarlet Letter and Other Writings*. Ed. Leland S. Person. New York: Norton, 2005. 7–166.

Hoffman, Daniel. *Form and Fable in American Fiction*. New York: Norton, 1961.

Nudelman, Franny. "'Emblem and Product of Sin': The Poisoned Child in *The Scarlet Letter* and Domestic Advice Literature." *Yale Journal of Criticism* 10.1 (1997): 193–213.

Powers, Douglas. "Pearl's Discovery of Herself in *The Scarlet Letter*." *Nathaniel Hawthorne Review* 16.1 (1990): 12–15.

Saxon, A. H. *P. T. Barnum: The Legend and the Man*. New York: Columbia UP, 1989.

"The Accurst, the Tainted, and the Innocent": *The Strange Case of Dr. Jekyll and Mr. Hyde* and the Fragmentation of Personality in Late Victorian and Edwardian Scottish Fiction_____

Tom Hubbard

"The good ended happily, and the bad unhappily. That is what Fiction means" (Wilde 58). Such is the opinion of Miss Prism, the fussily dogmatic tutor of young Cecily Cardew in Oscar Wilde's comedy *The Importance of Being Earnest* (1895). Miss Prism expresses herself with a confident finality rendered all the more laughable by her boast that she had herself written a novel that followed her formula to the letter.

Wilde was mocking the heaps of artistically mediocre Victorian novels that combined simplistic morality with astute commercialism. Their production was machinelike. The publishers required their writers to work toward a length suitable for issue in three volumes; this was not so much permission as encouragement to be long winded. Stock narrative devices—coincidences, missing wills that turn up at just the right moment, handsome heroes and beautiful heroines who overcome improbable vicissitudes—mixed with a set of assumptions that society's established codes of attitude and behavior were not to be questioned.

During the last quarter of the nineteenth century, writers in the English-speaking world, influenced by developments in literary France, increasingly regarded the writing of fiction as an art requiring as much thematic and structural subtlety as painting, sculpture, or music. A developing regard for the shapeliness of a piece of fiction meant that the three-volume formula was held in disdain by the producers (if not yet the consumers) of novels. The American-born writer Henry James, a connoisseur of European literary refinement, famously mocked the "loose baggy monsters" of dominant modes of nineteenth-century fiction; he indicated his preference for "a deep-breathing economy and an organic form" (84). Novels (or at least "art" novels) would become shorter. Moreover, the linear story, conventionally told, would be re-jected in favor of experimental approaches involving a variety of nar-rative techniques and points of view. All of these modifications char-acterize Robert Louis Stevenson's *The Strange Case of Dr. Jekyll and Mr. Hyde*, first published in 1886.

These specifically artistic changes took place concurrently with growing skepticism about moral, political, and religious precepts that had long been taken for granted. Putting it crudely, Miss Prism's days were numbered. In Stevenson's native Scotland, however, there exist-ed a complex of thought, faith, and feeling that did not prevail south of the border, or at least not to the same degree. This complex we know as Calvinism.

In Scotland, Calvinism took a particularly extreme form. Else-where in Europe it was not so oppressive, though it could be op-pressive enough. The doctrine of predestination cast its shadow over Scottish life. According to the doctrine, one's future was decided—"predestined"—by God before one was born. This applied not only to life but also to the afterlife: you were already on a path to "salva-tion" or "damnation," and nothing you could do in life would alter that course. If your salvation was predestined, your evil acts, no matter how heinous, would not prevent your eventual passage to heaven; if damna-tion was your lot, no kindly or otherwise virtuous behavior would save you from the flames. Either way, there was no incentive to be "good."

Again, it should be emphasized that this is Calvinism at its most extreme; even in Scotland it did not necessarily tend toward such grim implications. As early as 1824, however, there appeared a short, tightly constructed Scottish novel with multiple points of view that exposed the fallacies of any black-and-white way of looking at the world. Writ-ten by James Hogg, the book focuses on Robert Wringhim, a hard-line Calvinist who believes that he is not only "saved" but also tasked with destroying God's enemies. In other words, in following the tenets of his religion, Wringhim is prepared to commit murder. It is not difficult here to find similarities to the religiously motivated terrorists of al-

Qaida, or indeed to certain Christian fundamentalists who have killed doctors whom they believe to be carrying out abortions. The last two words of the novel's title, *The Private Memoirs and Confessions of a Justified Sinner*, sum up its moral-philosophical explorations.

Already we can observe that the binaries of "good" and "evil" are muddied by those of "saved" and "damned." These two sets are not only not identical—they contradict each other. The motifs of Hogg's novel are strongly recurrent in his fellow Scotsman's tale, published some sixty years later, of the supposedly good Dr. Jekyll and the supposedly evil Mr. Hyde—not least in the presentation of a mentality by which an assumption of one's "salvation," or at least of one's moral or religious superiority, can lead to a dangerous sense of entitlement.

The novelist and critic Vladimir Nabokov expressed strong views on what he considered to be crude misconceptions of Stevenson's novella. "Please completely forget," he urges, "disremember, obliterate, unlearn, consign to oblivion any notion you may have that 'Jekyll and Hyde' is some kind of mystery story, a detective story, or movie" (179). Indeed, it is a much more subtle work than most works in the genres listed by Nabokov—though detective stories have arguably moved beyond the simple good-versus-bad formula since Nabokov's time. The thrust of much of Stevenson's work is that human beings, and the moral universe that they inhabit, are more complex than mass-market fiction would suggest.

In his poem "The Song of Rahéro," Stevenson writes, "Now hearken to me, my daughter, and hear a word of the wise: / How a strength goes linked with a weakness, two by two, like the eyes" (*Poems* 16). A leading motif in Stevenson—perhaps *the* leading motif—is that we often find "good" people boring and "bad" people attractive. Rogues are sexier than prigs. Among those of Stevenson's villains who exercise great charm are the pirate Long John Silver in *Treasure Island* (1883) and James Durie in *The Master of Ballantrae* (1889). In *Kidnapped* (1886), the gauche David Balfour possesses a certain moral code of right and wrong, but he finds this challenged by the various older (and often wiser) people with whom he comes into contact, especially the dashing Alan Breck. David forms a close but difficult friendship with Alan. He does not approve of Alan's moral code, which is different from his own, but it is a moral code nonetheless. Such a testing of one's assumptions, such negotiations with the nuances of other people's points of view, is essential for a young person's passage to maturity.

During the nineteenth century there was no shortage of children's books that would have earned the strong approval of the likes of Miss Prism. George Douglas Brown—who tends to be regarded as Stevenson's immediate successor as the most significant Scottish novelist of the day—encountered such an excessively goody-goody story as a child. The book in question had been presented to him by a Sunday school teacher. It was supposed to be a scary tale about a cave-dwelling ogre called Selfishness, but the young Brown found himself having a soft spot for this creature who clearly had been intended by the book's author to serve as a moral warning. Brown recalls his fury at being "got at":

> I had been hoaxed. I had been tricked into reading a story that was no story, but a sermon, and to swallow what was no jelly but a pill. I had been taught to loathe for a foul monster that which was really a fine brave quality of my own nature, making for true strength of character. And his big green tail did NOT Wallop from the far end of the cavern: THERE WAS NO CAVERN! (Qtd. in Veitch 147)

The crass misconceptions that people hold about *Dr. Jekyll and Mr. Hyde* are often not only misconceptions but also preconceptions—people may have seen a film version but never actually have read the book itself! Could that "foul monster" Mr. Hyde actually possess "a fine brave quality"? Perhaps not, but the proposition is at least worth consideration.

Outwardly, Henry Jekyll is a brilliant, conscientious doctor who cares for his patients and is rightly respected and loved by his peers. He has certain dark urges, however, that he finds difficult to repress. The solution is at hand—and it is a solution in more senses than one, for Jekyll's scientific knowledge enables him to create in his private laboratory a cocktail of drugs by which he can perform a biochemical operation upon himself. This mixture will break up the compound within him—that is, a compound of good *and* evil, or at least of benevolent and not-so-benevolent qualities. The experiment results in the creation of the new and supposedly distinct "evil" personality of Mr. Hyde, which occupies the same body as Dr. Jekyll. Jekyll can continue to be the "good guy" while Hyde in effect does Jekyll's dirty work for him, allowing Jekyll to maintain and even believe in his façade of innocence.

It is crucial that we view Dr. Jekyll in the context of his various friendships. The members of his social circle are all professional men, such as lawyer and confidant Utterson and fellow doctor Lanyon. (We learn early on that the latter relationship has deteriorated because of down-to-earth Lanyon's objection to Jekyll's research. This sounds a sour and sinister note, with implications later on in the novella.) They are all bachelors leading seemingly sexless lives, albeit with dark hints of a certain youthful wildness, which in middle age they would rather not dwell upon. They are a bunch of old fogeys—male equivalents, you might say, of Wilde's Miss Prism.

There are curiously few female characters in the work, or at least few who are specifically cited: these are the little girl whom Mr. Hyde tramples, the servant who witnesses the murder of Sir Danvers Carew, and the old housekeeper who gleefully learns that Hyde is in trouble. The book's lack of women and emphasis on secrecy have led some scholars to suggest that Jekyll and his friends are gay—active homosexuality was a criminal offence in late Victorian Britain, necessitating secrecy and perhaps even a sort of double life—but I find this line of inquiry, while understandable, to be too speculative. The homosexual dimension of Wilde's life and work, including his Jekyll-and-Hyde-like novel *The Picture of Dorian Gray* (1891), is much more tragically documentable.

Certainly, though, Jekyll's circle of well-heeled, stuffy pillars of the community has a tendency to be less concerned with its fall from grace, past or present, than with the dire consequences of getting caught. That is clear from the very first chapter, notably in Enfield's observations to Utterson, his cousin, as they stroll stiffly by an ominously shady building in an otherwise respectable neighborhood:

> "And you never asked about—the place with the door?" said Mr. Utterson.
>
> "No, sir: I had a delicacy," was [Mr. Enfield's] reply. "I feel very strongly about putting questions; it partakes too much of the style of the day of judgment. You start a question, and it's like starting a stone. You sit quietly on the top of a hill; and away the stone goes, starting others; and presently some bland old bird (the last you would have thought of) is knocked on the head in his own back garden, and the family have to change their name. No, sir, I make it a rule of mine: the more it looks like Queer Street, the less I ask." (5–6)

We must be clear that "Queer Street" has nothing to do with homosexuality—the word "queer" did not have that meaning in 1886.

There is an odd vagueness, at times evasiveness, about the nature of Dr. Jekyll's youthful antics and indeed about the rascalities that he enables Mr. Hyde to enjoy without fear of the consequences. To claim a homosexual dimension may be too speculative, but it is difficult to rule out something of a sexual nature. Women find Mr. Hyde repulsive (the handsome Dr. Jekyll, presumably and ironically, would be more to their taste), so he may resort to prostitutes or indeed be a rapist. Rape is, of course, where sex and violence come together, and Hyde is certainly violent; his physical aggression toward a small girl anticipates the even greater violence of a murder, which makes Hyde's criminality explicit as never before and turns him (and, eventually, his creator) into a fugitive. (Hyde may, creepily enough, presage the real-life serial killer of prostitutes Jack the Ripper, who stalked the London streets during the late 1880s.)

The narrated instances of evil are all the more shocking and dramatic for the very lack of precision about Hyde's unsavory activities. Inevitably, readers have assumed these to be of a hormonal nature, despite Stevenson's denial of such in the book; "people are so filled full of folly and inverted lust, that they can think of nothing but sexuality," he remarks in a letter dated November 1887 (qtd. in Maixner 231). We should not necessarily take authors' comments on their own words at face value, and I would suggest that here, Stevenson is being more than a little hysterical. He could be notoriously coy about sexual content in fiction and objected to that particular sort of realism in the work of writers such as Émile Zola. In a sense, Stevenson shares something of Enfield's anxious tendency to look the other way.

Indeed, in *Dr. Jekyll and Mr. Hyde* Stevenson dramatizes his own personal conflicts, which originated in his youth in Edinburgh. During the late 1860s and early 1870s, when he was at university in Scotland's capital city, he possessed a streak of rebelliousness. He questioned the religious puritanism and social authoritarianism of respectable middle-class Edinburgh, and he frequented bars and brothels. All this, however, would give way to the counterforce of his deep love of and respect for his father, who was a stern adherent to the old values. The prodigal son would return to the family home, ashamed and contrite. As one leading authority on the author puts it, "Stevenson . . . reveals a teasing mixture of the Tory [conservative] and the radical" (Calder 5).

It is that rebellious, radical side that might encourage us to look more favorably on Mr. Hyde even as we look less favorably on Dr. Jekyll. This is not to suggest that Hyde is one of Stevenson's "attractive" villains on par with Long John Silver and James Durie; Hyde is too ugly and creepy for that, and he certainly does not appeal to women. Nor would I claim that Hyde might actually be a "good guy" after all; that would be absurd as well as perverse. I do not want to replace one oversimplification (Jekyll is good; Hyde is bad) with the opposite oversimplification. Let us consider, however, these lines from Jekyll's own "full statement of the case," the last revelatory chapter of the story: "[Jekyll] thought of Hyde, for all his *energy* of life, as of something not only *hellish* but inorganic" (73, emphasis added).

Stevenson has brought the words "energy" and "hellish" into close proximity with each other on several occasions. One of Stevenson's more "attractive" villains is Richard Crookback—the future Richard III of England—in his adventure story *The Black Arrow* (1888). In a letter thanking a friend for appreciating his portrayal of Crookback, Stevenson notes that Crookback "is a fellow whose hellish energy has always fixed my attention" (*Letters* 266). Yet another juxtaposition of those words occurs in Stevenson's novel *The Wrecker* (1892). The main character, an American artist named Loudon Dodd, muses on what it takes to be successful in his field: "On my side, I would admit that a sculptor should possess one of three things—capital, influence, or an energy only to be qualified as hellish" (59). As an artist himself, albeit a writer rather than a sculptor, Stevenson might well have concurred; he was certainly furiously prolific throughout his short life.

The association of "energy" and "hellish" in such positive contexts suggests that in Hyde's case, there is a quality here that is redeeming, or at least extenuating. Hyde is the youthful rebel against the dried-up father figure Jekyll; the idea that the relationship between the two selves is akin to that between father and son is made relatively explicit in the story. Indeed, Hyde's physical agility is somewhat refreshing to the reader who feels wearied by all the pompous old codgers who dominate the early chapters. There they are, drinking their wine by Jekyll's fireside—don't they need to go out more, get a life?

It remains for us to examine a little more the nature of Jekyll-before-Hyde—or rather, Jekyll before he realized the full implications of having created Hyde. We might say that from his youth, Jekyll has suffered from a dangerous innocence that for a long time had not been severely tested. That is not to say that as a young man he may not have been "guilty" of actions of which his more "upright" nature has been ashamed; he tells us that much in his final statement. It is a dangerous and—paradoxically—*culpable* innocence that eventually destroys him. As a self-righteous, religious prig and a somewhat nerdy medical student, Jekyll has managed "working hard" more assuredly than "playing hard." Accordingly, when he makes choices for which he is not as morally equipped as he thought he was, he cannot pull back again; in a sense, the flaws in his chemical concoction are a metaphor for the inadequacies of his powers of self-judgment.

Several commentators have interpreted *Dr. Jekyll and Mr. Hyde* as a late nineteenth-century version of the old German legend of Faust, best known in the English literary tradition in the form of Christopher Marlowe's play *Doctor Faustus* (1604). Faust is an accomplished philosopher and scientist, a man who has spent his life in diligent study of a wide range of academic disciplines. Old and disillusioned, he comes to feel that he has missed out on the pleasures that less gifted people—the majority of his fellow beings—would take for granted. Accordingly he makes a pact with the devil, who supplies an elixir to restore his youth, and with his new companion—who will one day claim his soul—Faust sets out to explore various forms of pleasure.

Twentieth-century theories of psychology, as developed by Sigmund Freud in Austria and Carl Jung in Switzerland, have offered fresh perspectives on what we might call the Faust-Jekyll syndrome. Freudian and Jungian models of the psyche have in common the premise that repression of natural instincts can be disastrous; if we overdevelop certain aspects of our personality (for example, studiousness or religiousness) and underdevelop others (such as active sexuality or artistic creativity), such imbalances will catch up with us. Twentieth-century psychology therefore challenges nineteenth-century assumptions (such as those of Wilde's Miss Prism) of what is and is not morally acceptable.

Moreover, socioeconomic as well as psychological theories have also severely questioned the old certainties. As a middle-class boy and youth, Stevenson encountered, sometimes with fear but more often with fascination, the very different lives of working-class Edinburghers. Karl Marx's contention that the middle class exploited the working class, that the wealthy were wealthy because the poor were poor, again cut across a supposed good/evil divide. The wealthy might express charity in church on a Sunday but were ruthless slave drivers for the rest of the week; if the poor and oppressed fought back, violently and even bloodily, could we altogether blame them? *Dr. Jekyll and Mr. Hyde* has thus also been read as an allegory of class conflict, anticipating such slightly later novels such as H. G. Wells's *The Time Machine* (1895), with its vision of a future world in which the idle, pretty Eloi live in splendid palaces while the apelike Morlocks toil underground. In Stevenson's work, the description of Mr. Hyde as apelike amounts to more than a nod toward Charles Darwin's theories of evolution (even evolution-in-reverse), which again came as a shock to those who had assumed that their moral and religious values were beyond scrutiny.

With *The Master of Ballantrae*, Stevenson returned to the more "attractive" kind of villain; indeed, this would be his most probing and profound example of the type. Set in eighteenth-century Scotland at a time of civil war, the novel tells of two aristocratic brothers, James and Henry Durie, who have contrasting personalities. Henry is the dull, conscientious manager of the family estate, while James is a wild adventurer who is charismatic to women and whose wicked charm ensnares even hardened members of his own sex. James has no morals and is determined not to acquire any. A Faust or a Jekyll might make a pact with the devil or a devil-like double, but in a tale that exhibits deliberately vague traces of the supernatural, it is more than hinted that James Durie *is* the devil, albeit in apparently human form. Even the dry old family servant Mackellar, a partisan of the more virtuous brother, cannot resist James's spell. He likens James to the serpent in the Garden of Eden (149), but earlier in the same chapter he confesses to a more favorable view of this fiend incarnate: "He had all the gravity and something of the splendour of Satan in the *Paradise Lost*. I could not help but see the man with admiration" (144). Mackellar, diligent student of literature that he is, refers to John Milton's long poetic masterpiece (first published in 1667), in which, it is often claimed, the poet portrays Satan more vividly and alluringly than he portrays the forces of "good." The visionary romantic poet William Blake mischievously explains this phenomenon in *The Marriage of Heaven and Hell* (c. 1793): "The reason Milton wrote in fetters when he wrote on Angels & God, and at liberty when of Devils & Hell, is because he was a true Poet and of the Devil's party without knowing it" (44).

In this light, a number of Stevenson's literary contemporaries and successors could not qualify as "true Poets." During the last decades of the nineteenth century and the early years of the twentieth, there came to the fore a popular and thus commercially successful genre of Scottish fiction called the Kailyard (the Scots word for "cabbage patch") school. The Kailyard writers depicted small-town and rural Scotland as a cozy idyll in which all the inhabitants were unfailingly nice to one another, the local teacher always produced diligent young scholars who became the pride of the whole village, the minister was a wise spiritual leader, and the lower orders knew their place in the presence of the land-owning gentry. There was no jealousy or backbiting in this one-dimensional utopia. As the critic Silke Böger has observed of the Kailyarders' productions, "never is there is a conflict between good and evil because evil is nowhere to be found" (28). As there is no serious conflict in this fiction, it tends to lack energy, hellish or otherwise.

There emerged, however, a counterforce to all this—a number of writers who, predictably enough, have been labeled the "anti-Kailyard," though that obscures the artistic differences between them. George Douglas Brown wrote his novel *The House with the Green Shutters* (1901) as a conscious attempt to posit realism against sentimentality. He took the basic Kailyard formula and subverted it from within. The people of small-town Barbie despise each other, and their gossip is sheer venom. The young scholar returns in disgrace to the village, having been expelled from university. The minister is a long-winded, pompous old fool.

The opposite of Böger's remark, we might think, could be applied here: good is nowhere to be found, or if it tries to appear, it is too weak or ineffectual. There is, however, conflict aplenty in the novel, which is more than just a mechanical reversal of the Kailyard. There is no little hellish energy in the form of the almost satanically splendid John Gourlay, the sometime leading businessman of Barbie, and in the neurotic, alcohol-fueled imagination of his oversensitive son, John Gourlay Jr. The town delights in the downfall of both, and the final confrontation between father and son is one of the most intense scenes in Scottish literature.

Socioeconomic forces, which are merciless to those who cannot adjust to a changing Scotland, cause the elder Gourlay's business to become uncompetitive; psychological forces overwhelm Gourlay Jr., whose natural abilities are defeated by his emotional immaturity. Choices can be made, with the responsibility that accompanies choice, but for the most part, both Gourlays are not in control of their lives. If the possibilities for meaningful decision making can be so diminished, how can we speak of moral freedom? Don't the categories of "good" and "evil" sound hopelessly pious?

The successive "anti-Kailyard" novel is John MacDougall Hay's *Gillespie* (1914), and again it must be stressed that, like Brown's work, the novel goes beyond any simple formula; unlike Brown's work, it is a sprawling book, twice the length of *The House with the Green Shutters* and even more emotionally intense. There is a certain dry restraint in the way Brown tells his story; Hay, by contrast, creates a storm of words and images from the first page to the last. Moreover, Hay was a Church of Scotland minister, and a strongly Calvinist theology broods over and through the novel. Much more than in Brown's tale, determinism vanquishes free will.

The basic elements of *The House with the Green Shutters* reappear in *Gillespie*, with variations: hard-nosed businessman father, hypersensitive imaginative son, maliciously gossipy small town, murderous family violence. Certainly there is no lack of moral dimension or (as critic Ian Spring rightly stresses) moral choice: the father takes malevolent delight in goading his competitors and anyone else who tries to stand in his way, while the son reveals a vein of compassion for his fellow sufferers in a harsh world. "The solidarity of the human conscience" (Hay 74) does play its part in *Gillespie*. However, the fragmentation of the son's personality is represented more as a grim psychological process than as a moral phenomenon. In Brown's book, Gourlay Jr.'s decline does not completely rule out his degree of moral responsibility. Jekyll, of course, consciously and deliberately sets out on a course of self-fragmentation.

Over and above the psychological, there is also a socioeconomic determinism at work here. In *Gillespie*, changes to the fishing industry exacerbate tensions; new developments in transportation affecting the movement and supply of goods fill a similar role in *The House with the Green Shutters*. Events in the wider world affect small communities and the lives of the people who work there. From the 1880s to the time of *Gillespie*'s publication, just before the outbreak of World War I, fiction in Europe and North America took account of seemingly large, impersonal forces that operated socioeconomically as well as on the individual's psyche. The likes of Darwin and Marx provided concepts for the former; the insights of Freud, Jung, and even Darwin offered tools for understanding the latter.

Characters in fiction published at this time became increasingly helpless against all that was ranged against them; the standard hero of earlier novels, triumphing over various vicissitudes, was a less plausible option for writers at the end of the nineteenth century. The American writer Stephen Crane, who challenged smug middle-class moralizing about working-class prostitutes in his short novel *Maggie: A Girl of the Streets* (1893), wrote that the book tried to "show that environment is a tremendous thing in the world and frequently shapes lives regardless" (qtd. in Stallman 78).

All of this applies to Hay's *Gillespie*. However, in addition to various "modern determinisms" (as enunciated by the likes of Darwin, Marx, and Freud), this clergyman's novel still draws heavily on that "older determinism" of Calvin as interpreted in Scottish life and culture, with all the implications that carry over from Hogg's *Private Memoirs and Confessions of a Justified Sinner*. Stated bluntly, just about everyone in *Gillespie* is doomed—in some cases, effectively doomed even before they were born. One of the book's many strong images of inexorability comes in the shape of the small town's "spey-wife," an old fortune teller who predicts deaths that will be both untimely and gruesome. True, Hay manages to end the book on a more transcendently hopeful note: "the truth that is imperishable in the breast of man" (446). However, poor Eoghan Strang, the literate, reflective son of the monster Gillespie, finds all avenues to a better life—a woman's love, university success—utterly blocked to him. The final chapters recounting his descent into madness are among the most harrowing in Scottish fiction, indeed in all fiction:

> Of late he had ceased to think of or hope in the Deity. His soul was broken up in a vast ruin. He saw a large, impassive, determinate hand in the heavens shaking a dagger, beneath which the accurst, the tainted, and the innocent alike were driven. . . . He ran to the mirror and stared at his face. It was drained to a livid whiteness, and subtly underwent a transformation. He was looking in upon the very lair of life. "That's not me," he whispered in fear. "Eoghan! oh, Eoghan!" (408)

There is an enormous distance between that passage and the complacent pronouncement of Wilde's Miss Prism. It is as if the categories of "good" and "evil" have become drained of meaning—or at least of whatever meaning they had carried in earlier days.

Works Cited

Blake, William. *Blake's Poems and Prophecies*. Ed. Max Plowman. New York: Dutton, 1959. Everyman's Lib.

Böger, Silke. *Traditions in Conflict: John MacDougall Hay's Gillespie*. Frankfurt am Main: Lang, 1988. Scottish Studies 7.

Brown, George Douglas. *The House with the Green Shutters*. New York: McClure, 1901.

Calder, Jenni, ed. *Stevenson and Victorian Scotland*. Edinburgh: Edinburgh UP, 1981.

Hay, John MacDougall. *Gillespie*. Edinburgh: Canongate, 1979.

Hogg, James. *The Private Memoirs and Confessions of a Justified Sinner*. Ed. John Carey. London: Oxford UP, 1970.

Hubbard, Tom. *Seeking Mr. Hyde: Studies in Robert Louis Stevenson, Symbolism, Myth and the Pre-Modern*. Frankfurt am Main: Lang, 1995. Scottish Studies 18.

James, Henry. *The Art of the Novel: Critical Prefaces*. New York: Scribner's, 1934.

Maixner, Paul. ed. *Robert Louis Stevenson: The Critical Heritage*. Boston: Routledge, 1981.

Nabokov, Vladimir. *Lectures on Literature*. Ed. Fredson Bowers. New York: Harcourt, 1982.

Spring, Ian. "Determinism in John MacDougall Hay's *Gillespie*." *Scottish Literary Journal* 6.2 (1979): 55–68.

Stallman, R. W. *Stephen Crane: A Biography*. New York: Braziller, 1968.

Stevenson, Robert Louis. *Kidnapped*. London: Heinemann, 1924. Vol. 6 of *The Works of Robert Louis Stevenson*. Tusitala ed. Lloyd Osbourne et al., gen. eds. 35 vols. 1923–24.

_____. *The Letters of Robert Louis Stevenson*. Vol. 2. London: Heinemann, 1924. Vol. 32 of *The Works of Robert Louis Stevenson*. Tusitala ed. Lloyd Osbourne et al., gen. eds. 35 vols. 1923–24.

_____. *The Master of Ballantrae*. London: Heinemann, 1924. Vol. 10 of *The Works of Robert Louis Stevenson*. Tusitala ed. Lloyd Osbourne et al., gen. eds. 35 vols. 1923–24.

_____. *Poems*. Vol. 2. London: Heinemann, 1924. Vol. 23 of *The Works of Robert Louis Stevenson*. Tusitala ed. Lloyd Osbourne et al., gen. eds. 35 vols. 1923–24.

_____. *The Strange Case of Dr. Jekyll & Mr. Hyde*. London: Heinemann, 1924. Vol. 5 of *The Works of Robert Louis Stevenson*. Tusitala ed. Lloyd Osbourne et al., gen. eds. 35 vols. 1923–24.

_____. *The Wrecker*. London: Heinemann, 1924. Vol. 12 of *The Works of Robert Louis Stevenson*. Tusitala ed. Lloyd Osbourne et al., gen. eds. 35 vols. 1923–24.

Veitch, James. *George Douglas Brown*. London: Jenkins, 1952.

Wilde, Oscar. *The Importance of Being Earnest: A Trivial Comedy for Serious People*. London: Smithers, 1899.

From Mice to *Mickey* to *Maus*: The Metaphor of Evil and Its Metamorphosis in the Holocaust

Pnina Rosenberg

Introduction

In a manipulative scene of swarming rats in a sewer accompanied by provocative narration, the Nazi propaganda film *The Eternal Jew* (*Der ewige Jude*) clearly identifies the rat with the filthy, evil, and corrupt Jew, whose only intent is to destroy the world. This motif, derived from medieval anti-Semitic vocabulary, provides the logic that lies behind the need to eliminate the Jew in order to protect humankind. Ironically and perhaps deliberately, Walt Disney's most famous rodent, Mickey Mouse, appears in a work of Holocaust literature, Horst Rosenthal's *Mickey Mouse in Gurs Internment Camp* (1942). One of the victims of virulent Nazi propaganda, Rosenthal created the booklet while he was himself imprisoned in the French camp. In the work, Rosenthal unfolds the prisoner's (hi)story from the Disney character's point of view; Rosenthal knew only too well that a happy ending exists only in a fictional world.

Rosenthal's *Mickey* could be regarded as the forerunner of Art Spiegelman's comic *Maus* (1986–91), which narrates the "survivor's tale" of Spiegelman's father, Vladek. Spiegelman's allegorical story depicts the Holocaust as a cat and mouse struggle—Jews (mice) vs. Germans (cats). Vladek's survival can be interpreted as an ironic inversion of this eternal battle. By analyzing Rosenthal's and Spiegelman's graphic novels, this article will present the multifaceted image of the mouse/rat in the Holocaust lexicon—and its transformation from the emblem of all evil to the symbol of victims as well as survivors.

The Holocaust in Comics?!

A relatively large number of Holocaust comics have been published, but they have not always been viewed favorably. In 2005, a polemical debate arose when two comics were translated into German. In *Yossel*, the American artist Joe Kubert depicts life in the Warsaw ghetto as seen from the point of view of the fifteen-year-old Yossel. In *Auschwitz*, French artist Pascal Croci unfolds life and death in the camp as reconstructed by a pair of fictional survivors. Croci's graphic novel incorporates scenes taken from Steven Spielberg's film *Schindler's List* as well as Claude Lanzmann's documentary *Shoah* and in so doing demonstrates that "the memory of the Holocaust has become a blend" of real and imaginative images. In response to arguments that comics are not an appropriate, that is, serious, medium in which to portray the Holocaust, Croci has argued that "Auschwitz has to be placed in the framework of current politics and be described in a form that leaves little scope for the imagination: it is time, he believes, to be direct with the younger generation" (Boyes).

In 2008, the Anne Frank Foundation published the fictional comic *The Search*, in which a Dutch survivor recounts to her grandson her family's tragic fate and her own experiences as a hidden child during the Holocaust. Eric Heuvel, the book's illustrator, relied on photographs in order to capture the period's visual characteristics accurately (Sawicki). The book, which was translated into various languages and is used in high schools in countries such as the Netherlands, Germany, Hungary, and Poland, was received with mixed feelings. On the one hand, Julia Franz of the Anne Frank Foundation stated that "the comic book brings children closer to a difficult subject. Nazism and the Holocaust stop being abstract history. People begin to take these matters very seriously, as something real, which actually occurred, and not so long ago" (qtd. in Sawicki). On the other hand, opponents argued that the Holocaust was not a subject to be treated lightly and aesthetically, as is done in *The Search* (Ashenfelter). Ironically, the echo of the Holocaust in the American comic series *X-Men*, which focuses on a team of mutants, gave the popular comics a new aura. Cheryl Alexandre Malcolm explains this in her landmark research:

When a new series under Chris Claremont's authorship disclosed that [the character] Magneto was an Auschwitz survivor, the entire concept of outcast mutants gained new depth and complexity. As Magneto equates mutants with Jews and anti-mutantism with anti-Semitism, the *X-Men* Comics rapidly become an extended Holocaust narrative and meditation on the viability of assimilation in light of the near total destruction of the European Jewry. (144)

Furthermore, Magneto's background as a Holocaust survivor enables him to represent his past as a camp inmate and thus engage in a dialogue with other visual representations of the Holocaust.

An additional and different comic representation of this infamous concentration camp, which in itself became a post-Holocaust icon of evil, is presented in the joint venture of artist Neal Adams, who also contributed to the *X-Men* series, and Holocaust scholar Rafael Medoff. The duo created a six-page comic narrating and depicting part of the biography of the artist Dina Gottliebova-Babbitt, who was imprisoned in Auschwitz. Gottliebova-Babbitt created several works in the camp, among them murals in the children's barracks and portraits of Gypsy inmates, the latter commissioned by Josef Mengele for his infamous racial-medical experiments. Adams and Medoff recount Gottliebova-Babbitt's story up until her immigration to the United States, where she found work as an animator. By doing so they recuperate Gottliebova-Babbitt's artistic activities, which helped her to survive in the death camp (Gustines).

Although "graphic novels have become increasingly accepted over the past decade, as artists used the medium of comic books to tell more complex and sophisticated stories" (Lidji), the question of whether it is the proper medium for representing the Holocaust is still being asked. It seems that, as Andreas Huyssen states in his analytical essay on *Maus*, the Holocaust is for many people a subject that is not suited to all kinds of media; thus, the problem becomes "how to represent [it] 'properly' or how to avoid aestheticizing it" (124). The attitude that regards mass-cultural representations as improper or incorrect, thus rejecting comics as a popular media that is sometimes associated with pleasure and amusement, might be reconsidered in view of the fact that incarcerated artists produced caricatures and comics as a means of resistance (Rosenberg, "*Mickey au camp*"). Humor served Holocaust prisoners as a weapon in their ongoing struggle for self-affirmation. Both the existence of art in concentration camps and the prolificacy of humoristic manifestations are attested to by Viktor Frankl, a Jewish Austrian neurologist and psychiatrist as well as Holocaust survivor: "To discover that there was any semblance of art in a concentration camp must be surprise enough for an outsider, but he may be even more astonished to hear that one could find a sense of humor there as well. . . . Humor was another of the soul's weapons in the fight for self-preservation" (54).

Mickey, Maus and Mice on Stage / Reality, Fiction and Propaganda

A black-and-white hybrid image of Hitler-cat-swastika encircled by light appears on the cover of volume 1 of Spiegelman's *Maus*, a pair of graphic novels that narrate his father's testimony as a Holocaust survivor. Above this focal point on Spiegelman's covers appears the title, *Maus*, written in bold red "bleeding" typography. Below the "projected" spotlight is an image of two seated mice, replaced in volume 2 by a group of mice in striped uniforms, blocked by a yellow, zigzagged barbed wire fence. A very similar device was used by Rosenthal while depicting Mickey Mouse as a camp inmate several decades earlier (see fig. 1). The title page of Rosenthal's small booklet, created in 1942 in the Gurs internment camp in France, depicts the smiling face of Mickey Mouse against the background of a circled spotlight, resembling the image that appears at the beginning of cinema cartoons. Rosenthal's Mickey is "projected" onto a wall of the barracks, with a barbed wire fence, one of the visual symbols of the Holocaust (Amishai-Maisels 14; Rosenberg, *Images and Reflection* 99–100), in the background.

Figure 1. Horst Rosenthal, Mickey au camp de Gurs, Camp de Gurs, 1942. Title Page
(© Mémorial de la Shoah, Centre de Documentation Juive Contemporaine, Paris)

The juxtaposition of the cinematographic motifs and the allusion to Nazi regime emblems—Adolf Hitler's image, the swastika, and the barbed wire fence of the concentration camps—with reference to the mouse protagonists evokes the anti-Semitic outlook that identified Jews with rats, an image that was brutally and vulgarly visualized in the Nazi propaganda film *Der ewige Jude* (*The Eternal Jew*). The film was produced in 1940 under the aegis and close supervision of Hitler and his minister of propaganda, Joseph Goebbels, shortly after the German invasion of Poland (Hornshøj-Møller). The director, Fritz Hippler, presented it as a "documentary film" that "shows us Jews the way they really are, before they conceal themselves behind the *mask* of the civilized European," as is printed in rolling titles at the beginning of the film (*Der ewige Jude*, emphasis added).

Filmed in Nazi-occupied territory, the film depicts Polish Jews as estranged and alien to other nations, a people whose only purpose is to take control of the world via an international net of banking and commerce. Yet, despite the corrupt wealth already accumulated by them, they are said to be disgusting, filthy, and sickening. This characterization is visualized in a scene that depicts rats squirming from the sewer and leaping toward the spectator while the narrator emphasizes Jews' ratlike characteristics and behavior. The film was meant to legitimize the exclusion and consequently the destruction of those "inferior" specimens. In the film's program, which was written by the Nazi Ministry of Propaganda and distributed to the audience, its credo is stated very clearly:

> We are shown Jewish living quarters, which in our view cannot be called houses. In these dirty rooms lives and prays a race, which earns its living not by work but by haggling and swindling. . . . We are shown how the Jewish racial mixture in Asia Minor developed and flooded the entire world. We see a parallel to this in the itinerant routes of rats, which are the parasites and bacillus-carriers among animals, just as the Jews occupy the same position among mankind. (qtd. in "*The Eternal Jew*")

In titling his comic *Maus* (that is, "mouse" in German), Spiegelman creates an allusion not only to the Nazi view of the Jews but also to the Nazis' dislike of Disney's protagonist. Spiegelman references this dislike in the epigraph to his second volume, which quotes a mid-1930s German newspaper:

> Mickey Mouse is the most miserable ideal ever created. . . . Healthy emotions tell every independent young man and every honorable youth that the dirty and filth-covered vermin, the greatest bacteria carrier in the animal kingdom, cannot be the ideal type of animal. . . . Away with Jewish brutalization of the people! Down with Mickey Mouse! Wear the Swastika Cross! (qtd. in *Maus* 2)

Both Rosenthal and Spiegelman were conscious of such virulent defamation and ironically incorporated it into their works, thus criticizing the oppressors with their own weapon.

Mickey and *Maus*: An Inmate's (Hi)Story and a Survivor's Testimony

Mickey Mouse in Gurs Internment Camp is one of three comic booklets created by Rosenthal in Gurs, all narrating, from different points of view, his suffering and hardship as a camp inmate as well as his sense of frustration and betrayal. The booklets create a constant contradiction between the humoristic and pseudoidyllic text and illustrations and the subtly implied ruthless reality. This juxtaposition produces satire and irony, which are the only means of protest and resistance left to the author-inmate (Rosenberg, "*Mickey Mouse*"). Rosenthal, who was born in 1915 in Breslau, Germany (now Wrocław, Poland), fled his hometown after the Nazis rose to power. He immigrated to France in 1933, hoping to find a haven in the country, the motto of which is "Liberty, Equality, Fraternity." Mickey Mouse arrived in France a year later as the result of the initiative of Paul Winkler, a Hungarian Jew émigré, who established the newspaper syndicate Opera Mundi. In 1934 Winkler began to publish the comic magazine *Le Journal de Mickey*, which became an immediate success (Grove).

Following the outbreak of World War II, Rosenthal was detained in the Gurs internment camp. In 1942 he was deported to Auschwitz, from which he never returned (Rosenberg, "*Mickey Mouse*"). The hardship he experienced as an inmate in Gurs camp, situated near the Pyrenees, is vividly depicted in the fifteen-page booklet he created while imprisoned. Rosenthal recounts the story of his internment from the point of view of a fictional protagonist known worldwide, Mickey Mouse; this narrative choice enhances readers' awareness of the surrealistic situation that for thousands of human inmates was an actual reality (Rosenberg, "*Mickey Mouse*"). After describing various aspects of life in Gurs, a life characterized by arbitrary cruelty and lack of humanity, Mickey comes to the inevitable conclusion that this place does not suit him and he wants to return to his own "reality" (see fig. 2).

Figure 2. Horst Rosenthal, Mickey au camp de Gurs, *Camp de Gurs, 1942. Mickey's Departure to the USA* (© Mémorial de la Shoah, Centre de Documentation Juive Contemporaine, Paris)

Still, the air of the Pyrenees no longer suited me at all. As I am no more than a cartoon, I simply erased myself with a stroke of an eraser, and . . . hop . . . !!

The guards can always come and look for me in the land of [Liberty], [Equality] and [Fraternity].

(I mean America!). (Rosenthal 229)

Mickey replaces the disillusioning France with the United States, which is not only a synonym of freedom but also Mickey's fatherland. The moral of the final episode is that only a cartoon protagonist, employing the same artistic devices by which he himself was created, can "erase" himself from the camp. Thus Rosenthal bitterly hints that mortal inmates, contrary to fictive heroes, rarely live to see the "Happy End."

The United States, Mickey's anticipated haven at the end of Rosenthal's story, is the setting of the very beginning of Spiegelman's *Maus.* It is not a coincidence that one story's (envisioned) point of departure serves as the other's starting point. Rosenthal unfolds his own experience through the story of Mickey, while Spiegelman transmits his father's survival story, told to his son in the "promised land" of America. Spiegelman's allegorical "animal fable" seems to be derived from, even as it complements and extends, Rosenthal's booklet.

Despite the similarity of the factual sources, there are crucial differences between Rosenthal's and Spiegelman's works. Both artists depict barbed wired fences, but while those on the cover of volume 2 of *Maus* are very stylized and are situated in front of the mice inmates (that is, seen from an outsider's point of view), the undulating fences on Rosenthal's front page are placed behind Mickey and so create our awareness that the scene was drawn by an insider. The different artistic concepts of inmates, as understood by those who experienced the Holocaust and saw it firsthand and those who did not, are derived from the artists' different experiences and manifest in their works "even when the same iconography [is] used" (Amishai-Maisels 15).

Cinematic Devices

Both Rosenthal and Spiegelman create cinematic allusions in their graphic novels, incorporating references to Nazi propaganda and American cartoons. *Mickey* maintains an ongoing dialog with its source of inspiration by means of the text and illustrations, the latter of which switch between long-distance, panoramic views and close-ups and in the process create a cinematic sense of movement. This transition between two registers—the reality of the camp and the fantasy of animated films—increases the satire and subtly sharpens the criticism. It also underscores the sense of total alienation between the world of fantasy, with its stable laws, and the world of reality, in which all accepted laws and norms had been overturned. Mickey Mouse cartoons are based on an unwritten agreement with the viewers, who understand the laws of the medium—the bad guys will be punished and the story will have a happy ending. In light of the author's fate, the irony of Rosenthal's paraphrase of this convention has a heartrending, tragic effect.

Spiegelman's transmission of his father's testimony moves the narrative of *Maus* through space and time—from the United States to Europe and from then-contemporary times to the 1930s and 1940s. The oral testimony is quite often interrupted by mundane trivialities, sometimes ironic or despairing, showing the constant presence of the past that has not passed. The transitions in time and space, depicted through the use of cinematic zooms, force very close reading and viewing and evoke cinematic flashbacks. Huyssen states that this dualism, which is established at the beginning of the first graphic novel, enables Vladek, the father, to create a "safe distance between the two temporal levels; actually the tale of his past is visually framed by Spiegelman as if it were a movie projected by Vladek himself" (126).

When Vladek begins his testimony about his life as a young man in Czestochowa, Poland, he mentions that at that time, "people always told [him he] looked like Rudolph Valentino" (*Maus* 1: 13); a large poster of Valentino's 1921 film *The Sheik*, on which Valentino and his costar are depicted as mice, can be seen in the background. Why are they depicted as Jews, when neither of them was? Is it another bitter, ironic reference to the anti-Semitic Nazi propaganda that constantly stated that Jews controlled mass communications, including Hollywood, as part of their plot to conquer the world? Huyssen observes that Vladek's "exercycle mechanism looks remotely like a movie projector with the spinning wheel resembling a film reel and Vladek, as narrator, beginning to project his story" (126). This, in turn, resembles Rosenthal's artistic device, whereby Disney's protagonist narrates his own story. Despite the generation gap and the different circumstances of their creative production, both artists, from the very beginning, establish dialogues with the symbols and metaphors of anti-Semitic Nazi propaganda as well as the most effective channel for its dissemination—film.

Maus/Mickey Mouse—(Copy)Right Violation

Spiegelman's provocative epigraphs have been discussed by various scholars (Huyssen 139–40; Mulman 85). Huyssen remarks that "the very top of *Maus I*'s *copyright page* features a Hitler quote: 'The Jews are undoubtedly a race, but they are not human'" (129, emphasis added); after citing the second epigraph, he states that "*Maus* thus gives *copyright* where it is due: Adolf Hitler and the Nazis" (emphasis added). Contrary to Spiegelman, who credits his references, Rosenthal "confesses" on the cover page of his booklet that in creating *Mickey*, he breached Disney's copyright, since he made the booklet "without Walt Disney's permission" (see fig. 1). His "confession" has a certain irony. Rosenthal's booklet depicts a bureaucratic and illogical world in which hardship is legally based on and derived from the inhuman decrees of Vichy and Nazi regimes, which declared thousands of people "undesirable." The arbitrary bureaucratic formalities are apparent in the dialogue between Mickey, who is "strolling idly somewhere in France," and the gendarme who arrests him:

> . . . your papers!!!
>
> My papers!?? I never had any
>
> Me, no papers! Me international!
>
> Ah! You are a foreigner! That settles your case. Come on, to the headquarters
>
> And that's how I got to . . . GURS!!! (Rosenthal 227).

It is, therefore, ironic that Rosenthal himself is so pedantic with copyright formalities. He is ironic about his felony—which is regarded as quite a severe misdeed in the normal world—and also implies that despite everything, he tries to cling to "old-fashioned" rules and standards. Rosenthal's "confession" also indicates that the world of the camps functions according to laws that bear no similarity to the laws of his former life.

Mouse/Maus: Allegory and Imagination, Guise/Dis-guise

As discussed earlier, the racist Nazi imagery of the interchangeable components of the unholy trinity—Mickey Mouse/vermin/Jew—is the reason for the artists' allegorical choices. Both Rosenthal and

Spiegelman "identify" themselves with the vermin, but while Rosenthal refers only to his own persona, Spiegelman extends the metaphor to a whole ethnic group, emphasizing it in the subtitle of *Maus*, volume 2, "From Mauschwitz to the Catskills and Beyond," and bonding it with the annihilation of millions of the defamed race.

Maus tells a complex story of Spiegelman's parents' lives in Poland before, during, and shortly after the Holocaust, as told to him by his father, Vladek, in various interviews over a period of time. Spiegelman creates a correlation between the various ethnic/national groups and the animal kingdom. Thus Jews are mice; Germans, cats; Poles, pigs; Americans, dogs; and the French, frogs. This division expands the scope of the family biography and puts the intimate narration into a wider and older context, the eternal cat-rat quarrel. The use of animals is meant to enable Spiegelman to create the needed poetic distance from his family's story and to transmit it in a more "objective" and measured manner. A similar device is used by Rosenthal, who, in "disguising" himself as Mickey, an artist-made animal, distances himself from his own narrative. Creating a temporary haven through one's imagination was a quite common strategy among inmate-artists, who sought refuge in their artistic world, the only world in which they could create the rules (Rosenberg, *Images and Reflections* 105–6).

Yet, even the strategy of an imaginative haven has its limits, as can be seen in *Mickey*'s closing panel. The last episode (fig. 2) depicts Mickey merrily walking toward an American metropolis, accompanied by text noting that as a cartoon, he can escape the camp simply by erasing himself. He escapes to the Land of Liberty. The text is signed "Mickey," with a postscript: "p.s.s. Horst Rosenthal, Camp de Gurs 1942" (see fig. 2). At this crucial point Rosenthal discards his mask; he "discloses" the fact that he is the one who is behind the work's creation and puts an end to the literary/artistic make-believe. It is Rosenthal who fathered the inmate Mickey, and it is he who is staying in the camp; only free-spirited, fictional Mickey may appear and reappear in different roles and places as he pleases. The artist in the camp world can find refuge in his imaginative sphere only to a certain point, at which he finally realizes that the evil of the Holocaust is more powerful than anything imagined before.

This double signature turns the whole playful comic booklet upside down. It obliges us to reread it from a different point of view, from a new angle revealing that the artist is aware of the fact that he has been playing a role while wearing an allegorical mask. Yet, Rosenthal knows all too well that his repertoire is very limited: he can be the author and director of his autobiographical play only in his imaginative-artistic space.

Spiegelman's sophisticated camouflage also falls apart at a very crucial point in his life and in so doing reveals that the schematic of *Maus* was only a guise. "Time flies, Vladek died of congestive heart failure on August 18, 1982" (*Maus* 2: 41), writes Spiegelman, portraying himself near his drawing table, working on the second volume of *Maus*. The volume narrates his father's life in Auschwitz as well as his own life since the publication of volume 1:

> Vladek started working as a tin man in Auschwitz in the spring of 1944. . . .
> I started working on this page at the very end of February 1987. In May
> 1987 Françoise and I are expecting a baby. . . . Between May 16, 1944 and
> May 24, 1944, over 100,000 Hungarian Jews were gassed in Auschwitz. . . .
> In September 1986, after 8 years of work, the first part of *Maus* was published. It was a critical and commercial success. (*Maus* 2: 41)

Here, when the artist exposes himself, he is depicted wearing a mask that enables us to see parts of his face and the back of his head. Ironically, this seemingly intimate exposure, as we understand at the end of this page, is meant for a television crew. This practice goes on in the subsequent pages (42–47), in which he represents himself, the television crew, and his visits to his psychiatrist. At the very moment that "the culture industry's obsession with the Holocaust almost succeeds in shutting down Spiegelman's quest . . . this moment of extreme crisis, as close as any in the work of traumatic silence and refusal to speak" (Huyssen 134) causes Spiegelman to reveal his artistic devices, understanding that he cannot hide completely behind his artistic persona. Marianne Hirsch, while analyzing the scene, says of Spiegelman the following: "No longer isolated, he is surrounded both by the world of his imagination (a Nazi guard is shooting outside his window) and that of his craft (a picture of *Raw* and the cover of *Maus* are on the wall). For him to enter his book has become more problematic and overlaid, the access of his mouse identity more mediated" (27).

Depictions of a painter's self-portrait and his source of inspiration are derived from a long tradition in the history of art. (One thinks, for example, of Velazquez's *Las Meninas* and Rockwell's *Triple Self Portrait*, to name only two.) Spiegelman's, though, presents a new, complex situation: he is both the artist, the creator of the oeuvre—who theoretically dominates it—and its "victim," trapped and entangled in his familial Holocaust history and his current life events. This double exposure forces him to reveal his artistic devices as well as his real self.

Rosenthal, personified as Mickey Mouse, underwent a similar process of "self-exposure" when he realized that his hope of fleeing the camp was not feasible; this is subtly underlined in *Mickey*'s last episode. However, while Rosenthal's postscript reveals the real person behind the artistic disguise, Spiegelman goes one step further. Toward the "Happy End" of *Maus*, when husband (Vladek) and wife (Anja) are eventually about to be reunited, the artist inserts Vladek's photograph as a camp prisoner, which Vladek sent to Anja as a token of survival (*Maus* 2: 134). The juxtaposition of Vladek's photograph with the drawings of father and son as mice might lead to the assumption that Spiegelman means to raise the curtain from his allegorical animal fable, to reveal the mouse's human identity. Yet, Vladek's photograph is problematic; it not an authentic document but an artistic, staged scene, as Vladek himself attests: "I passed once a photo place what had a camp uniform—a new and clean one—to make souvenir photo" (134). Does Spiegelman's use of the photo mean that even "authentic" documentation should be deciphered cautiously? Does it mean that artistic documentation is no less valuable than archival/historical relics?

Both Rosenthal and Spiegelman, when exposing the human being behind the stigmatized mouse, do so very cautiously, as if implying that it is difficult to come to terms with one's self after witnessing such prolonged, virulent propaganda and the atrocities it incites. The first epigraph of volume 1 quotes Hitler: "The Jews are undoubtedly a race, but they are not human." Mickey and the mice of *Maus* are the ironic incarnated victims of the propaganda that singled them out.

Conclusion

Unlike most contemporary Holocaust graphic novels, the forerunners created by Rosenthal and Spiegelman are nonfictional accounts of firsthand experience and family testimony, respectively. Yet, instead of narrating them as "realistic" stories, the authors preferred to produce analogical spheres that recall the folktale, a device that creates a poetic distance from the twisted and abnormal Holocaust world either experienced or memorized and marked through the familial legacy.

In a deconstructive mode, both authors ironically allude to the directives and purposes of Nazi propaganda that, as manifested in *The Eternal Jew*, not only equated Jews with mice but also intended to show the real diabolism of Jews, who "conceal themselves behind the *mask* of the civilized European" (emphasis added). Indeed, the comics' protagonists as well as their creators wear masks and thus create a constant tension between their fictive personae and the historical (auto) biographies they relate. It is not their mouselike selves they conceal but their human, "civilized European" identities, which could not otherwise endure the unimaginable consequences of the Nazi propaganda machinery—mass murder and genocide.

By metamorphosing their protagonists into mice, the artists create a bond not only with the metaphors of Nazi propaganda but also with the absurd, arbitrary, Kafkaesque world in which people are accused and sentenced without knowing why and human beings are transformed into bizarre creatures or exiled to "penal colonies." Thus, Rosenthal and Spiegelman extend the prophetic, accurate vision of the evil world of the Holocaust.

Notes

Horst Rosenthal's booklet, *Mickey Mouse in Gurs Internment Camp, 1942* (*Mickey au camp de Gurs 1942*), is part of the archives of the Mémorial de la Shoah, CDJC, Paris (DL xvi–92). The booklet consists of fifteen 7.5 × 13.7 cm (2.95″ × 5.39″) pages of ink watercolor illustrations.

I would like to express my sincere gratitude to Madame Karen Taieb, director of archive services, for her amiable and invaluable assistance.

Works Cited

Amishai-Maisels, Ziva. *Depiction and Interpretation: The Influence of the Holocaust on Visual Arts*. Oxford: Pergamon, 1993.

Ashenfelter, Morgan. "Holocaust Comics for Students." *Graphic Novels/Comics* 101.28 (2008). Web. 2 July 2011.

Boyes, Roger. "Comic Book Depiction of Holocaust Upsets Jews." *Times* 21 June 2005. Web. 2 July 2011.

Croci, Pascal. *Auschwitz*. New York: Abrams, 2003.

Der ewige Jude. Dir. Fritz Hippler. Berlin: Deutsche Film Gesellschaft, 1940. Film.

"*The Eternal Jew*, Film Program." *The Holocaust History Project*. The Holocaust History Project, n.d. Web. 11 June 2011.

Frankl, Viktor, E. *Man's Search for Meaning: An Introduction to Logotherapy*. New York: Simon, 1984.

Grove, Laurence. "Mickey, Le Journal de Mickey and the Birth of the Popular BD." *Belphégor* 1.1 (2001). Web. 15 July 2011

Gustines, George Gene. "Comic-Book Idols Rally to Aid a Holocaust Artist." *New York Times* 8 Aug. 2008. Web. 11 July 2011.

Heuvel, Eric, Ruud van der Rol, and Lies Schippers. *The Search*. New York: Farrar, 2009.

Hirsch, Marianne. "Mourning and Postmemory." *Family Frames; Photography, Narrative and Postmemory*. Cambridge: Harvard UP, 1997. 17–40.

Hornshøj-Møller, Stig, "The Role of 'Produced Reality' in the Decision-Making Process which Led to the Holocaust." *The Holocaust History Project*. The Holocaust History Project, 1997. Web. 11 June 2011

Huyssen, Andreas. "Of Mice and Mimesis: Reading Spiegelman with Adorno." *Present Pasts: Urban Palimpsests and the Politics of Memory*. Stanford: Stanford UP, 2003. 122–37.

Kubert, Joe. *Yossel: April 1943; A Story of the Warsaw Ghetto Uprising*. New York: IBooks, 2003.

Lidji, Eric. "Using Comics to Teach the Hardest Subject: The Holocaust." *Jewish Chronicle* Dec. 2009. Web. 2 July 2011.

Malcolm, Cheryl Alexandra. "Witness, Trauma and Remembrance: Holocaust Representation and X-Men Comics." *The Jewish Graphic Novel: Critical Approaches*. Ed. Samanta Baskind and Ranen Omer-Sherman. New Brunswick: Rutgers UP, 2008. 144–62.

Mulman, Lisa Naomi. "A Tale of Two Mice: Graphic Representation of the Jew in the Holocaust Narrative." *The Jewish Graphic Novel: Critical Approaches*. Ed. Samanta Baskind and Ranen Omer-Sherman. New Brunswick: Rutgers UP, 2008. 85–93.

Rosenberg, Pnina. «Mickey Mouse in Gurs: Graphic Novels in a French Internment Camp.» *Rethinking History: The Journal of Theory and Practice* 6.3 (2002): 272–93.

_____. "*Mickey au camp de Gurs* by Horst Rosenthal: Humor in the Art of the Holocaust."

Internment and Liberation: Two Views of War Time France. Ed. William Kid. Stirling: U of Stirling, 2003. 1–16. Stirling French Pub. 10.

_____. *Images and Reflections: Women in the Art of the Holocaust*. Israel: Ghetto Fighters Museum, 2002.

Rosenthal, Horst. *Mickey Mouse in Gurs Internment Camp 1942. The Last Expression: Arts and Auschwitz*. Ed. David Mickenberg, Corinne Granof, and Peter Hayes. Evanston: Northwestern UP, 2003. 226–29.

Sawicki, Paweł. "Holocaust Comics. A Story in Drawings." *Memorial and Museum Auschwitz-Birkenau*. Memorial and Museum Auschwitz-Birkenau, 5 Mar. 2008. Web. 10 July 2011.

Spiegelman, Art. *Maus: A Survivor's Tale*. 2 vols. New York: Pantheon, 1986, 1991.

Understanding Communal Violence: Khushwant Singh's *Train to Pakistan*

Patrick Colm Hogan

Societies have paradigms of good and evil. These are socially definitive cases, often historical instances that embody what the society most
admires or despises. In the West, perhaps the most prominent paradigm
of evil is the Holocaust, personified in Adolf Hitler. If one wants to cite
a definitive case of personal evil, the most likely candidate is Hitler. If
one wants to evaluate the evil of an event or policy, one's standard is
likely to be the Holocaust. In the case of evil, such paradigms are commonly historical traumas, events so socially devastating that they seem
to defy coherent representation and explanation (see Kacandes and ci-
tations on recent views of history, trauma, and literature). As such, the
paradigms of evil often become prime cases for historical analysis and
literary representation—attempts to give a coherent, meaningful representation to the horrors and explain them in satisfying ways.

In modern India, perhaps the most salient paradigm of evil is the violence that broke out between religious communities at the time of the
partition of the subcontinent. British rule of India ended in 1947 with
the division of the country into the Muslim-majority nation of Pakistan and the secular, Hindu-majority nation of India. Large numbers
of Hindus and Sikhs left areas that were designated for Pakistan, and
large numbers of Muslims left areas assigned to India. In the course
of this massive exchange of populations (about ten million people
were displaced [Wolpert 348]), violent conflicts broke out between the
Hindus and Sikhs and the Muslims. The result was devastating and
traumatic communal violence—a million deaths as well as staggering
rates of rape, abduction, arson, theft, and other forms of violence and
cruelty (348). (Since the opposed groups were religious communities,
this is referred to as "communal violence," and the associated attitudes
of anger, hate, bias, and so on are referred to as "communalism.")

The legacy of Partition violence has been enduring. It has in many ways shaped the subsequent histories of both nations. Though much less extensive than the Holocaust in its human devastation, the Partition is comparably baffling, seemingly "unnarratable" in the sense of resisting a coherent causal account. Nonetheless, historians, novelists, political scientists, and filmmakers have sought to make sense of Partition violence. One of the earliest and most influential novels to treat this issue is Khushwant Singh's *Train to Pakistan* (1956). Singh was in his early thirties when India was partitioned and his "family was uprooted from its ancestral home" (Lall). Within a decade of the terrible events, Singh had integrated his personal experiences, historical knowledge, and journalistic skills to produce this short novel. He set himself the task of depicting how and explaining why, over the course of a few weeks in late 1947, enduring communal harmony ("It had always been so" [5]) was destroyed in a small Indian village.

One of the most haunting images of Partition violence is that of a silent train with no visible occupants pulling into a station. Indian trains are notoriously crowded—prototypically overflowing with brightly clothed passengers who not only crowd the compartments but also cover the tops of the trains. The silent train, with no discernible people inside or on top, is already ominous, unnatural. When the officials at the station enter, they find compartments piled with corpses—Hindu and Sikh victims of Muslim militants in Pakistan, or Muslim victims of Hindu and Sikh militants in India, depending on the origin of the train. The experience was repeated again and again. It became a symbol of Partition violence generally. In a sense, it is this silent train that Singh sets out to explain in his novel. (There are, of course, many ways in which one might interpret the train in Singh's novel. For a discussion in relation to themes of modernity, for example, see Aguiar.)

The Story of Jugga and Nooran

Singh's novel is not a generalized treatment of historical events. Rather, it is a particular story with many individual characters, perhaps the

---

most important of whom are the ill-fated lovers Jugga, a Sikh criminal, and Nooran, the daughter of the local mullah (Muslim cleric)—lovers who, as is so often the case in romantic stories, cross acceptable social boundaries and suffer tragically as a result.

The events of the novel take place in the small village of Mano Majra. The town's population is roughly half Sikh and half Muslim, with one Hindu family living there as well. Singh is careful to represent the different communities as closely interrelated in what we might call their "practical identity." One's practical identity is one's knowledge and practice of integration with a group, one's interlocking interconnection with other members of a society. Muslims, Hindus, and Sikhs are not three separate societies who happen to share one space. They are a single society integrated at countless points. Thus, we find that even the activities of the mullah and his counterpart, the bhai (or "brother") in charge of the Sikh gurdwara (place of worship) are inseparable from one another. The morning prayer of the mullah serves as a signal to the bhai to begin his morning prayer (4). Indeed, the three religions are not even entirely distinct in worship. They share "the local deity," the object of reverence and petition "to which all villagers—Hindu, Sikh, Muslim . . . repair secretly whenever they are in special need of blessing" (2). Such deviation from sectarian orthodoxy and sharing of local beliefs is a crucial feature of the villagers' practical identity.

The problem is that categorial identity can be so readily called into play. Categorial identity is the social self-definition that labels a person as essentially this or that—"Sikh" or "Muslim," "male" or "female," "Pakistani" or "Indian." Such labeling is easy to trigger (see Hirschfeld 1) and is highly consequential. The result of identity categorization is severe prejudice in favor of one's own group (the "in-group") and against the other group (or "out-group"). The prejudice is both a matter of evaluations (e.g., seeing the out-group's work as inferior [Duckitt 68–69]) and a matter of motivations (e.g., preferring dominance of the in-group over the out-group, even if that means an absolute reduction in benefits for both groups [85]). (For more on practical and categorial identity, see Hogan 23–65.) One main concern of Singh's novel is tracing this transformation from shared practical identity to antagonistic categorial identity.

The novel begins with a group of Sikh criminals murdering a Hindu man during a robbery. The group is led by Malli, who arranges to frame Jugga for the crimes. Jugga is eventually arrested for the murder and robbery. In addition to being framed by Malli, he is a "natural" suspect because his father had been convicted of precisely these crimes (59). The assumption of virtually everyone in the novel—except the communist Iqbal (41)—is that a propensity toward crime is heritable, and Jugga has inherited this propensity from his father. The assumption is continuous with the view that particular propensities are shared within a religious community—a view crucial to the rationalization of communal violence.

After Malli, Singh introduces Jugga and Nooran. He then goes on to introduce Hukum Chand, the magistrate and deputy district commissioner, who has been sent to Mano Majra with the task of preventing communal violence. He is an ambiguous character. He does try to prevent the killing of Muslims, but he is not very effective at his job. Moreover, his efforts seem to be driven by a combination of greed and fear of punishment (22); in some areas, "officials were disciplined if they failed to deter communal violence" (Talbot and Singh 82).

Another major character, Iqbal, is introduced soon after this. Iqbal is a political activist whose mission is similar to that of Chand. Though not a member of the Communist Party proper, Iqbal does belong to an organization with parallel ideas. As scholar Yasmin Khan points out, the Communist Party of India was one of the few groups to have a realistic assessment of the communal situation in India, recognizing "the Muslim right to self-determination" (31). This is in keeping with Iqbal's non-communalist views. At the same time, Iqbal's relative ineffectiveness recalls the fact that communists were "sidelined from mainstream . . . politics" (31) and were much more consequential in Bengal than in the Punjab, where Singh's novel takes place (176–77).

In keeping with the secularism of the party he represents, Iqbal's religious affiliation is ambiguous. As Singh explains, Iqbal "was one of the few names common to the three communities" (35); that is, it could be Hindu, Sikh, or Muslim. While Singh clearly sympathizes with many of Iqbal's attitudes and analyses, he portrays him as hardly Indian at all. For example, Iqbal refuses to eat the local food (45–46) and relies on canned goods (35). More significantly, when there is a threat to the Muslim community of Mano Majra, he fails to engage in any sort of productive action. Singh may be suggesting that this is related to Iqbal's lack of religious commitments (35). His lack of religion is what makes him relatively neutral among the opposed communities, but it also marks him as foreign to them.

Iqbal's ambiguous identity serves him well in some situations (e.g., when Sikhs assume he is Sikh and Muslims assume he is Muslim). However, it proves dangerous elsewhere, as when he is arrested and accused of working for the Muslim League—an accusation seemingly (though, of course, not really) supported when he is stripped and found to be circumcised, unlike a typical Hindu or Sikh.

While Iqbal and Jugga are in prison, one of the death trains arrives from Pakistan. The introduction of Chand and Iqbal represents the entry of outside elements into the ordinary life of the village; however, they are relatively inconsequential. This is the first moment in which something occurs that could have a genuine impact on the village. Chand determines that he must get the Muslims out of Mano Majra at all costs. To do this, he devises a bizarre scheme that involves spreading rumors about Muslim League activities in the village and insinuating that the recent murder in the village may have been communally motivated.

Whether due to Chand's manipulations or the spread of rumors from other sources, the leading Sikhs of the village eventually decide that it would indeed be best for the Muslims to leave. The Sikh police and military explain that the Muslims cannot take their property with them. Rather, they should entrust their property to a village representative.

Malli is appointed as that representative, and the implications for the security of the Muslims' property are obvious.

Following this, Sikh militants join with Malli's gang to kill the Muslims passing on a train to Pakistan—including the Muslims from Mano Majra—putatively as an act of revenge. Scholars Ian Talbot and Guharpal Singh note that Sikh militant groups were often "ruthlessly efficient killing machines" (49). Chand realizes that he does not have sufficient police forces to do anything effective (Singh 158). Finally, he decides to release Jugga and Iqbal so that they may learn about the planned attack and, he hopes, do something about it. Iqbal does nothing; however, Jugga resolves to do whatever he can. In part, this is because he realizes that Nooran is one of those endangered. Certainly, his strong feelings for Nooran are the primary motivational force here—an unselfish force, because he is saving her so that she can live somewhere else, without him. But it is important to note that his concern is not only for Nooran but also for the Muslims generally. Jugga's attachment to Nooran has served to broaden his sympathies to her entire community. As one character reports early on, due to Jugga's relation with Nooran, "no one dares say a word against the Muslims" (23). However, this intercommunal sympathy does not mean that Jugga abandons Sikh practices. Indeed, he goes to the gurdwara for prayers before he sets out to try to stop the massacre.

The plan of the militants is a simple one. They have tied a thick rope over the tracks, just a bit above the top of the train. When the train passes, the rope will kill many of those riding on the tops of the compartments and knock others to the ground. If the train stops, the militants will kill the passengers systematically; if it does not, they will shoot through the windows. Jugga determines to climb up to where the rope is tied and sever it before the train arrives. He manages to cut the rope just before Malli's men see and shoot him. His body falls beneath the train that now passes safely on toward Pakistan.

Explaining Evil

At a very general level, Singh suggests two necessary conditions for Partition violence: individual motivations must converge with developing social dynamics to produce the killing. This is just what one would expect. Indeed, the argument is uncontroversial to the point of banality. What is significant about Singh's account is the way in which he specifies both factors.

As to individual motivation, revenge is often a force in cycles of violence. Singh certainly indicates this. However, there are two complications to Singh's treatment. First, in Singh's account, it appears that impassioned calls for revenge are often rationalizations or even mere lies that serve to conceal cooler motives of greed. In the chaotic conditions of Partition, material goods became readily available. Malli's involvement with the scheme to kill the Mano Majra Muslims is the most obvious case of this. Having been appointed caretaker of the Muslims' property, he has every reason to wish to ensure that they do not return. But the same sort of rationalization appears in more moderate cases as well. For instance, Chand instructs the police inspector to have the Muslims "get out, but be careful they do not take too much with them. Hindus from Pakistan were stripped of all their belongings" (21). This seems to suggest that Chand is interested in revenge or in compensating Hindus who have lost their belongings (though refugees begin to arrive in Mano Majra only after this, and they "have not lost much in Pakistan" [97]). But he goes on to note that "magistrates have become millionaires overnight" (22), clearly suggesting his own self-interest.

Second, as the preceding example already suggests, Singh reveals something about the operation of revenge in these conditions and more generally about the operation of human cognition and emotion. We may understand revenge very simply as an anger-driven activity in which one seeks to victimize someone in retaliation for real or perceived harm. Note that this involves causal attribution. One can only retaliate against a target person or group that is blameworthy, and a target is blameworthy to the extent that he/she/they caused the prior harm. We generally think of this in individual terms: Smith harmed Jones, and Jones takes revenge by harming Smith. This is in keeping with one form of human causal reasoning, reasoning based on particulars. But we also engage in category-based causal inference. If a lion eats a gazelle, we do not explain this action by referring to anything specific about that particular lion. We attribute it to the nature of lions.

Humans readily expand categorial explanation to blame. They do so with particular ease in relation to racial, sexual, ethnic, and religious identity groups as well as other groups commonly taken to share definitive properties. Singh suggests this expansion of blame, so to speak, at both ends. First, the initial harm need be suffered not by the revenger but by someone in the revenger's identity group. Second, and more disturbingly, the target of revenge need not be the person who actually committed the act. Rather, the target becomes the causally "explanatory" group, thus potentially any member of that group. We see this in the case of Chand when he speaks about Muslim property. Even if his case for revenge (or retribution) were sincere, it would be invalid. Clearly, the Pakistani Muslims who took the property of Hindus are not the same people as the Mano Majra Muslims. Moreover, the lost property of the Mano Majra Muslims would not compensate deprived Hindu refugees from Pakistan. Rather, some Muslims would be punished for the misdeeds of other Muslims and some Hindus or Sikhs would be compensated for harm done to other Hindus or Sikhs.

But how does someone come to adopt categorial rather than particular causal inference? To a great extent, it is simply a matter of identity categories becoming more salient than individual properties in a given context. Singh makes it clear that ordinary village life involves a sort of nonequilibrium steady state, a relatively stable though continually active condition (like, for instance, a whirlpool). A system in such a state has a number of conditions to which it might readily change. But the change needs to be initiated. Often, that occurs by the entry of some external element into the system. Such an external element may have limited effects, if it does not conduce toward the more readily accessible states of the system. However, if the direction of causal alteration is properly oriented, it may lead to a shift in the entire system. For example, ice is a readily accessible state from purified water at thirty-one degrees. But ice probably will not form unless some impurity is introduced into the water, which provides a site for "ice 'nucleation'" (Ball 163). Clearly, the same point does not hold if the water temperature is at thirty-three degrees. Singh's novel suggests that blame based on identity categorization is a persistently accessible condition. Thus it is always relatively easy to foster systematic identity categorization—even when the alien factors introduced to the system have only a small bias in that direction. The events of Partition had far more than a small bias.

Of course, not all forms of identity categorization are as equally accessible. Singh suggests that there are, for example, class categories that could have been activated for the villagers but were not. Rather, specifically religious identities become an issue. This is not because religious identity categories are more true or essential than class or other categories. Indeed, they seem to be relatively arbitrary when compared with the practical interests and competences of the people involved. However, religious categories have a long history of motivational force and social functionality in India. (On this and other reasons why a particular identity category may become predominant, see Hogan 66–123.)

Moreover, as Singh stresses, the opposition between Sikhs and Muslims has been important within Sikhism itself. The last of the great Sikh gurus, Gobind Singh, saw members of his family martyred by Muslim rulers (Nesbitt 60–61). He made it "part of a baptismal oath that no Sikh was to touch the person of a Muslim woman" (Singh 150), thereby precluding romantic attachment. He also constrained the friendship of Sikhs and Muslims by limiting the possibilities for sharing meals (Nesbitt 58). These rules inhibited the development of motivationally consequential relations of practical identity. Late in the novel, the bhai argues against Sikh militancy by insisting that "only people who have committed crimes should be punished" and that it is wrong to kill "the Muslims here . . . in revenge for what Muslims in Pakistan are doing" (149). In response, he is told that Guru Gobind Singh said, "Only befriend the Turk [thus a Muslim] when all other communities are dead" (150). After Guru Gobind Singh, anything that heightened religious categorial identification for Sikhs was, at the same time, likely to heighten intergroup antagonism with Muslims.

Singh points to two sorts of external elements that may enter into otherwise-stable social systems: information (including false information) and people. In the case of Partition, the information often took the form of rumors spreading vivid and emotional stories of massacres. In itself, the effect of this could go in any direction. However, there is a standard bias in the communication of news. In effect, Sikhs, Hindus, and Muslims faced two sorts of stories. One concerned violence *by* people with whom they shared an identity category; the other concerned violence *against* people with whom they shared an identity category. Stories of the former sort were largely irrelevant to them (after all, they had not engaged in violence themselves). However, stories of the latter sort represented potential threats. This and other preferences were likely to make stories of massacred Sikhs far more widely circulated among Sikhs and stories of massacred Muslims far more widely circulated among Muslims.

Singh presents clear instances of such rumors. After the train of corpses arrives in Mano Majra, the two communities divide physically and talk among themselves. Among the Muslims, "rumors of atrocities committed by Sikhs on Muslims in Patiala, Ambala and Kapurthala, which they had heard and dismissed, came back to their minds" (120). In this case, the rumors appear to be more or less spontaneous. However, Singh also stresses that rumors may be spread directly or indirectly by political leaders who set out to create communal tension. Thus, while the Muslims are contemplating the threat from Sikhs, Sikhs are considering the hints dropped by the police that the murder of a Hindu in Mano Majra was communally motivated (121).

Similar points hold for the influx of people. Two sorts of people were likely to enter into a village at the time of Partition. The first were refugees. Refugees as a whole would bring with them anger against a range of individuals and communities. However, the refugees entering a particular village were not a random selection. Hindu and Sikh refugees entered Hindu and Sikh areas; Muslim refugees entered Muslim areas. This has two effects. First, there is a further biased circulation of information. Second, there is an intensification of possible emotional contagion. When faced with angry or suffering people, we are likely to "catch" their mood to some degree (see Hatfield, Cacioppo, and Rapson). The more people with the same or related emotions we encounter, the more likely this effect becomes. As hurt and angry refugees enter a small society, the likelihood increases that sorrow and anger will spread across that community. More exactly, the likelihood increases that the emotional contagion will reach some critical threshold and have systemic consequences.

Singh somewhat downplays the role of refugees, at least in instigating violence directly. Nonetheless, both Chand and the police subinspector suggest the importance of refugees in the initiation of violence. For example, the latter warns of refugees "who have been through massacres and have lost relations," and Chand expresses concern that refugees "may start the killing in Mano Majra" (97). Moreover, the refugees take part in theft from Muslim homes in the village (139). More significantly, they make up the majority of volunteers who join Malli's gang and the militants in the final attempted attack on the train to Pakistan (152). Still, they are depicted as followers rather than leaders. Their presence does in a sense "start the killing," but it does so through the mechanisms of emotional contagion, intensified by the manipulations of political leaders.

Once emotional contagion occurs and communal violence results, systemic factors will probably exacerbate the condition. For one thing, it is likely that other violent elements in the society will be reoriented. For example, it becomes increasingly likely that criminal violence will take on a communal coloring. In addition, the prominent motivation of greed acquires a possible systemic outlet in communal violence leading to theft. This is evident in the actions of Malli's gang. Assigned to care for the property of the Muslim refugees, they immediately loot the carts of the Muslims (137) and "ransack Muslim houses" (139).

As the reference to criminal violence suggests, such disruptions in the steady state of a social system are not inevitable even with a strong systemic bias (here, toward identity categorization with identity-based blame) and an influx of appropriate influences (such as communalist rumors and refugees). Rather, there are agencies whose function is, precisely, to preserve the steady state of society even in the face of potential disruptions. These include the local leadership, thus the putatively neutral political stratum (as opposed to the various disruptive partisan leaders), as well as the legal system, prominently the police and military. But here, too, there is a problem. At the time of Partition, there was likely to be an overrepresentation of Hindu police and military in Hindu areas, Sikh police and military in Sikh areas, and Muslim police and military in Muslim areas. The situation was only worsened by the fact that non-Hindu police and military were more likely to leave Hindu areas, and so on. Thus an initial disproportion was almost certain to increase. Moreover, in addition to refugees, at the time of Partition, there was likely to be an influx of military personnel in border areas. In Pakistan, these were likely to be Muslim; in India, they were likely to be disproportionately Sikh and Hindu. (Singh notes that, at one point, "A unit of Sikh soldiers arrived" in Mano Majra [77].) Police and soldiers are subject to the same tendencies as other people: the same identity categorizations, emotional contagion, etc. Thus they are unlikely to correct disruptions in the initial steady state of the village fully. Indeed, their own communal biases may be a further force pushing the system toward categorial identification and blame, thus communal violence (cf. Talbot and Singh 86–87). Precisely the same points apply to political leaders. As Talbot and Singh explain, Partition "violence evinced a high degree of planning and organisation by para-military groups . . . assisted by the quiescence, if not active involvement of state agents" (66). We see all this clearly when Malli's gang loots Muslim homes. As Singh notes, while they were stealing the refugees' goods, "Malli's men . . . saw Sikh soldiers come and go" (139), indifferent to the blatant violation of law.

Singh presents this range of factors to account for the violence of Partition. What, then, accounts for the nonviolence? What explains the fact that some districts were relatively peaceful and some individuals were devoted to preventing violence, even risking and sacrificing their own lives?

There are several obvious possibilities here. For example, one might imagine that a government official's commitment to his or her official duty might inhibit the violence. However, Singh's novel does not present us with any cases in which the government officials are in fact neutral between communities and prevent violence for reasons of duty. Officials and other leaders all appear to be biased by their categorial identifications or corrupted by greed. Similarly, political commitments have little effect in leading Iqbal to engage in any beneficial actions. Local loyalties and ethical arguments are further possibilities. But these have virtually no effect on the majority of Sikhs in Mano Majra. In the case of the bhai, they certainly contribute to his refusal to be complicit in the violence. However, they do not lead him to any positive action.

Again, there is only one case of such positive action—that of Jugga. Singh suggests that there are two key factors in Jugga's self-sacrifice on behalf of the Muslims of Mano Majra. The first is attachment. His bond with Nooran inspires him to wish to protect her. (For a critical interpretation of this, see Daiya.) But it also inspires him to think about and respond to other Mano Majra Muslims, not as impersonal and identical members of an out-group but as individual people with whom he has concrete relations. In effect, attachment particularizes and helps to reorient thought and attitudes from categorial to practical identity— prominently including the concrete, particularistic connections one has with other people in one's sphere of action and acquaintance. Singh's suggestion here is that sincere and consequential commitment to opposing communal violence can come most significantly from violating at least one proscription of Guru Gobind Singh—the proscription on sexual relations across Sikh and Muslim identity categories. Only deep relations of attachment—perhaps necessarily the sort of familial relations that we find between Jugga and Nooran—are sufficient to inspire courageous and self-sacrificing opposition to communal violence. Perhaps the best way to prevent such violence initially is through the development of many such cross-identity bonds.

Works Cited

Aguiar, Marian. "Making Modernity: Inside the Technological Space of the Railway." *Cultural Critique* 68 (2008): 66–85.

Ball, Philip. *Critical Mass: How One Thing Leads to Another*. New York: Farrar, 2004.

Daiya, Kavita. "Postcolonial Masculinity: 1947, Partition Violence and Nationalism in the Indian Public Sphere." *Genders* 43 (2006). Web. 18 June 2011.

Duckitt, John. *The Social Psychology of Prejudice*. New York: Praeger, 1992.

Hatfield, Elaine, John Cacioppo, and Richard Rapson. *Emotional Contagion*. Cambridge: Cambridge UP, 1994.

Hirschfeld, Lawrence. *Race in the Making: Cognition, Culture, and the Child's Construction of Human Kinds*. Cambridge: MIT P, 1996.

Hogan, Patrick Colm. *Understanding Nationalism: On Narrative, Identity, and Cognitive Science*. Columbus: Ohio State UP, 2009.

Kacandes, Irene. "Trauma Theory." *Routledge Encyclopedia of Narrative Theory*. Ed. David Herman, Manfred Jahn, and Marie-Laure Ryan. New York: Routledge, 2005. 615–19.

Khan, Yasmin. *The Great Partition: The Making of India and Pakistan*. New Haven: Yale UP, 2007.

Lall, Arthur. Preface. *Train to Pakistan*. By Khushwant Singh. New Delhi: Time, 1981. n. pag.

Nesbitt, Eleanor. *Sikhism: A Very Short Introduction*. Oxford: Oxford UP, 2005.

Singh, Khushwant. *Train to Pakistan*. New Delhi: Time, 1981.

Talbot, Ian, and Gurharpal Singh. *The Partition of India*. Cambridge: Cambridge UP, 2009.

Wolpert, Stanley. *A New History of India*. 4th ed. Oxford: Oxford UP, 1993.

Unfinished Evil and Benevolent Community in Edwidge Danticat's *The Farming of Bones*_____

Katharine Capshaw Smith

Unearthing a moment of devastating historical evil, *The Farming of Bones* (1998) describes the 1937 massacre of Haitians and people of Haitian descent living in the Dominican Republic. Edwidge Danticat's novel explores the problem of explaining evil as the main character attempts to understand the political and social forces that create the conditions for genocide. A Haitian woman working as a domestic servant in the Dominican Republic, Amabelle Désir finds herself thrust into a crisis of national political upheaval. The reader of the text discovers the causes of the genocide only through indirection, as does Amabelle. But as the book explores the larger ideological causes of the massacre, the narrative becomes interested in the role of individual choice in perpetuating evil, focusing on specific characters who act on the distorted and malicious ideas advanced by the state. Danticat embraces an ethos of the unfinished in *The Farming of Bones*, for just as there is no straightforward closure for the main character in the face of the massacre, the process of remembering and representing evil is continuous rather than discrete. The unfinished representation of evil signifies the ethical imperative to recognize the permanence of evil as a feature of human existence as well as the need to tell continuously the stories of those erased from the historical record by virtue of social class, nationality, and race. When characters discover good in the wake of catastrophe, satisfaction comes through creating community and connection by sharing stories of loss and building relationships with others. There can be no simplistic triumph of good over evil in the wake of genocide. But what can survive and provide comfort are connections with others, particularly with those who have a memory of the atrocity and who can acknowledge and validate loss.

Shadowing Amabelle's story is the deep and conflicted history between Haiti and the Dominican Republic. The two countries share the island of Hispaniola, with Haiti to the west and the Dominican Republic to the east. In the northern part of the island, the border between the nations is marked by the Massacre River (named for a seventeenth-century brutality), which is central to Danticat's text. Since their separation in 1697 by colonial powers, with France claiming Haiti and Spain claiming the Dominican Republic, the two countries have had a tense, often oppositional relationship, especially after Haiti threw off French rule in 1804 to become the first black republic in the New World. Because of three hundred years of the slave trade, both countries contained large populations of African descent as well as classes of mixed heritage and those claiming lineage from colonial powers. The Dominican Republic was ruled by Haiti for several decades during the nineteenth century. Because of racism and fear of slave rebellions, the international community shunned Haiti and thereby caused political and financial instability that rendered Haiti more economically precarious than the Dominican Republic.

The two countries were also occupied by the United States at virtually the same time in the early twentieth century, although the US government did not galvanize its occupational forces, preferring again to keep the countries and campaigns separate. Because of supposed fear of German invasion, the United States occupied Haiti from 1915 to 1934 and the Dominican Republic from 1916 to 1924. The "Yankis" (Danticat 239) helped propel the disintegration of the Haitian peasant economy, as Danticat indicates in the story of Sebastien and Mimi's dispossession. The US occupation also helped create the conditions for the rise of Rafael Trujillo, the dictator who ruled the Dominican Republic from 1930 to 1961 and engineered the 1937 massacre. Trujillo ascended through the ranks to become the leader of the Dominican military under US occupation and was trained by US Marines; after the Americans retreated from the Dominican Republic, a reactionary nationalistic impulse allowed Trujillo to rise to political dictatorship. His campaign to rid the country of its Haitian presence, which he imagined as a contaminant, resulted in part from a distorted patriotic impulse in the wake of American occupation and in part from profound cultural racism. In truth, Haiti and the Dominican Republic had always been intertwined, particularly at the border, which laborers and traders regularly crossed. People of Haitian descent were born on the Dominican side, often without tangible linguistic or familial roots in Haiti. In fact, people of African descent populated the Dominican Republic as well as Haiti, and Trujillo himself was descended on his mother's side from African ancestors, a fact he tried to suppress by wearing lightening makeup in public.

In October 1937, Trujillo launched a two-week campaign to kill Haitians living in the Dominican Republic, ordering his soldiers to use machetes rather than guns so that it would seem as though peasants, supposedly defending themselves from attacking Haitians, rather than the government had committed the massacre. Between twenty and thirty thousand Haitians were ruthlessly murdered. Also killed were many dark-skinned Dominicans and people of Haitian background whose families had lived in the Dominican Republic for generations. Dominicans referred to the massacre as "El Corte," the cutting; in Haitian Kreyòl (or Creole), the event took the name "kout kouto," the stabbing. While Trujillo paid some financial reparations to the Haitian government, virtually no money was offered to the victims, and Trujillo would not admit that the event occurred. US president Franklin Delano Roosevelt also largely ignored the massacre, seeking to maintain peaceful relationships between the United States and the various Caribbean nations. The event dropped out of the public historical record in Haiti and the Dominican Republic. Danticat herself carried out interviews, archival research, and historical reading in order to construct her story. *The Farming of Bones*, then, intervenes in the writing of history even as it is a work of fiction. The novel offers the story of a peasant woman caught up in a moment of atrocity, and by envisioning the events through Amabelle's perspective, it allows the record of history to be constructed through the seemingly powerless voice of a poor Haitian woman.

In Danticat's text, evil is associated with difference and separation. Remembering that Hispaniola is one island with two national identities, we can recognize that many pairings in the text can be read as comments on the divided and unequal relationship between Haiti and the Dominican Republic. Amabelle was orphaned as a young child when her parents drowned crossing the river as they tried to return to Haiti after marketing in the Dominican Republic. Taken in by Don Ignacio, Amabelle grows up alongside Señora Valencia, his daughter, who is close in age to Amabelle and who also has lost her mother. They share the same virtual family—Amabelle refers to Don Ignacio as "Papi"—but their statuses are profoundly dissimilar. One could consider their familial relationship as akin to the political and economic relationship between the Dominican Republic and Haiti: sharing the same space, one becomes wealthy and powerful and the other dependent and vulnerable.

Soon after Danticat introduces the family, Valencia gives birth to twins, a dark-skinned girl who appears small and weak and a light-skinned boy who seems stout and hearty. Danticat presents these twins as another analogue to the national relationship, and in the family's response to the children, malevolent cultural concepts become readily apparent. At first Valencia seems to acknowledge that her daughter's skin manifests an African heritage, although she employs magical thinking in order to ascribe the color to Amabelle's presence rather than to the background of her family or that of her husband, saying, "My daughter is a chameleon. She's taken your color from the mere sight of your face" (11). Soon after, Valencia worries, "Amabelle do you think my daughter will always be the color she is now? . . . My poor love, what if she's mistaken for one of your people?" (12). Valencia struggles to place her daughter's skin color within her own prejudiced definition of family. In other words, she refuses to believe that a black child could have been born to the Dominican elite. Later in the book, Valencia even recasts her daughter's color so that it confirms rather than challenges Dominican national heritage. Valencia says to Amabelle, "See what we've brought forth together, my Spanish prince and my Indian princess. . . . Look at that profile. The profile of Anacoana, a true Indian queen" (29). By casting Rosalinda, her daughter, as descended from people indigenous to Hispaniola, Valencia creates a mythologized familial (and national) narrative, one that erases an African presence. While Valencia strains to interpret dark skin color within culturally acceptable narratives, her husband, Pico, refuses entirely to accept or acknowledge his black daughter. The example of the twins allows us to consider the weight of the particular kind of evil that will come in the massacre; though Amabelle and Valencia should be as sisters, and the twins should be equally embraced, the evil of racism causes separation and rejection. With the twins serving as a metaphor for the relationship between Haiti and the Dominican Republic, the massacre that comes later takes on a familial character.

Other dimensions of Haitian life in the Dominican Republic connect explicitly to the evil of the massacre. Most prominent is the depiction of the effects of labor in the cane fields. When Amabelle visits the cane workers as they wash in a stream behind the sugar mill, a description of Kongo, a man whose son was recently killed, points to the exploitation of labor by linking it subtly to the massacre to come: "He moved slowly as he scrubbed his wide shoulders and contorted himself to allow the parsley to brush over the map of scars on his muscular back" (62). Sugarcane is harvested with machetes, which makes it dangerous work, and the cane itself can cut brutally. Danticat describes Kongo's back as a "map of scars," one that presumably could be read in order to discover the sources of his injuries and that again indicates the novel's investment in national spaces. Also important to this description is the mention of parsley, the herb that will be used as a test of national identity during the massacre. Here it retains one of its primary functions within Haitian and Dominican peasant cultures, that of cleansing. (The use of parsley later will be distorted to indicate national cleansing of Haitians from the Dominican Republic.) In the cleansing scene we also meet women whose damaged bodies speak of the cruelty of cane work.

Early in the text, then, Danticat draws parallels between the evil of labor exploitation and the horror of the genocide to come. Even the title of the work, *The Farming of Bones*, points to both experiences, as cane cutting is likened to the mowing down of bodies in the massacre.

Haitians have been separated out by the labor of the cane fields, a condition that promotes exploitation and mistreatment. Language becomes another vehicle through which Dominican authorities attempt to separate Haitians in order to exclude and disempower them. From a distance, it would seem that language would offer a discrete line between the cultures: Dominicans largely speak Spanish, having been colonized by Spain, while Haitians speak Kreyòl, a language created from French and African sources. However, the boundaries between the two languages are fluid, as Danticat indicates at various moments, such as when a woman speaks to Father Romain and Father Vargas early in the book: "'I pushed my son out of my body here, in this country,' one woman said in a mix of Alegrían Kreyòl and Spanish, the tangled language of those who always stuttered as they spoke, caught as they were on the narrow ridge between two nearly native tongues" (69). Even for characters who do not combine Spanish and Kreyòl, language does not necessarily separate Haitian from Dominican, since the cane workers and domestic workers such as Amabelle speak fluent Spanish. In order to use language to separate Haitians and render them targets of the massacre, Dominican authorities (in life and in the novel) asked people to pronounce the word "parsley" (or "perejil") in Spanish. A Kreyòl accent would render the word "pewegil" and identify the speaker as Haitian. Valencia, who espouses the malevolent separatist cultural concepts of the Dominican elite, concludes her explanation of the parsley test by asserting, "On this island, you walk too far and people speak a different language. Their own words reveal who belongs on what side" (304). Valencia is incorrect, of course; Haitian workers speak both languages, and even Amabelle can pronounce "perejil" with a Spanish accent, as she explains during the massacre. Danticat demonstrates that the machinations of evil come through distinctions and separations that are imagined rather than real. Language itself is fluid, permeable, and dynamic. Danticat uses language in the novel to emphasize cultural interdependence rather than segregation; the Dominican military sought clear lines of linguistic distinction, an impossibility given the way the two countries are intertwined, and instead turned toward Spanish pronunciation in order to isolate and injure Haitians.

In life and in the novel, Trujillo used a flawed logic of division to rationalize the massacre. Of course, one person cannot kill tens of thousands without the complicity of others. Danticat is as much interested in the role of individual choice within the massacre as in the larger ideologies behind the event. Danticat constructs Pico, Valencia's husband, as the most straightforwardly evil character in the text. An ambitious member of the military, he aims to follow in Trujillo's footsteps toward political success. Like the historical Trujillo, Pico has African ancestry about which he is ashamed. The narrator tells us, "With his honey-almond skin and charcoal eyes, he was the one that baby Rosalinda resembled most" (35). He is also the most explicitly racist character in the text, as he rejects his dark daughter and smashes the tea set Valencia uses to serve the cane workers during her son's funeral. Perhaps in order to compensate for his vexed status as a person of mixed background under Trujillo, Pico executes the orders to kill without hesitancy. Importantly, Pico is also the most isolated character in the book. His marriage to Valencia is shallow and superficial, and by the end of the book he has taken up residence in the city rather than in the country with his wife. In a book that emphasizes the importance of community, Pico stands outside even marriage, the most intimate of personal connections.

Valencia herself participates in evil through passivity and silence about her husband's racism and murderous actions. When Pico rejects Rosalinda, Valencia will not stand up for her daughter. The narrator explains, "She chose to ignore his avoidance of their daughter and of herself, as she did all the other things he did that were not pleasing to her" (137). Danticat makes clear in this passage that Valencia's passivity is a choice, a personal decision that will ensure her continued status as a married woman of privilege. W. Todd Martin, Lynn Chun Ink, and April Shemak, among other critics, discuss Valencia's acceptance of patriarchal and classist ideas. The more thoughtful and resistant Dominican figures in the text, Papi and Beatriz, challenge Valencia's constant refusal to recognize her husband's immorality:

> "There is a side to Pico that I never liked," confessed Beatriz. "He's always dreamt that one day he would be president of this country, and it seems to me he would move more than mountains to make it so."
>
> "He is a good man," Señora Valencia said, using her customary defense of her husband.
>
> "Many good men commit terrible acts these days," Beatriz said. (150)

Using platitudes to soothe her conscience and divert the conversation, Valencia reveals her complicity in an ideology that produces racial violence. After the massacre, when Valencia explains her position, she turns toward her national and marital status: "If I denounce this country, I denounce myself. I would have had to leave the country if I'd forsaken my husband. Not that I ever asked questions. Not trusting him would have been like declaring that I was against him" (299). Here Valencia identifies herself with the national agenda: her identity and voice are completely subsumed in her place as a married woman, and she maintains her status within Dominican culture by blindly following its demands. Valencia is entirely obedient to a system that exploits the poor (including Amabelle) for labor and initiates the horrific slaughter of innocent people. Once faced with the massacre, Valencia protects several Haitian individuals even though she is hemorrhaging from childbirth, but she steadfastly refuses to see her investment in the political system. She says, "I did what I could in my situation" and argues for her personal motivations in order to gain forgiveness from Amabelle: "I hid them because I couldn't hide you, Amabelle. I thought you'd been killed, so everything I did, I did in your name"

(299). She explains her action as justified by personal affection rather by an awareness of the injustice of massacre. Valencia even concludes by again excusing her husband and ignoring the motivations behind the event: "Amabelle, Pico merely followed the orders he was given. . . . We lived in a time of massacres" (300). Such dismissive explanations are more than just inadequate: they reiterate Valencia's investment in the evil social structure of separation, exploitation, and prejudice that fueled the massacre. Valencia again decides to preserve her privilege rather than recognize the truth.

Individual choice is at the heart of the depiction of the massacre as well. Amabelle and her friends Yves, Tibon, Wilner, and Odette reach the border town of Dajabón, where Amabelle hopes to find her lover, Sebastien, and his sister, Mimi. Members of the military and upper-class people have gathered to listen to Trujillo give a speech in a church, while people of various classes and backgrounds crowd the plaza. Some seem sympathetic to Amabelle and Yves, offering "looks that showed they pitied us more than they despised us" (190), while others are overtly hostile. Five Dominican teenagers attack Amabelle, Yves, and Tibon, killing Tibon with Yves's machete and then carrying the three of them into a crowd, past two laughing soldiers. More people become involved in the attack, lining up to force parsley down Amabelle's and Yves's throats. They throw rocks at the pair and brutally kick them. The attack begins with Amabelle noticing particularities among the five teenagers, including the details of their reddened faces and the probable age of one of the attackers. By the end, the attackers have lost particularity and become a mob. What begins as individual choice ends in mass violence. While soldiers may be literally and figuratively behind the attack on Amabelle and Yves, local people execute the assault. Instead of constructing evil as a distant, governmental affair, Danticat emphasizes the participation of individuals—not necessarily the people in power or even the economically and socially privileged—in the execution of evil. By emphasizing the specific details of the attack, Danticat forces the reader into an intimacy with violence. The reader must recognize that individual blows come from individual people who have made the choice to support such a malevolent ideology.

If evil is connected to separation and isolation, impulses toward good in the novel all cohere around community and continuity. Such a construction fits with the novel's emphasis on the intertwined histories and experiences of Haiti and the Dominican Republic. One of the first instances of an attempt at building connection comes through the relationship between Don Ignacio (Papi) and Kongo. When Valencia's twins are born, Pico and Papi drive recklessly toward home, hitting and killing Kongo's son, Joël. Papi later wishes to meet with Kongo, initially to pay for the young man's funeral. When Amabelle brings this message to Kongo, he replies, "Tell him I am a man. . . . He was a man, too, my son" (109). Kongo asserts a relationship of equality between himself and Papi. Later in the book, Papi seeks out Kongo in the cane fields, and together they walk into the woods. Kongo describes their conversation to Amabelle and Yves: "Misery makes us appear small, . . . but we are men. We spoke like men. I told him what troubled me, and he told me what troubled him. I feel perhaps I understood him a trace and he understood me" (145). This conversation is one of the few moments in the book in which Haitian and Dominican individuals interact as equals, and it tellingly takes place in the woods, a site away from the town and the cane fields, a place unmediated by the culture of oppression. What Papi and Kongo have in common is sorrow and a willingness to build understanding and connection by talking about loss.

A similar moment occurs between Kongo and Valencia while Valencia's son, who is named Rafael after Trujillo, is being buried. Valencia invites cane workers to take tea with her while her husband is at the funeral. Such a gesture emphasizes Valencia's desire to acknowledge the Haitian workers, though only through the formal style of European social practice, a gesture empty of true empathy. Kongo and Valencia have both just lost their sons, and the opportunity for connection becomes apparent to Kongo, who strides "boldly into the parlor" (115), where Valencia blocks Kongo's fingers from touching baby Rosalinda. Kongo grabs Valencia's hand and kisses her fingernails, a gesture that sarcastically extends the European social performance Valencia has initiated through the tea. He then speaks, in Spanish, frankly and sympathetically with her. Like his exchange with Papi, Kongo's talk with Valencia holds out the promise of connection and empathy. Given Valencia's deep investment in racism and classism, however, such a promise cannot come to fruition. While Papi and Kongo speak in the woods, Valencia and Kongo talk in the parlor, immersed in a culture based on uneven social power. Crossing the boundaries between Haitian and Dominican contexts remains desirable but nearly impossible.

Perhaps the most elemental instance of good within the text comes through the relationship between Sebastien and Amabelle. Deeply in love, the two have a connection that is expressed through telling stories about their losses, particularly the loss of Amabelle's parents and Sebastien's father. Also important to their relationship is its affirmation of physical beauty. In the first dreamlike section of the novel, Sebastien asks Amabelle to remove her clothing: "'Your clothes cover more than your skin,' he says. 'You become this uniform they make for you. Now you are only you, just the flesh'" (2). While an erotic scene, the exchange also highlights the way in which Amabelle's physical body signifies cultural value. When clothed as a domestic servant, Amabelle takes on that exploited identity. Sebastien recognizes the value of the black body: "'Look at your perfect little face,' he says, 'your perfect little shape, your perfect little body, a woman child with deep black skin, all the shades of black in you, what we see and what we don't see, the good and the bad'" (3). Since the narrative will describe the destruction of black bodies, his comments are particularly resonant: "Everything in your face is as it should be." His comments anticipate what will happen to Amabelle, her jaw broken and face cut at Dajabón, and help explain why Amabelle returns so often in her dreams and memories to a time in which her body was in its innocent state and Sebastien could confirm her body's perfection. The connection between Sebastien and

Amabelle speaks to the good of physical as well as emotional affirmation and bonds.

After the massacre, Amabelle appears haunted by memories of Sebastien and their physical relationship, so much so that she refuses to build a relationship with another man or connect substantively with her community. In Father Romain, the book provides an example of the need for physical connection even after violence, even with a body that is imperfect. Father Romain explains why he left the priesthood: "It took more than prayers to heal me after the slaughter. . . . It took holding a pretty and gentle wife and three new lives against my chest. . . . It took a love closer to the earth, closer to my own body, to stop my tears. Perhaps I have lost, but I have also gained an even greater understanding of things both godly and earthly" (272).

His description emphasizes the need for movement forward in the "new lives" of his children and also the importance of physical validation through sexuality. Soon after hearing this from Father Romain, Amabelle wishes she had built such a relationship with Yves, saying, "He and I both had chosen a life of work to console us after the slaughter. . . . I regretted that we hadn't found more comfort in each other" (274). In refusing to embrace another lover, Amabelle does not accept the value of her own body, even when it has been injured, and refuses to create a connection that could sustain her physically.

In addition to sexual physical validation, the best good in the novel comes through emotional connection. As in Kongo's conversations with Papi and Valencia before the massacre, individuals build relationships through sharing stories of pain. How can remembering a massacre be a good thing? In a wide sense, the event was lost to public knowledge, and remembering therefore bears palpable justice to those who have suffered and died. One might consider Danticat's book itself as an effort to bring voices erased by history into the present historical consciousness. In terms of the characters themselves, telling their stories enables them not to be silent or ashamed about the devastation. It also permits a kind of resurrection of the people who have been lost, since they become present in memory, as Amabelle's repeated dream-like meditations on Sebastien make clear. Danticat uses Father Romain again as a kind of ideal with regard to memory. As a priest, Romain would speak to his parishioners about their histories in Haiti and about their shared culture: "His creed was one of memory, how remembering—though sometimes painful—can make you strong" (73). Remembering the massacre, then, does not invoke what we might think of as good, which often implies pleasure; instead, as April Shemak has argued, remembering calls up pain and is therefore ambivalent. It becomes apparent that memory must be shared with others for the good of emotional connection to happen. Without an auditor for memory, individuals such as Amabelle are adrift in a sea of dreams.

After the massacre, many survivors wish to tell their stories to the authorities in order to seek recognition and justice. A crowd waits outside the office of the justice of the peace and eventually becomes frustrated when the stories will not be heard. When that satisfaction is denied people, they turn to the church, which is taking stories for the media, perhaps to sell them. Amabelle meets the priest, and he assumes she wishes to tell her story, saying, "To all those who tell us of lost relations, we can offer nothing, save for our prayers and perhaps a piece of bread. So we have stopped letting them tell us these terrible stories. It was taking all our time, and there is so much other work to be done" (254). The people seek to tell their experiences to the church and state, but neither is a willing or adequate auditor. Perhaps this is because some characters seek closure through money or justice, and Danticat's novel argues that testimony will not expunge memory, as critic Amy Novak's work cogently explains.

Stories of the massacre are best shared between survivors, the book argues, as a means to build solidarity and connection. Part of the reason that Yves and Amabelle seem to be living in stasis for thirty years after the event is their refusal to communicate their pain with each other; such communication was the foundation of Amabelle and Sebastien's love, which was formed through sharing stories of the loss of their respective parents. In the description of the clinic after the massacre, Danticat offers the best example of the solace that can come through communication with someone who also has experienced suffering. When the group at the clinic first starts to talk, they urgently tell their particular stories: "Taking turns, they exchanged tales quickly, the haste in their voices sometimes blurring the words, for greater than their desire to be heard was the hunger to tell" (209). The individual telling shifts subtly toward an appreciation of others' experiences. The speakers repeat the phrase, "I was there when . . ." (210), emphasizing that they witnessed other people's suffering as well as endured their own. The group validates elements of particular stories, as when a man describes vultures above a pit of cadavers: " 'Oh, the vultures,' everyone chimed in" (211). When the man says that he smiled when he thought of his lover even though he was surrounded by the dead, the group affirms him: "The people around him smiled too, at the beauty of such an innocent moment, when a young woman wakes up in her new man's bed for the first time and forgets how she came to be there" (211).

The conversation then moves toward cultural memory as the group defines Haiti through collective memory of Haitian revolutionaries and leaders, and the narration switches from noting the particular speaker to presenting the scene through a collective voice: "They wondered what would happen to their relations who had disappeared. . . . What could have been done differently? Whatever became of our national creed, 'L'union fait la force'? Where was our unity? Where was our strength? And how can we not hate ourselves for the people we left behind?" (213). Eventually Amabelle becomes part of this collective voice, even as an auditor; the narration moves from the outside perspective of "they" to the affirmative, interior, collective voice of "our." It is striking that the group questions the unity of the state and the ability of the state to act on their behalf within a passage that demonstrates the formation of their own viable unified group of survivors. Unity will come not through political leadership, the text suggests, but through collaborations among citizens. The group imagines reunions with family members, looking forward rather than recalling the massacre: "They dictated step by step what the first domino games and cockfights with their fathers and compadres would be like, the first embraces given to lovers and children" (213). Sharing stories with each other, first individually and then collectively, enables the group to move toward the future, as critic Lynn Chun Ink argues.

Amabelle is unable to share her experience with others touched by violence, even though she seeks out Sebastien's mother and builds a companionate friendship with Yves's mother. She explains her desire to tell her story: "The slaughter is the only thing that is mine enough to pass on. All I want to do is to find a place to lay it down now and again, a safe nest where it will neither be scattered by the winds nor remain forever buried beneath the sod" (266). This passage suggests the unfinished nature of memory, for telling the story is something she wishes to do not once but "now and again" so that it will remain safe and undisturbed. The image of a nest suggests protection and nurturance rather than dissipation; she wishes her memories to live and not be entombed in the earth or scattered as ashes after a cremation. This passage permits us to appreciate that telling the past does not mean dismissing or moving beyond it. Telling the past can build community and connection, for the historical memory is alive and present in Amabelle's mind. Memories will not pass away, just as the presence of evil in the world is not something that can be eradicated or erased. Telling stories of the past permits those memories to live for a moment in the world, bringing pain but also the profound good of acknowledgement, visibility, and empathy.

The first line of the book and the line repeated in the last dream sequence is "His name is Sebastien Onius" (1, 281). Amabelle wishes to tell Sebastien's story in order to recover him and make his experience more concrete. She explains that "men with names never truly die. It is only the nameless and faceless who vanish like smoke into the early morning air" (282). The narrative itself is a form of naming, for, in telling the story of Amabelle and Sebastien, Danticat gives life to names unwritten in history books. Amabelle seeks connection with the spirit of Sebastien when she travels back to the Dominican Republic at the book's conclusion; instead of entering the waterfall in which she and Sebastien used to meet, Amabelle enters the river, the same river that drowned her parents, separates the two countries, and became the scene of the massacre. Instead of Sebastien, she meets another survivor of the massacre, the Professor, a man still mentally disturbed by the event, who emerges from the river "a ghost with a smile on his face" (309). Amabelle explains her desire to connect with him: "I wanted to call him, but only by his proper name, not by the nickname, Pwofesè, the replacement for 'crazy man,' that he had been given" (309–10). She wishes to address him as an equal rather than as a pariah, much as Kongo insisted that he be treated as a man by Papi earlier in the text. Amabelle asks the Professor to take her into the past by naming those she has lost—Sebastien and her parents—but she envisions them through the joy that the relationships have brought her. The ending of the novel is deliberately ambiguous with regard to Amabelle's fate, and some readers have suggested that her entering the river evokes a suicide attempt. Given that the river is "warm and shallow" (310), such intention seems unlikely. The Professor gazes at Amabelle "cradled by the current, paddling like a newborn in a washbasin." The language here suggests new life rather than death, as if remembering her past and connecting with the Professor, if only through a gaze, has transformed Amabelle. She envisions the Professor's sandals through an image that corresponds to the two of them: he walks away with "his sandals flapping like two large birds fluttering damp wings, not so much to fly as to preen themselves." Amabelle and the Professor, wet from the river, are like these birds that will not fly, for they cannot escape the past and instead must use it to renew themselves. The novel concludes optimistically, "He, like me, was looking for the dawn." Amabelle sees herself in the Professor, acknowledges the connection between them, and with him welcomes the new day.

Danticat's *The Farming of Bones* considers evil as rooted in the embrace of separation, both as cultural norm and as individual practice; the book also leads us toward a definition of good that requires communication and connection, a sense of solace that can come through sharing the past in story. Evil is not discrete and cannot be expunged or contained, and it is ever present in memories of the massacre. But just as the event lives on in memory, so too do the stories of lost loved ones that remind Amabelle of her value to them and their importance to her. Danticat's novel insists on the need to tell stories of good and evil, of innocence and loss, particularly when the historical record fails. We may not know the names of the tens of thousands of individuals massacred in October 1937, but through Danticat's work, we can arrive at a better understanding of the significance of their lives and the weight of their deaths.

Works Cited

Calder, Bruce J. *The Impact of Intervention: The Dominican Republic during the US Occupation of 1916–1924*. Austin: U of Texas P, 1984.

Danticat, Edwidge. *The Farming of Bones*. New York: Soho, 1998.

Ink, Lynn Chun. "Remaking Identity, Unmaking Nation: Historical Recovery and the Reconstruction of Community in *In the Time of the Butterflies* and *The Farming of Bones*." *Callaloo* 27.3 (2004): 788–807.

Martin, W. Todd. "'Naming' Sebastien: Celebrating Men in Edwidge Danticat's *The Farming of Bones*." *Aetna* 28.1 (2008): 65–74.

Novak, Amy. "'A Marred Testament': Cultural Trauma and Narrative in Danticat's *The Farming of Bones*." *Arizona Quarterly* 62.4 (2006): 93–120.

Roorda, Eric Paul. *The Dictator Next Door: The Good Neighbor Policy and the Trujillo Regime in the Dominican Republic, 1940–1945*. Durham: Duke UP, 1998.

Sagás, Ernesto. *Race and Politics in the Dominican Republic*. Gainesville: UP of Florida, 2000.

Shemak, April. "Re-Membering Hispaniola: Edwidge Danticat's *The Farming of Bones*." MFS: *Modern Fiction Studies* 48.1 (2002): 83–112.

Wucker, Michele. *Why the Cocks Fight: Dominicans, Haitians, and the Struggle for Hispaniola*. New York: Hill, 1989.

Revisiting the Gothic: *Buffy the Vampire Slayer* and *Angel* as Contemporary Gothic_____

Erin Hollis

Typically characterized by "imperiled heroines, dastardly villains, ineffectual heroes, supernatural events, dilapidated buildings, and atmospheric weather" (Spooner and McEvoy 1), the gothic genre has a long history within art, literature, film, and television. This essay will examine the genre and its literary history in order to explore how Joss Whedon's television shows *Buffy the Vampire Slayer* and *Angel* are examples of a contemporary and updated gothic genre. Whedon uses humor to poke fun at gothic conventions, encouraging his audience to reexamine the genre and its typical characteristics, and employs numerous tropes and figures of speech from the genre, including the uncanny and the haunting past. In so doing, he prompts viewers to engage in a more nuanced exploration of the apparently simple distinctions between good and evil so often depicted within the genre.

The Gothic Genre: A Brief Overview

Most critics agree that the gothic genre originated in the late eighteenth century with texts such as Horace Walpole's *The Castle of Otranto* (1764) and Ann Radcliffe's *The Romance of the Forest* (1791), *The Mysteries of Udolpho* (1794), and *The Italian* (1797). Indeed, *The Castle of Otranto* is often considered the first gothic novel, and Walpole even "provided the new subgenre with its future name when he subtitled the second edition [of *The Castle of Otranto*] 'A Gothic Story'" (Miles 11). In his preface to the second edition of *The Castle of Otranto*, Walpole provides a definition of the genre as "an attempt to blend the two kinds of romance, the ancient and the modern" (65), a definition that highlights that his "new species of romance" is itself a collision of earlier genres (70). As scholar E. J. Clery argues, "Walpole wanted to combine the unnatural occurrences associated with romance and the naturalistic characterization and dialogue of the novel" (24).

This collision of different aspects of other genres creates a dual quality within the gothic genre:

> Still classified for many as betwixt and between "serious" and "popular" literature and drama, the Gothic is thus continuously about confrontations between the low and the high, even as the ideologies and ingredients of these change. It is about its own blurring of different levels of discourse while it also concerned with the interpenetration of other opposed conditions—including life/death, natural/supernatural, ancient/modern, realistic/artificial, and unconscious/conscious—along with the abjection of these crossings into haunting and supposedly deviant "others" that therefore attract and terrify middle-class characters and readers. (Hogle 9)

Thus, because gothic fiction was a popular genre that was consumed quickly by its audience but was also one that experimented with the relatively new form of the novel, it has pushed against the boundaries between high and low culture from its inception.

In addition to this combination of high and low forms, gothic literature generally employs several common tropes, including supernatural themes and situations and archetypal good and evil characters. Beyond these stereotypical tropes of the genre, more recent critics have described the genre as having an "emphasis on the returning past, [a] dual interest in transgression and decay, [a] commitment to exploring the aesthetics of fear, and [a] cross-contamination of reality and fantasy" (Spooner and McEvoy 1). The oft-noted ineluctable presence of the past in gothic fiction has often been related to the genre's reactionary style. Many critics have argued that the genre simply wishes to reinforce the status quo by looking to the past for inspiration on how to live in the present. Because the gothic was initially so closely related to the aristocracy, many pieces of gothic literature seem to seek merely to reify or make concrete traditional socioeconomic and religious hierarchies. Yet, other gothic literature seems to seek to subvert such hierarchies, questioning the status quo and embracing progress. For example, while many gothic novels include a conventional damsel in distress, novels such as Charlotte Brontë's *Jane Eyre* (1847) and Jane Austen's *Northanger Abbey* (1818) either parody the typical damsel in distress or depict an atypical female character who demonstrates a desire for a change in the status quo. Scholar Jerrold E. Hogle discusses the tension within the genre between reactionary and progressive stances:

> Most often . . . Gothic works hesitate between the revolutionary and conservative, as when Radcliffe allows her heroines independent property and ultimate freedom of choice within the fervent worship of their fathers and an avoidance of all direct political action, rebellious or reactionary. Partly because it comes from mixing discourses and postures so blatantly, often with their incompatibilities fully in view, the Gothic can both raise the sad specters of "othered" and oppressed behaviors, crossings of boundaries, and classes of people and finally arrange for the distancing and destruction of those figures or spaces into which the most troubling anomalies have been abjected by most of the middle class. (13)

The gothic genre thus encompasses a variety of texts with different approaches to tradition and hierarchy; because the genre began as a combination of other genres and so consistently marries high and low culture, it has been particularly open to shifts in style and perspective. These shifts and the ability of the genre both to reinforce and to subvert the status quo have led critics to refer to the genre as "gothics" rather than "gothic," implying that while there are many similarities within the genre, there are a great deal of differences between individual texts. The gothic genre has thus changed over the years as different authors have updated it to reflect the tropes and concerns of their times.

Unsurprisingly, then, representations of good and evil within the gothic genre tend to blur the boundaries between the two even as they introduce good and evil stereotypes. Such blurring is most clearly demonstrated by "one of the most characteristic—and charismatic— figures of the period": "the hero-villain":

The years 1790–1830 give us a whole crop of hero-villains, and these younger Satanic heroes are often portrayed from within. Many texts demand empathy with the agonised villain who is now a warped hero . . . and we are asked more explicitly to focus through his or her desire and passion. Most significantly, many of these heroes and heroines have fallen beyond the pale. They are outsiders and tend not to be associated with institutionalised power. (McEvoy 24)

The figure described here closely resembles the Byronic hero—a literary figure that also grew in popularity during the romantic period. Named after Lord Byron, a well-known romantic poet, the Byronic hero is a figure who is outside of society, seeking his own redemption while flouting societal conventions. Usually, such a hero has a dark past for which he is trying to atone. Such figures complicate clear distinctions between good and evil, as they encourage readers to sympathize with characters whose actions cannot always be deemed good. Thus, gothic literature has played with the boundaries between good and evil since the genre's inception, complicating simplistic ideas of what is good and what is evil by presenting readers with multifaceted characters whose disparate actions make them difficult to categorize.

At the same time, however, the gothic genre plays on the audience's stereotypical ideas of good and evil by depicting exaggerated characters, supernatural occurrences, and heightened emotions. The reader's expectations about certain characters are often satisfied within the gothic genre. For example, in *Dracula* (1897), which is often considered an example of the Victorian gothic, Bram Stoker depicts the vampire Dracula as a character who possesses typically evil characteristics. Dracula's desire for blood and his demonic nature receive more attention in the text than his human characteristics. Indeed, Dracula is made all the more frightening because, with his ability to adopt human characteristics, he is initially able to trick Jonathan Harker and many of the other characters in the novel into believing he is human. Additionally, the use of supernatural beings or events in gothic literature encourages readers to anticipate the presence of evil. Because the supernatural is so difficult to explain, the idea of evil easily comes to the fore as an explanation for such occurrences. In Mary Shelley's *Frankenstein* (1818), the mob that attacks Frankenstein's creature immediately assumes that the creature is evil because his existence is difficult to understand. Underlying *Frankenstein* is a criticism of this response, but the novel also exploits people's willingness to judge something unexplainable. The heightened emotions so common in the gothic genre also may encourage quick categorization on the part of the reader. If the reader is caught up in fear while reading, it may be more difficult to make subtle distinctions between good and evil. In the most frightening moments of *Dracula*, for example, Dracula seems to possess no nuance; he appears to be entirely evil. Thus, the gothic genre both exploits the readers' willingness to categorize and encourages the readers to examine their own reactions to depictions of good and evil within the text.

Buffy the Vampire Slayer and *Angel* as Contemporary Gothic

Buffy the Vampire Slayer (1997–2003) and *Angel* (1999–2004), two televisions series created by Joss Whedon, reflect many of the characteristics of gothic fiction. Indeed, when Whedon created *Buffy the Vampire Slayer*, he took as his inspiration a variety of genres, including the gothic genre. In part, he wanted to take genres such as horror and the gothic and subvert them by pushing against his viewers' expectations. In his commentary on the opening episode of the series, Whedon discusses how he rewrites genre conventions:

> The first thing I ever thought of when I thought of *Buffy* the movie was the little . . . blonde girl who goes into a dark alley and gets killed in every horror movie. The idea of *Buffy* was to subvert that idea, that image, and create someone who was a hero where she had always been a victim. That element of surprise . . . [and] genre-busting is very much at the heart of both the movie and the series.

Thus, from its inception, the series sought to "bust" typical conventions of the gothic and horror genres, and this desire to reinvent these genres paradoxically reflects the gothic genre's play with boundaries and ability to shift easily between ideologies. Indeed, Buffy herself is a fantastic example of a certain kind of atypical gothic heroine who appears in such novels as *Jane Eyre* and Emily Brontë's *Wuthering Heights* (1847). Both *Buffy the Vampire Slayer* and *Angel* regularly employ the conventions of the gothic genre even as they poke fun at such conventions or seek to subvert them. Furthermore, famous pieces of gothic literature are often reflected in each series as Whedon and his cohorts pay tribute to the one of the genres that served to inspire them.

Classic Gothic Literature in *Buffy* and *Angel*

Both series regularly make references to earlier texts that are often categorized as gothic. Within the first season of *Buffy* alone, there are allusions to *Frankenstein*, Robert Louis Stevenson's *The Strange Case of Dr. Jekyll and Mr. Hyde* (1886), and a variety of vampire stories. *Frankenstein* also becomes the background for the entirety of the show's fourth season, during which a government agency seeks to create cyborg monsters that will help to control the demon population. The series updates Shelley's story by turning the creature into a being who is part human, part demon, and part machine. This updated creature, whose name is Adam, possesses an unmatched intellect and ability to read people but shares none of the humanity that the creature of *Frankenstein* possesses. Thus, while *Frankenstein* has as one of its focuses the transformation of a creature who is subjected to intolerant treatment by both his creator and the other characters that he meets, the version of the creature represented on *Buffy* never cares what others think of him and only desires to control humanity by creating more creatures like him. While both the show and the novel explore the troubling issue of creating life, the show focuses more on the evil nature of the creature and his threat to civilization rather than on the potentially evil acts of the creature's creator, Maggie Walsh. This emphasis reflects the persistent trend in popular culture representations of the novel to focus on the creature rather than the creator. The creature, as a representation of the manipulation of science and technology, reflects the cultural anxieties of the specific time period during which each adaptation is created. Thus, the portrayal of Adam highlights anxieties about technological innovation and genetic mutations, whereas the original creature is more of a response to early nineteenth-century scientific thought. Nonetheless, both depictions of the creature demonstrate the gothic genre's ability to forecast cultural anxieties about progress in the fields of science and technology and the sorts of evil acts that might be spawned by such fields.

The Victorian gothic also appears in *Buffy*. Most notably, Dracula himself makes an appearance in the episode "Buffy vs. Dracula." First published in 1897, *Dracula* updates the gothic genre so that it addresses the cultural anxieties of the late nineteenth century. In *Dracula*, images of the past collide with images of progress. Most of the images of the past occur during Jonathan Harker's stay at Dracula's castle in Transylvania. As Harker makes his journey there, even the mode of transport becomes increasingly antiquated; he begins his trip on a train and ends it in a horse-drawn carriage. By associating Dracula so clearly with the past, Stoker situates his work within a gothic context, since gothic works almost always have a focus on a resurgence of the past or on the past coming back to haunt a work's characters. Stoker updates the gothic genre not only by suggesting a return to the past but also by depicting technology that indicates progress throughout the text. His frequent references to new technology such as the typewriter, steam trains, and blood transfusions demonstrate not only how the past might haunt the reader but also how the present, with all its innovations, can be haunting as well. Further, the figure of the vampire provides readers with an example of someone who can never escape the past—Dracula, after all, lives for hundreds of years—but who must always adapt to the future. Dracula *is* the past coming back to haunt the other characters, even as he embraces the technological present in his business dealings. The frightening villain of Stoker's novel has the power of both the past and the present.

"Buffy vs. Dracula" pokes fun at the character of Dracula and the ways in which he is depicted not only in the original novel but also in subsequent adaptations. Just as Stoker updates the gothic in his treatment of the past and the present in his novel, this episode of *Buffy* engages with the interplay between a late twentieth-century television series and a late nineteenth-century literary character. "Buffy vs. Dracula" acts, in part, as a parody of the *Dracula* story, mimicking many of the major characters and events of the novel. At the beginning of the episode, Buffy and her friends are playing at a very sunny beach when a storm suddenly starts to roll in. This storm, mirroring the events of the novel, brings Dracula to the town of Sunnydale, where he immediately finds an old, somewhat dilapidated mansion in which to live. Xander, one of Buffy's friends, takes on the role of *Dracula*'s Renfield, whom Dracula uses to carry out his plans; Xander begins to eat bugs and quote Renfield's lines from the novel, providing comic relief. The three female vampires from Dracula's castle also make an appearance and seduce Buffy's mentor, Giles. Thus, the episode is rife with references to the original story, providing humorous parallels that function as a sort of homage to the novel.

The episode, however, also takes the traditional view of Dracula and turns it on its head. Early in the episode, Buffy is unable to resist Dracula's thrall; she even lets him bite her and risks becoming a typical damsel in distress. This is rare for Buffy, who usually has the ability to defeat almost any demon. As the episode progresses, however, Buffy begins to resist his thrall, and finally, in the end of the episode, she defeats Dracula. In their final battle, Buffy relentlessly mocks Dracula to such a degree that he looks ridiculous. She returns to her usual witty and punning self, telling him that the "thrall" has gone out of their relationship. Dracula is no longer a scary demon or even a romantic figure, as some movies have represented him; rather, he is a ridiculous and exaggerated figure who serves to highlight the absurdity of gothic conventions. The episode calls attention to Dracula's love of transporting himself in the dirt from his native country as well as his attraction to old-world clothing and ruined castles, and, in doing so, it exposes as ridiculous the gothic conventions of setting novels or other works in ruins and focusing on the past. Such conventions are further parodied at the end of the episode, after Buffy has killed Dracula with a stake. When Dracula begins to come back to life, Buffy stakes him again, saying, "You think I don't watch your movies? You always come back." Referencing the common gothic and horror genre convention of villains who repeatedly come back from death, the episode pokes fun at the staking, which usually serves to inspire fear in the viewer/reader; the moment causes the viewer/reader to rethink such tropes and conventions.

The Uncanny in *Buffy* and *Angel*

Other gothic conventions and tropes are frequently referenced throughout both *Buffy* and *Angel*. The gothic genre commonly employs what Sigmund Freud famously named the "uncanny." Critic David Punter describes the uncanny:

> It represents a feeling which relates to a dialectic between that which is *known* and that which is *unknown*. If we are afraid, then more often than not it is because we are experiencing fear of the unknown: but if we have a sense of the uncanny, it is because the barriers between the known and the unknown are teetering on the brink of collapse. We are afraid, certainly; but what we are afraid of is at least partly our own sense that we have *been here before*. It is perhaps easy to guess how Freud pursues this argument: namely into the idea that the uncanny is occasioned when an event in the present reminds us of something in the (psychological) past, but something which cannot by fully remembered, a past event, or situation, or feeling, which should have been locked away or buried but which has emerged to haunt the current scene. (Punter 130)

Thus, the uncanny represents the feeling of experiencing something one has already experienced but in an unfamiliar way, a feeling similar to déjà vu. Combining the familiar and unfamiliar, the uncanny serves to produce discomfort as well as fear. *Buffy* employs this trope throughout its seven-season run. During the first three seasons, the show takes common high school experiences that would be familiar to the viewer and makes them uncanny. In the show, such experiences are often transformed into supernatural events or caused by literal monsters. Whedon takes the idea of high school being hell and actually makes the events during the characters' high school lives hellish. Sunnydale High School even sits atop a "hellmouth," a sort of portal to the demon dimension that affects anyone who comes into contact with it. A girl actually becomes invisible because no one ever pays attention to her, and vampires attack parent-teacher night, causing Buffy to get into trouble. Taking anxieties common to high school students and wrapping them in the guise of the supernatural, the show renders them at once familiar and unfamiliar—they become uncanny.

Buffy addresses the uncanny in other ways as well. In two episodes, "The Wish" and "Doppelgangland," one of the show's main characters, Willow, is made uncanny for the viewer. Throughout the early years of the series, Willow is a bookish, nerdy type who embraces her love of knowledge. In the episode "The Wish," another character wishes that Buffy had never come to Sunnydale, and, as a result, Sunnydale becomes a town run by vampires, of which Willow is one. By creating this alternate Sunnydale, the show produces the effect of the uncanny and so creates an unfamiliar familiar experience. Willow especially manifests this effect, as she becomes the exact opposite of herself even as she still resembles herself; she becomes cruel and evil yet retains her intelligent curiosity.

In "Doppelgangland," this effect is further developed. In this episode, the alternate-universe Willow is brought over into the Sunnydale with which the viewer is familiar. The original and alternate-universe versions of Willow occupy the space of one universe for one episode.

This creation of a doppelgänger, or double, is a common occurrence in gothic novels and usually serves to evoke a feeling of the uncanny. Both the viewer and the characters in the show experience the uncanny effects of this doppelgänger. The characters at first assume that the Willow they know has turned into a vampire. Hijinks ensue as this assumption causes Buffy and her friends to react humorously to the overtly sexual vampire Willow. The show parodies similar appearances of the uncanny doppelgänger in gothic works by using humor in the situation rather than fear. Though the characters are at first saddened by Willow's apparent plight, the viewer always knows that vampire Willow is not the "real" Willow; this awareness allows the viewer to see the humor in the situation rather than the fear and tragedy. *Buffy* once again turns a trope on its head: what is meant to inspire fear instead becomes humorous and, in the process, provides viewers with both the experience of a typical gothic trope and the ability to laugh at and develop a more critical stance toward such conventions.

Angel, who first appeared as Buffy's major love interest in *Buffy* and then went on to be the focus of the spin-off series *Angel*, also reflects an experience of the uncanny. From the beginning of *Buffy*, Angel is depicted as an atypical vampire. Cursed by a family of Gypsies for killing one of their beloved daughters, Angel has a soul, which makes him at once both human and vampire, both familiar and unfamiliar. Because he has a soul, he feels remorse for the cruel acts he performed before he was cursed and seeks redemption for those acts. Angel's curse comes with a caveat: if he experiences one moment of true happiness, he will revert to his former, soulless self. In season 2 of *Buffy*, he experiences such a moment of happiness while he is having sex with Buffy for the first time; as a result, he reverts to his evil self and becomes the villain of the season. Angel's double nature creates an uncanny experience for both the viewer and the characters. Angel is suddenly unfamiliar even as he remains entirely familiar; a character who once was represented as unquestionably good becomes evil, and viewers must confront the effects of such a change. Later, in the spin-off series *Angel*, Angel loses his soul again in an attempt to gain knowledge of a particularly difficult enemy. He again becomes uncanny as he uses his familiarity with the other characters in order to torture them. Unlike moments in the two series in which the uncanny is subverted and made absurd, the scenes depicting the unfamiliar familiarity of the soulless Angel inspire fear. In this instance, at least, the shows use a gothic convention in a straightforward manner. In general, however, both series take such conventions and revise them in order to encourage viewers to approach typical conventions in a critical manner.

The Haunting Past in *Buffy* and *Angel*

Another common gothic convention that the two series usually depict straightforwardly rather than with humor is the persistent presence of the past. Whedon still seeks to question this convention; indeed, each series creates an interesting dichotomy between the present and the past in terms of setting. *Buffy* takes place in the fictional Sunnydale, a town that, on first appearance, seems to have no remnants of the past; rather, Sunnydale appears to be a typical suburban town with new houses and a shiny new high school. *Angel* takes place in Los Angeles, a city well known for its embrace of the present and not known for its abundance of ruins. Unlike the typical settings of gothic literature, the settings for these series make the past seem invisible. Both series take place in California, which is typically associated with the sun, further indicating the contrast that Whedon sought to create between conventional gothic literature, which is so often set in gloomy and sunless locales, and his own gothic series. Yet, each series also seems haunted by events in many of the characters' pasts, and there are frequent references to artifacts from the past. The old and musty books in which Buffy and her friends discover information about the evil demons they must fight are often written in ancient languages, providing a complete contrast to the sunny and modern setting of the series. Indeed, in the first three seasons, the group regularly meets to do research in the library, and Giles, the librarian, objects to computers and modern technology in general.

By having the group do research in this manner and referencing earlier stories and legends, Whedon and his cohorts bring the past into the present of the series and provide a contrast between bright, modern-day Sunnydale and the past represented in the old books.

Other examples of the presence of the past are the frequent forays that are made into Angel's past as an evil vampire and also as a human. In several different episodes, viewers are made privy to the past events of his life, including the moment when he became a vampire, the moment when he regained his soul, and the moment when he first saw Buffy. In one episode of *Angel*, "Why We Fight," Angel's involvement with the US military during World War II is revealed. The episode details an event in Angel's past that took place after he was cursed with his soul but before he began to seek redemption by fighting the forces of evil. The show intersperses the present-day narrative with scenes from the past; as a mysterious figure from Angel's past holds his friends hostage in the present, the story of Angel's mission during World War II unfolds. Angel is asked by the US government to rescue a submarine that the Americans had commandeered from the Nazis. When he arrives on the submarine, he quickly discovers that it contains secret Nazi weapons: vampires, including Spike, a main character on both *Buffy* and *Angel*, and a character known as the Prince of Lies, who is an obvious caricature of the vampire Nosferatu from the classic 1922 German horror film of the same name. The vampires had been feasting on the American crew, and only a few members of the crew remain locked in a room. An attack renders the submarine inactive, and one of the crewmembers, Lawson, who is the mysterious figure in the present, must fix the leaks and other mechanical problems in order to rescue the entire submarine. A Nazi prisoner stabs Lawson fatally with a screwdriver, and because Lawson is the only person who can fix the submarine, Angel turns him into a vampire so he can carry out the needed repairs. Angel lets Lawson go free after he saves the ship, telling him that if he ever sees him again, he will kill him. In the present, Lawson confronts Angel for turning him into a vampire; unhappy as a vampire, he seeks revenge. Angel's literal confrontation with the consequences of his past actions emphasizes the ways in which his past both haunts him and defines his present actions. Such frequent references to Angel's past highlight how he carries those events around with him throughout his daily life. In having the past invade Angel's life so often, the writers on both shows employ the common gothic technique of exploring the past and its relationship to the present. The frequent resurfacing of the past in each series gives weight to Angel's struggle for redemption and also demonstrates for the viewer the inability to escape past misdeeds.

Both *Buffy the Vampire Slayer* and *Angel* frequently employ gothic tropes and references to gothic literature in order to pay tribute to a genre that served as a partial inspiration for both series and prompt viewers to confront the conventions of the genre and question how such conventions may create a particular perspective about topics such as good and evil. All too often, gothic characters can be easily (and flatly) categorized as good or evil, but both *Buffy* and *Angel* complicate such a reductive approach to the genre. By parodying gothic tropes and highlighting the permeability of the genre, Joss Whedon and his colleagues ask viewers to reconsider binaries such as good and evil and recognize that good and evil exist on a continuum rather than a simple hierarchy. Easy categorization simply does not work: characters who might typically be categorized as good sometimes do things that might be considered evil, and characters who might be easily assumed to be evil often turn out to be good. What each series makes clear is that it is our daily lives and daily actions that matter. Each day is a struggle to be good and not to embrace a negative attitude toward life. Every day is an opportunity for redemption. Representing a contemporary approach to the gothic, *Buffy* and *Angel* complicate the tropes of the genre and, in the process, encourage viewers to develop a nuanced understanding of the genre and a critical engagement with their own conceptions of good and evil.

Works Cited

Buffy the Vampire Slayer Season 4 DVD Collection. Dir. Joss Whedon et al. Twentieth Century Fox, 2003. DVD.

"Buffy vs. Dracula." *Buffy the Vampire Slayer Season 5 DVD Collection.* Dir. David Solomon. Twentieth Century Fox, 2004. DVD.

Clery, E. J. "The Genesis of 'Gothic' Fiction." *The Cambridge Companion to Gothic Fiction.* Ed. Jerrold E. Hogle. Cambridge: Cambridge UP, 2002. 21–40.

"Doppelgangland." *Buffy the Vampire Slayer Season 3 DVD Collection.* Dir. Joss Whedon. Twentieth Century Fox, 2003. DVD.

Hogle, Jerrold E. "Introduction: The Gothic in Western Culture." *The Cambridge Companion to Gothic Fiction.* Ed. Hogle. Cambridge: Cambridge UP, 2002. 1–20.

McEvoy, Emma. "Gothic and the Romantics." *The Routledge Companion to Gothic.* Ed. Catherine Spooner and McEvoy. London: Routledge, 2007. 19–28.

Miles, Robert. "Eighteenth-Century Gothic." *The Routledge Companion to Gothic.* Ed. Catherine Spooner and Emma McEvoy. London: Routledge, 2007. 10–18.

Punter, David. "The Uncanny." *The Routledge Companion to Gothic.* Ed. Catherine Spooner and Emma McEvoy. London: Routledge, 2007. 129–36.

Spooner, Catherine, and Emma McEvoy. Introduction. *The Routledge Companion to Gothic.* Ed. Spooner and McEvoy. London: Routledge, 2007. 1–3.

Walpole, Horace. Preface to the Second Edition. *The Castle of Otranto.* Ed. Frederick S. Frank. Orchard Park: Broadview, 2003. 65–71.

Whedon, Joss. Commentary. "Welcome to the Hellmouth." *Buffy the Vampire Slayer Season 1 DVD Collection.* Twentieth Century Fox, 2000. DVD.

"Why We Fight." *Angel: The Series Season 5 DVD Collection.* Dir. Terrence O'Hara. Twentieth Century Fox, 2006. DVD.

"The Wish." *Buffy the Vampire Slayer Season 3 DVD Collection.* Dir. David Greenwalt. Twentieth Century Fox, 2003. DVD.

The Touch of Evil and the Triumph of Love in Harry Potter_____

Vera J. Camden

"There is no good or evil, there is only power, and those too weak to seek it." (Quirinus Quirrell, *Harry Potter and the Sorcerer's Stone*)

For the generation of children who spent nights in bookshop doorways waiting for each new Harry Potter novel to appear, Harry's death and resurrection in J. K. Rowling's *Harry Potter and the Deathly Hallows* signify a bittersweet coming-of-age. In this final book of her seven-book series, "the boy who lived" (*Sorcerer's Stone* 1) through a brutal attack in his infancy is now a young adult. In Rowling's novel, Harry bravely surrenders to death in an inexorable confrontation with his evil nemesis, Voldemort, magically returns to finish Voldemort off, and lives happily ever after. Rowling's fans, both children and adults, breathlessly followed the young wizard from his traumatic childhood in *Harry Potter and the Sorcerer's Stone* to this final victory over Voldemort in the seventh book. "Really, the entire series of Potter books and motion pictures has been leading us to this final showdown between Harry and Voldemort. It could easily have been a letdown. But the fight here between good and evil is more than satisfying. It's thrilling" (Bamignoye). Harry's triumph is a hard-won victory based on elaborate and intricate magic. Yet the moral psychology Harry heroically exemplifies in this triumph is, I suggest, simple and self-fulfilling. It goes like this: human love overcomes evil.

This essay will argue that the victory Harry enjoys at the end of Rowling's epic saga is itself premised on a moral psychology that has been explicated throughout the series, but nowhere more powerfully than in the third novel, *Harry Potter and the Prisoner of Azkaban*. His physical victory over both Voldemort and death itself is founded upon a moral and psychological achievement that prepares him for his flourishing finish. Rowling's most intense, explicit exploration of

Harry's psychological battles and breakthroughs occurs in *Prisoner of Azkaban*. Thus, while it is impossible to consider Rowling's individual works in isolation from the epic sweep of her series, this essay will primarily concern itself with Harry's journey in *Prisoner of Azkaban*. Here Rowling takes him into traumatic memory only to discover the holy grail of his mother's love beneath the rubble of his shattered infancy. In thus modeling Harry's inner triumph over the evil that infected him in his infancy, Rowling has created a contemporary mythology for the generation that has come of age with Harry Potter. I will thus conclude this chapter with reflections on how Rowling has provided this generation with an "old" magic to offer "some protection" from individual traumas as well as the terrors of their own troubled times (*Half Blood Prince* 510).

Who Is Harry Potter?

Sorcerer's Stone begins in medias res: a sleeping infant with a note pinned to his blanket is left at the door of his aunt and uncle's home on Privet Drive. We come to learn that this infant, Harry Potter, is a wizard who lived through his parents' murder. His aunt and uncle are fearful of magic and mystery. They defame the memory of Harry's parents and abuse Harry. At the age of eleven, Harry is rescued from their domination and whisked off to Hogwarts School of Witchcraft and Wizardry by the gentle giant Hagrid. At Hogwarts, Harry learns that the tyrannical Lord Voldemort murdered his parents, James and Lily Potter, in an effort to kill Harry himself; he later learns that Voldemort believes (from a prophesy he has overheard) that Harry is destined to destroy him. The headmaster at Hogwarts, Albus Dumbledore, explains in the fifth book of the series, *Harry Potter and the Half Blood Prince*, that while this prophesy indeed set Voldemort's murderous mission in motion, it is not to be conferred objective significance:

> "But Harry, never forget that what the prophecy says is only significant because Voldemort made it so. . . . If he had not forced your mother to die

for you, would he have given you a *magical protection* he could not *penetrate*? Of course not, Harry! Don't you see? Voldemort himself created his worst enemy, just as tyrants everywhere do!" (509–10, emphasis added)

Voldemort's self-fulfilling prophecy thus predicates his disempowerment. By forcing Lily's self-sacrifice, he set in motion the protective power of love. Harry's traumatic beginning in turn predicates his triumphant ending. He is granted special powers and a special destiny. Because he is saved by love, he is capable of love:

"Yes, Harry, you can love," said Dumbeldore. . . . "Which, given everything that has happened to you, is a great and remarkable thing. You are still too young to understand how unusual you are, Harry."
    "So, when the prophecy says that I'll have 'power the Dark Lord knows not,' it just means—love?" asked Harry. (509)

In this explanation to young Harry—who is trying to figure out who he is, who he has been, and who he will be—Dumbledore identifies the power within Harry that will in fact destroy Voldemort and define Harry. Dumbledore offers Harry the following interpretation of the utter impermeability of his skin in *Sorcerer's Stone*:

"Your mother died to save you. If there is one thing Voldemort cannot understand, it is love. He didn't realize that love as powerful as your mother's for you leaves its own mark. Not a *scar*, no visible sign . . . to have been loved so deeply, even though the person who loved us is gone, will give us some protection forever. It is in your very *skin*." (299, emphasis added)

Harry learns that his mother invoked a deep, "old" magic when she died for him. The love of his mother infuses his body and covers his skin. Conversely, the lightning bolt scar that Harry famously bears on his forehead is the sign of Voldemort's slashing curse. Harry will eventually discover the terrifying truth that this scar actually contains a parasitical fragment of Voldemort's very soul that shattered like shrapnel—a touch of evil—into Harry's flesh. It is also a mark of the traumatic loss of his mother. Thus the power of his mother's love and the traces of the trauma that took her from him each make a living claim on his memory. They wage a war—a psychomachia—within Harry. Harry's capacity to remember this infantile trauma in *Prisoner of Azkaban* allows him to overcome the fear of annihilation located in the repressed memory of his parents' brutal murder. Underneath that trauma he recovers the memory of his mother's voice and love.

"The Boy Who Lived"

The story of Harry's magical rebuke of Voldemort's killing curse is foundational to the whole series, yet it occurs before the opening of the novel—offstage, as it were. Much of the mystery of the series depends upon the gradual reveal of what happened when Harry first met Voldemort in his home village of Godric's Hollow—and why. He will hear many versions as he develops relationships at Hogwarts, but the first story he hears about that fateful night comes from Hagrid: "Somethin' about you finished him, Harry. There was somethin' goin' on that night he hadn't counted on—*I* dunno what it was, no one does—but somethin' about you stumped him" (*Sorcerer's Stone* 57).

Harry's own recovered memory becomes his truest guide as the series unfolds. Its fundamental importance emerges in bits and pieces throughout the series. Harry gradually reconstructs the content and import of this ur-encounter through memory and his moment-by-moment reexperiencing of Voldemort's renewed assaults. Harry's scar remains a tormenting trace of the fateful night; its full vitality only gradually is disclosed in the novels. Dumbledore, who functions as Harry's guide and "interpreter," explains to Harry that he and Voldemort are locked together by his scar, among other connections. Harry learns that the two are destined to struggle to the death: "Neither can live while the other survives" (*Order of the Phoenix* 841). What begins in *Sorcerer's Stone* as a graduated series of incidents in which Harry's forehead throbs inexplicably whenever he is around the mysterious Professor Quirrell (who turns out to be host to the then-parasitical Voldemort) intensifies and multiplies as the saga unfolds. Harry discovers to his horror that the scar he bears on his forehead has a life of its own. It allows Harry literal insight into the Dark Lord's mind and emotions. His final revelation will be that his scar actually bears a split-off portion of Voldemort's soul; he must die if he wants to destroy Voldemort once and forever. The core irony of the novels is that Harry's survival sets him apart as a "chosen" wizard, yet his growing identity, power, and destiny are inextricably interwoven with his would-be destroyer. Rowling draws mysterious and eerie parallels between her hero and her villain. Each novel offers an inevitable, climactic confrontation between these enemies, whose first unresolved encounter is variously reenacted in scenes of graduated intensity and violence until the culmination of the final encounter in *Deathly Hallows*.

The recovery of this memory in the context of his evolving relationships at Hogwarts gives Harry the narrative of his own traumatic past. Rowling quite elegantly makes the following point about trauma and memory: Harry's ultimate triumph over Voldemort's parasitical greed and hunger is fostered by an emerging understanding and awareness of his own history, a history he shares with his attacker. He ensures his future survival and the survival of his world by his brave capacity to remember and listen to his memories. The menacing, shrill voice and laugh of the one who murdered his mother and plots to slay him recur in his mind; overcoming this memory becomes the central psychological battle of the series, preliminary to any and all armed encounters. Interestingly, Rowling has underscored her moral conviction that the real battles in life are "inward" in autobiographical reflections about her own youth: "One of the many things I learned at the end of that Classics corridor down which I ventured at the age of eighteen, in search of something I could not then define, was this, written by the Greek author Plutarch: What we achieve inwardly will change outer reality" (Rowling, "Fringe").

Parasites of the Mind

The nineteenth-century French neurologists Pierre Janet and Jean Charcot theorized that when the individual experiences "vehement emotions" following trauma, his or her mind is not capable of placing the experience into existing meaning schemes. The experience thus is not integrated into personal awareness, resulting in dissociation from consciousness of the trauma. Janet explained that when individuals do not, or rather cannot, integrate traumatic events, they are halted in emotional development. If they never integrate the trauma into their conscious awareness, they become "'attached' . . . to the trauma as to an insurmountable obstacle" (660). In effect, they become ruled by a trauma they are not consciously aware of but to which they are attached. Charcot first described traumatic memories as "parasites of the mind" (Van der Kolk et al. 49–52). Sigmund Freud later took up Janet's theories in his idea of "fixation." Contemporary psychologists follow Charcot and Janet's emphasis on the reality or "history" of traumatic events in creating a dissociated state of consciousness, or what is now termed post-traumatic stress disorder (PSTD); this disorder requires both memory and a narrative "testimony" to overcome or work through such experiences, usually in sustained psychological treatment. In terms very relevant to Harry Potter's legacy of survival, Cathy Caruth asks of traumatic testimony: "Is the trauma the encounter with death, or the ongoing experience of having survived it? At the core of these stories [of trauma is] . . . the oscillation between *a crisis of death* and the correlative *crisis of life*: between the unbearable nature of an event and the story of the unbearable nature of its survival" (*Unclaimed Experience* 7).

The metaphor of the "parasites of the mind" resonates with Rowling's characterization of Harry's traumatic memory whereby the traumatic remnant of Voldemort's curse remains unintegrated and attached to his victim and feeds off of the victim's life's blood symbiotically. In terms of Harry's trauma, Rowling sets up a hideous logic. The mother/infant relationship entails a natural and nurturing symbiosis.

For Harry, this mother/infant pairing is supplanted by the imbedding of Voldemort's parasitical sliver in the infant Harry's skin and mind. In an uncanny echo of psychological theories of trauma, Rowling creates Harry's scar as a location of living memory: a parasite. It marks the place of his loss, leaving a residue that insists he return to banish its power. The abuser in this case, Voldemort, has left his mark, and in the image of his wand's lightning bolt, Rowling concretizes the dynamics that trauma theorists know to be true: memory is housed almost unmediated in the body and mind of the victim. This anguished irony determines Harry's destiny. The depiction of childhood misery and abuse in *Sorcerer's Stone*, however powerful for the young reader, contains none of the dark, politically inflected and psychologically penetrating dramatization of the later books. As Harry matures, so do the demands placed upon him, demands that lead him to confront despair, torture, and death itself. In *Prisoner of Azkaban*, Harry takes lessons with the remarkable Remus Lupin, the Hogwarts professor of the Dark Arts who guides Harry into the realms of memory and the feelings of his early losses. Here Rowling actually depicts Harry's "treatment," offering him a place for what Caruth describes as the testimony to traumatic memory in the presence of a witness who can tolerate the recollection and narration of the memory (*Trauma*).

Rowling clarifies some of the origins of her fictional preoccupations in her 2008 Harvard University commencement speech. She underscores her personal awareness of political and psychological trauma in social as well as psychological history. The tyranny and terror that she acknowledges "informs" Harry Potter's internal and external worlds.

One of the greatest formative experiences of my life preceded Harry Potter, though it informed much of what I subsequently wrote in those books. This revelation came in the form of one of my earliest day jobs. . . . working at the African research department at Amnesty International's headquarters in London.

There in my little office I read hastily scribbled letters smuggled out of totalitarian regimes by men and women who were risking imprisonment to inform the outside world of what was happening to them. . . . I read the testimony of torture victims and saw pictures of their injuries. I opened handwritten, eyewitness accounts of summary trials and executions, of kidnappings and rapes. . . .

I shall never forget the African torture victim, a young man no older than I was at the time, who had become mentally ill after all he had endured in his homeland. . . .

And as long as I live I shall remember walking along an empty corridor and suddenly hearing, from behind a closed door, a scream of pain and horror such as I have never heard since. . . . [A young man had just heard] that in retaliation for his own outspokenness against his country's regime, his mother had been seized and executed. ("Fringe")

Rowling's encounter with the suffering of the victims of oppressive regimes became attached to her mind and in some ways traumatized her memory: "Every day, I saw more evidence about the evils humankind will inflict on their fellow humans, to gain or maintain power. I began to have nightmares, literal nightmares, about some of the things I saw, heard, and read." This radical encounter with evil finds its way into her young hero, Harry, who fights his own internal oppression and in the process liberates the wizarding world.

Nothing to Fear but Fear Itself

It is not until Rowling's third book, *Prisoner of Azkaban*, that Harry truly returns to the scene of his parents' murder and his clash with the Dark Lord, Voldemort. Harry's memory revives through the effect of the demonic figures Rowling calls dementors: "the foulest creatures that walk this earth. . . . They glory in decay and despair, they drain peace, hope, and happiness out of the air around them. . . . You'll be left with nothing but the worst experiences of your life" (187). For all of their life-sucking horror, the dementors operate as agents to Harry's deepest encounter with his own traumatic history. The dementors counterpoint the Mirror of Erised—"desire" spelled backward—in *Sorcerer's Stone*, which reveals Harry's deepest desire: to see the mother and father whose memory he has repressed. The dementors, in turn, reveal to Harry that his deepest fear is not of Voldemort but of fear itself. Rowling's knowing reference to US president Franklin D. Roosevelt's famous caution to the American people in the midst of the Great Depression—"the only thing we have to fear is fear itself"—seems apropos to the word "depression." Rowling herself has tied the dementors to her own depression following the death of her mother ("A Year"), and this fear of fear directly points Harry to the repressed memory of the night he lost his mother. When he encounters the dementors, he is taken back in memory to that night and actually hears his mother's voice and the violence surrounding his parents' death. Indeed, the psychological centerpiece of *Prisoner of Azkaban*, arguably the most psychological of all the novels, is Harry's recovery of the memory of his trauma. Harry's reconstruction of that night and the feelings he experiences as he reencounters his mother and the memory of his loss are revived in the presence of a witness, Professor Lupin. Rowling's depiction of this internal battle within Harry begins early in the series with glimmers of memory and becomes more pronounced as the series progresses. Here Harry actually meets his mother in an aural memory.

Harry revisits the night of his parents' murder through the influence of dementors, who prey on human fear. Ironically, Harry's confrontation with his greatest fear allows him to discover its origins: his infantile panic at the loss of his mother. To capture the scope of what psychologists call "annihilation fear," pediatrician and psychoanalyst D. W. Winnicott famously asserted, "There is no such thing as a baby alone." The human baby cannot survive outside the "maternal environment" (*The Child* 88). Winnicott emphasized the role of the breast and the infant's cultivation of a transitional space between the mother and the emerging world ("Transitional" 89–97). Psychoanalyst Didier Anzieu highlights this symbiosis in the mother/infant dyad through the recognition of the skin as the organ of connection, and, with loss of touch, as the source of enveloping dread:

> It seems that by clinging to the breast, hands, body, and clothing of the mother, [the infant] can elicit from her a kind of response [of] . . . utopian notion of the maternal instinct. The catastrophe haunting the nascent psyche of the human baby would then be that of letting go of this clinging grip. When that happens the child is plunged into a . . . "nameless dread" (23).

Harry actually revisits the memory he had repressed in stages, administered by gradually intensified encounters with dementors who seek him out, hungry for his buried terror and despair:

> The cold went deeper than his skin. It was inside his chest, it was inside his very heart. . . . He was drowning in cold. . . . He was being dragged downward, the roaring growing louder. . . . And then, from far away, he heard screaming, terrible, terrified, pleading screams. He wanted to help whoever it was, he tried to move his arms, but couldn't . . . a thick white fog was swirling around him, inside him. (*Prisoner of Azkaban* 84)

This first memory will be fleshed out with Harry's full-blown recollection and reconstruction in subsequent encounters. But in some ways this is the most primitive and most vivid glimpse of his infantile experience because it is the most bodily, and it captures the blurring of the inner and outer worlds of the infant: a catastrophe beyond the skin, the sense of drowning and dread.

With Lupin's help, Harry gradually reconstructs bursts of traumatic memory filled with the vivid exactness one expects of memory that is locked in through post-traumatic stress disorder. The sudden onset of memory is like being there again. It is unintegrated, fresh, "just like it was": "Memories of the trauma tend . . . to be experienced as fragments of the sensory components of the event: as visual images; olfactory, auditory, or kinesthetic sensations; or intense waves of feelings that patients usually claim to be representations of elements of the original event" (Van der Kolk et al. 49–52). Harry's next encounter with the dementors takes him straight back to the night in Godric's Hollow:

> It was as though freezing water were rising in his chest, cutting his insides. And then he heard it again. . . . Someone was screaming, screaming inside his head . . . a woman. . . .
>
> *"Not Harry, not Harry, please not Harry!"*
>
> *"Stand aside, you silly girl . . . stand aside, now. . . ."*
>
> *"Not Harry, please no, take me, kill me instead—"*
>
> Numbing, swirling white mist was filling Harry's brain. . . . He needed to help her. . . . She was going to die. . . . She was going to be murdered. . . .
>
> He was falling, falling through the icy mist.
>
> *"Not Harry! Please . . . have mercy . . . have mercy. . . ."*
>
> A shrill voice was laughing, the woman was screaming, and Harry knew no more. (*Prisoner of Azkaban* 179)

Harry's memory here is entire, though it takes him some revisiting to understand its content and the uniqueness of his encounter with the dementors: "No one else heard echoes in their head of their dying parents. . . . He heard the last moments of his mother's life, her attempts to protect him . . . and Voldemort's laughter before he murdered her" (184). His dreams begin to fill with the clammy hands of the dementors, while he dwells upon his mother's voice, now riveted by the sound he had long forgotten. What he had once forgotten he can now not forget; the voices and the sights haunt him. As psychiatrist Lenore Terr remarks of the traumatized children that she studies, "psychic trauma victims are cursed with an unstoppable tendency to 'see' their traumas. They are indeed 'haunted'" (140).

"Expecto Patronem": The Power of Positive Memory

When Harry discloses this experience to Lupin, the Dark Arts professor commences their "anti-dementor" lessons. These passages of Harry's lessons with Lupin are among the most powerful in the entire saga, offering the moral psychology that undergirds the birth of Harry as hero. Here, Harry learns how to conjure a Patronus, a force conjured magically from within that enables one to fight the fear instigated by the dementors. Harry's anguished work with Lupin enables his eventual victory, volumes later, over Voldemort. Lupin explains that Harry must learn to perform the incantation "expecto patronum," which conjures a "guardian that acts as a shield between you and the dementor. . . . The Patronus is a kind of positive force, a projection of the very things that the dementor feeds upon—hope, happiness, the desire to survive—but it cannot feel despair, as real humans can, so the dementors can't hurt it" (237). In order to learn this spell, Harry must descend into the darkness of his memory. With each descent Harry hears and learns more:

> White fog obscured his senses. . . . Then came a new voice, a man's voice, shouting, panicking—
> "*Lily, take Harry and go! It's him! Go! Run! I'll hold him off—*"
> *The sounds of someone stumbling from a room—a door bursting open— a cackle of high-pitched laughter—* . . .
> "I heard my dad," Harry mumbled. "That's the first time I've ever heard him—he tried to take on Voldemort himself, to give my mum time to run for it. . . ." (240)

As Harry's capacity to conjure the Patronus grows, so does the depth of his penetration of memory. Though his lessons with Lupin are titrated so that he is not overwhelmed, his mind remains fixated at the place of his renewed awareness. Harry's thoughts wander back to his mother and father, and though it was terrible to hear his parents' last moments replayed inside his head, these were the only times Harry had heard their voices since he was a very small child. If he wants to hear his parents again, he must reenter the agony of the dementor's domain. Harry considers the conflict: "He'd never be able to produce a proper Patronus if he half wanted to hear his parents again. . . . 'They're dead,' he told himself sternly. 'They're dead and listening to echoes of them won't bring them back.'" Harry later confesses guiltily to a secret desire to hear his parents again that renders his efforts to conjure a powerful Patronus rather lame (243).

Here again Rowling shows remarkable insight into the dynamics of memory as Harry's return to his infantile encounter with Voldemort also returns him to an affective bond with a mother and father whom he now remembers and, in particular, to a longing to linger with those who once loved him so much. Rowling shows the parasitical nature of trauma: its capacity to pull its victim into a repetition of the violation in an attempt at mastery but also in an attempt to return to the innocence of life before the traumatic shock. Nanette Auerhahn and Dori Laub write about "memory as a self-healing process" and the Holocaust victim's desire to return to the memory of the trauma in order to find not only the lost relationships with those who loved him but also the self that was lost through the trauma. It is the positive hope contained in that return that promises a rediscovery of some continuation of that loved object and loved self in the current life post trauma. Thus they insist that the dwelling on the past prevalent in PTSD cases is not an "inability to mourn" so much as a search for a foundation upon which to recover and rebuild:

> The need is to . . . redress the imbalance created in the psyche between good and evil, form and meaninglessness. After a holocaust, to heal a person must be able to relink with what has been destroyed so as to combat a sense of annihilation. . . . Holding on to first love objects represents holding onto the basic landmarks according to which the self was originally established (329–30).

Present hope is contingent on such historical realignment with the beloved objects that are lost, now remembered precisely to be found in a new—restored, perhaps redeemed—relation to the world and to the self. Rowling offers a similar foundation in the "anti-dementor" lessons that teach Harry to find a positive *memory* from which to resist despair and annihilation. His successful Patronus is precisely drawn from the power of his father in the past, the promise of his godfather, Sirius Black, in the future—*"We'll be okay—I'm going to live with him—'Expecto patronum!'"* (*Prisoner of Azkaban* 383)—and the integration of both positive figures into Harry's sense of himself and his new sense of being by the novel's end.

In a crucial scene of Harry's confrontation with the dementors, he saves himself with the successful invocation of a Patronus, Prongs the stag: the plot "turns" on this scene because Rowling creates a "time-skew" (Terr 160). Harry at first believes that somehow his father has come back to save him. The scene is rendered with deliberate ambiguity. The dementors confront Harry in a true assault, not in the studied safety of Lupin's office:

> He could feel its putrid breath. . . . His mother was screaming in his ears. . . . She was going to be the last thing he ever heard—
>
> And then, through the fog that was drowning him, he though he saw a silvery light growing brighter and brighter. . . .
>
> Something was driving the dementors back. . . . Harry tried to make out what it was. . . . It was as bright as a unicorn. . . . Fighting to stay conscious, Harry watched it canter to a halt as it reached the opposite shore. For a moment, Harry saw, by its brightness, somebody welcoming it back . . . someone who looked strangely familiar . . . but it couldn't be. (*Prisoner of Azkaban* 385)

Harry thinks the person whom he sees in the distance, strangely familiar, is his father come back from the dead to help him: "I think it was my dad," Harry later tells his friend Hermione (407).

Using a device called a "Time-Turner," Harry is able to revisit and review this contemporary moment of terror and make it his own. Harry later learns by revisiting this powerful scene of salvation that the savior who conjures the Patronus is not his father but himself. In this scene Rowling allows Harry, her trauma victim, a chance to redeem time and thus redeem himself by watching himself, from a distance, as if in a film: "Harry began to run. He had no thought in his head except his father. . . . If it was him . . . if it really was him . . . he had to know, had to find out. . . ." He waits for his father to appear:

A terrified excitement shot through him—any moment now—

"Come on!" he muttered, staring about. "Where are you? Dad, come on—"

But no one came. Harry raised his head to look at the circle of dementors across the lake. One of them was lowering its hood. It was time for the rescuer to appear—but no one was coming to help this time—

And then it hit him—he understood. He hadn't seen his father—he had seen *himself*—. . .

"*EXPECTO PATRONEM!*" he yelled.

And out of the end of his wand burst . . . a blinding, dazzling silver animal. . . .

The dementors were falling back, scattering, retreating into the darkness. . . . They were gone.

The Patronus turned. . . . Slowly, it bowed its antlered head. And Harry realized . . .

"*Prongs,*" he whispered. (410–12)

This scene is Rowling's coup de grâce in *Prisoner of Azkaban*, a moment that indulges the understandable obsession with meeting his parents that has dominated Harry since his encounter with the Mirror of Erised but also instructs him in terms more powerful than Dumbledore's removal of the offending temptation. Rowling allows Harry to "become" the father for whom he longs in a positive identification with his Patronus, Prongs. In doing so, he can leave the fear of that night in Godric's Hallow behind him and move forward into the future. "*I* saw me but I thought it was my dad! It's okay!" Harry tells Hermione. "I knew I could do it this time . . . because I'd already done it. . . . Does that make sense?" (412).

Rowling's rendering of Harry's victory over memory and fear captures the peculiar pressure of time that is experienced by the trauma victim. Once again, her metaphor of the Time-Turner allows Harry to overcome the dissociation that typifies the victim of PSTD. Terr, following Freud's speculations about the ways in which psychic trauma is a "breach in the protective shield against stimuli," explains that "time goes awry" for trauma victims (Terr 136). Harry's use of the Time-Turner to return to his father through memory facilitates his progression toward himself, his destiny, and ultimately his defeat of Voldemort, the destroyer of time. The traumatized person's time sense undergoes damage that resembles "flood lines on the walls of Venetian churches. . . . As a 'stimulus barrier,' in other words, 'time' functions both as a protection against damage and as a marker of the damage" (149). Trauma victims often experience paranormal and uncanny events—"the sense of telepathy, prescience, and powers" (155)—in an attempt to recover the sense of power over time that they lost when the catastrophe broke the rhythm of their expected life and its routines." A child's tale of trauma often becomes a tale in which the uncontrollable might have been controlled. . . . Kids will retroactively put things that followed a traumatic event into places that precede it. . . . We all wish to turn back time. . . . [It is] a universal wish, the wish for a second chance" (160–62).

Thus, in inventing the Time-Turner in *Prisoner of Azkaban*, Rowling allows Harry a measure of control when he most needs it. He meets his father in memory, recognizing James's support for Lily's valiant effort to save her baby; experiences his "father" saving him from the dementors in the form of Prongs, the Patronus he believes James conjures for him; and then, with the aid of the Time-Turner, goes back to that moment and recognizes that he conjured the Patronus himself, fueled by the positive associations he has allowed to return through the replaying and deepening of memory. This is sheer brilliance on Rowling's part. It perfectly enacts the fantasy that Terr explains the trauma victim needs while allowing Harry, the "victim," the measure of control and liberation from past trauma *he* needs to move forward into his new, heroic identity.

Wizards and Woe: Harry Potter in the World

In a September 12, 2011, issue of *The New Yorker* commemorating the tenth anniversary of the September 11, 2001, terrorist attacks, Lorrie Moore reflects upon her experience of the attack on New York's World Trade Center. She titles her piece "Wizards" because she recognizes that the generation that came of age following 9/11 also came of age in the light—and the darkness—of Harry Potter and the "good-versus-evil wizardry of J. K. Rowling." She thinks sadly about her brother, who walked covered in ash to his home in Queens the afternoon of the attack only to return to work the next day, where he sat alone at his desk, waiting for normality to return. Clearly in a dissociated state, Moore's brother was, she remarks, revealing the "universal human desire to return to the fictional normal; the normal and the everyday are often amazingly unstoppable, and what is unimaginable is the cessation of them. The world is resilient, and no matter what interruptions occur, people so badly want to return to their lives and get on with them" (28). Moore does not connect her brother to Harry Potter, though she might have. Rather, she seems astonished that the "brilliant university students" whom she teaches named "Harry Potter" as their desert-island book and laments that the moral vision imbuing the series seems to have trumped the more subtle prognostications of her fellow *New Yorker* writers. She imagines that the generation that was "the same age as Harry Potter, having begun middle school exactly when he began Hogwarts" somehow is subject to a "magical, Manichean, neo-Biblical view of the world" (28), as if its members are groping in a fog of idealism that is slated to lift once they mature. I believe she misses the point.

The Harry Potter generation is far from idealistic; indeed, I would suggest, that it has many of the dissociated characteristics of PSTD victims who fear for the future: "Psychic trauma destroys a child's sense of the future. . . . A sense of limited future, in other words, appeared to be a good indicator of childhood psychic trauma" (Terr 163–65). I have taught the Harry Potter books throughout the last two decades, and I asked students about their experience of growing up with Harry. One student writes, "I have become so intertwined with these books that I can no longer remember what life was like before them or how I survived," while another notes, "I do not remember first reading Harry Potter because he has just always been there. I do not remember living before Harry Potter." Another student writes, "As his story ended, so did my childhood . . . . It is like a piece of my childhood that I have been able to hold onto for so long is tearing away. Nothing is sadder to me." Yet another writes: "J. K. Rowling gave me something to look forward to and something to enjoy. . . . I have always wanted to thank her for that. She changed my life and the life of so many kids who . . . felt like they were locked up in a cupboard under the stairs. Harry Potter is not a fad, and the older I get, the prouder I am to say: 'I am from the Harry Potter generation.'" Another student explains:

When I was a child I suffered severe trauma from abuse that my father inflicted. Harry's trauma showed me that as long as he was true to himself he would not become the vicious murderer Voldemort was. So I realized that my father was a horrible part of my past but I did not have to be like him, drunken and cruel. When the series came to a conclusion I was very sad. The last chapter took me so long to read because of the tears that could not seem to be held in. I was happy that the story ended for Harry's sake. That his scar did not hurt anymore. That was the way Rowling said she was going to end it. I wanted Harry to live a normal life after the tragedy that he had faced for the first seventeen years, but I did not want the story to end for me. I still hold the hope that Hogwarts exists, at least in the hearts of readers. . . . It is wonderful that J. K. Rowling created such magic with paper and ink.

This student's testimony captures as well as anything I have read or could write how the wizard Harry Potter has helped the current generation. These children who came of age with Harry are not so much Manichean as they are woebegone. Among the many marvelous and magical reasons that the Harry Potter series has captured the zeitgeist of an entire generation, perhaps one of the most significant is Harry's capacity to rebound the touch of evil with the triumph of love.

Works Cited

Anzieu, Didier. *The Skin Ego*. New Haven: Yale UP, 1989.

Auerhahn, N. C., and Dori Laub. "Annihilation and Restoration." *International Review of Psychoanalysis* 11.3 (1984): 329–30.

Bamigboye, Baz. "How Will We Survive When Harry's Gone?" *Daily Mail*. Associated Newspapers, July 2011. Web. 19 Sep. 2011.

Caruth, Cathy. *Unclaimed Experience: Trauma, Narrative, and History*. Baltimore: Johns Hopkins UP, 1996.

_____, ed. *Trauma: Explorations in Memory*. Baltimore: Johns Hopkins UP, 1995.

Janet, Pierre. *Psychological Healing*. Vol. 1. New York: Arno, 1976.

Moore, Lorrie. "Wizards." *The New Yorker* 12 Sep 2011: 28.

Roosevelt, Franklin D. "First Inaugural Address." *Inaugural Addresses of the Presidents of the United States*. Washington: US GPO, 1989.

Rowling, J. K. *A Year in the Life*. Dir. James Runcie. IWC Media, RDF Television, ITV, 2007. Television.

_____. "The Fringe Benefits of Failure, and the Importance of Imagination." Harvard University, Cambridge. June 2008. Address.

_____. *Harry Potter and the Deathly Hallows*. New York: Scholastic, 2007.

_____. *Harry Potter and the Half Blood Prince*. New York: Scholastic, 2005.

_____. *Harry Potter and the Order of the Phoenix*. New York: Scholastic, 2003.

_____. *Harry Potter and the Sorcerer's Stone*. New York: Scholastic, 1998.

_____. "Oprah and Harry Potter Phenom Billionaire J. K. Rowling." Interview by Oprah Winfrey. *The Oprah Winfrey Show*. CBS, 1 October 2010. Television.

Terr, Lenore. *Too Scared to Cry: Psychic Trauma in Childhood*. New York: Harper, 1990.

Van der Kolk, Bessel A., Alexander C. McFarland, and Lars Weisaeth, eds. *Traumatic Stress: The Effects of Overwhelming Experience on Mind, Body, and Society*. New York: Guilford, 2007.

Winnicott, Donald. *The Child, the Family, and the Outside World.* Harmondsworth: Penguin, 1964.

_____. "Transitional Objects and Transitional Phenomena." *International Journal of Psychoanalysis* 34 (1953): 89–97.

Zalon, Lily, ed. *Dear Mr. Potter.* Dear Mr. Potter, n.d. Web. 19 Sep 2011.

RESOURCES

Additional Works on Good and Evil _____

Drama
Titus Andronicus by William Shakespeare, 1594
The Good Soul of Szechuan by Bertolt Brecht, 1943
The Crucible by Arthur Miller, 1952
Aunt Dan and the Lemon by Wallace Shawn, 1985
Death and the Maiden by Ariel Dorfman, 1991

Graphic Novels
Watchmen by Alan Moore, 1986–87
Hellblazer by Jamie Delano et al., 1988–
The Sandman by Neil Gaiman, 1989–96
Preacher by Garth Ennis, 1995–2000

Long Fiction
The Divine Comedy by Dante Alighieri, 1308–21
The Monk by Matthew G. Lewis, 1796
Frankenstein; or, The Modern Prometheus by Mary Shelley, 1818
Demons by Fyodor Dostoevsky, 1872
Anna Karenina by Leo Tolstoy, 1877
Dracula by Bram Stoker, 1897
The Turn of the Screw by Henry James, 1898
Heart of Darkness by Joseph Conrad, 1902
The Sea-Wolf by Jack London, 1904
The House on the Borderland by William Hope Hodgson, 1908
The Space Trilogy by C. S. Lewis, 1938–45
America Is in the Heart by Carlos Bulosan, 1946
Cry, the Beloved Country by Alan Paton, 1948
Nineteen Eighty-Four by George Orwell, 1949
Charlotte's Web by E. B. White, 1952
Lord of the Flies by William Golding, 1954
The Lord of the Rings by J. R. R. Tolkien, 1954–55
The Cairo Trilogy by Naguib Mahfouz, 1956–57
No-No Boy by John Okada, 1957
The African Trilogy by Chinua Achebe, 1958–64
One Hundred Years of Solitude by Gabriel García Márquez, 1967
In the Fog of the Season's End by Alex La Guma, 1972
The Conservationist by Nadine Gordimer, 1974

The Patternist series by Octavia Butler, 1976–84

Sitt Marie Rose by Etel Adnan, 1977

In the Heart of the Country by J. M. Coetzee, 1977

The Stand by Stephen King, 1978

Ghost Story by Peter Straub, 1979

The House of the Spirits by Isabelle Allende, 1982

Schindler's Ark by Thomas Keneally, 1982

Hawksmoor by Peter Ackroyd, 1985

Ender's Game by Orson Scott Card, 1985

Blood Meridian; or, The Evening Redness in the West by Cormac McCarthy, 1985

Sozaboy: A Novel in Rotten English by Ken Saro Wiwa, 1985

Beloved by Toni Morrison, 1987

The Messiah of Stockholm by Cynthia Ozick, 1987

The Silence of the Lambs by Thomas Harris, 1988

When Heaven and Earth Changed Places by Le Ly Hayslip, 1989

Good Omens: The Nice and Accurate Prophecies of Agnes Nutter, Witch by Neil Gaiman and Terry Pratchett, 1990

The Devil's Advocate by Andrew Neiderman, 1990

The Quorum by Kim Newman, 1994

His Dark Materials series by Philip Pullman, 1995–2000

Comfort Woman by Nora Okja Keller, 1997

The Harry Potter series by J. K. Rowling, 1997–2007

Disgrace by J. M. Coetzee, 1999

A Gesture Life by Chang-Rae Lee, 1999

Black House by Stephen King and Peter Straub, 2001

The Stone Virgins by Yvonne Vera, 2002

Jonathan Strange & Mr. Norrell by Susanna Clarke, 2004

Mr. Shivers by Robert Jackson Bennett, 2010

The Surrendered by Chang-Rae Lee, 2010

Nonfiction

The Diary of a Young Girl by Anne Frank, 1952

Motiveless Malignity by Louis Auchincloss, 1969

First They Killed My Father: A Daughter of Cambodia Remembers by Loung Ung, 2000

Short Fiction

"Young Goodman Brown" by Nathaniel Hawthorne, 1835

"The Great God Pan" by Arthur Machen, 1890

"The Beckoning Fair One" by Oliver Onions, 1911

"Night Fears" by L. P. Hartley, 1924

"The Dunwich Horror" by H. P. Lovecraft, 1929

"Wings in the Night" by Robert E. Howard, 1932

"The Lottery" by Shirley Jackson, 1948

"Where Are You Going, Where Have You Been?" by Joyce Carol Oates, 1966

"I Have No Mouth, and I Must Scream" by Harlan Ellison, 1967

Bibliography

Arendt, Hannah. *Eichmann in Jerusalem: A Report on the Banality of Evil*. New York: Viking, 1963.

Aristotle. *The Nicomachean Ethics*. Trans. W. D. Ross. New York: Oxford UP, 1998.

Athanasopoulos, Constantinos. "Good and Evil in Human Nature: Some Preliminary Ontological Considerations." *Philosophical Inquiry: International Quarterly* 22.3 (2000): 103–15.

Baudrillard, Jean. *The Transparency of Evil: Essays on Extreme Phenomena*. Trans. James Benedict. London: Verso, 1993.

Bellett, Alan. "Evolution, Process and the Tree of the Knowledge of Good and Evil." *Process Studies* 32.1 (2003): 121–41.

Bentham, Jeremy. *An Introduction to the Principles of Morals and Legislation*. Oxford: Oxford UP, 2009.

Bhabha, Homi. *The Location of Culture*. New York: Routledge, 1994.

Breen, Margaret Sönser, ed. *Minding Evil: Explorations of Human Iniquity*. New York: Rodopi, 2005.

_____. *Truth, Reconciliation, and Evil*. New York: Rodopi, 2004.

_____. *Understanding Evil: An Interdisciplinary Approach*. New York: Rodopi, 2003.

Butler, Judith. *Frames of War: When Is Life Grievable?* London: Verso, 2009.

_____. *Precarious Life: The Powers of Mourning and Violence*. London: Verso, 2004.

Cahalan, John. "Natural Obligation: How Rationally Known Truth Determines Ethical Good and Evil." *Thomist: A Speculative Quarterly Review* 66.1 (2002): 101–32.

Card, Claudia. *The Atrocity Paradigm: A Theory of Evil*. Oxford: Oxford UP, 2002.

Cheliotis, Leonidas K. *Roots, Rites and Sites of Resistance: The Banality of Good*. New York: Macmillan, 2010.

Coleman, Richard J. *Eden's Garden: Rethinking Sin and Evil in an Era of Scientific Promise*. Lanham: Rowman, 2007.

Cooper, Terry D. *Dimensions of Evil: Contemporary Perspectives*. Minneapolis: Fortress, 2007.

Crosby, Donald. "Both Red and Green but Religiously Right: Coping with Evil in a Religion of Nature." *American Journal of Theology and Philosophy* 31.2 (2010): 108–23.

De Marneffe, Peter. "The Problem of Evil, the Social Contract, and the History of Ethics." *Pacific Philosophical Quarterly* 82.1 (2001): 11–25.

Dewey, John. *Human Nature and Conduct: An Introduction to Social Psychology*. New York: Holt, 1922.

_____. *Theory of Valuation*. Chicago: U of Chicago P, 1939.

Eagleton, Terry. *On Evil*. New Haven: Yale UP, 2010.

Epstein, Greg M. *Good without God: What a Billion Nonreligious People Do Believe*. New York: Morrow, 2009.

Fleming, Richard. *Evil and Silence*. Boulder: Paradigm, 2010.

Garçon, Maurice. *The Devil: An Historical, Critical, and Medical Study*. London: Gollancz, 1929.

Gini, Al. *Why It's Hard to Be Good*. New York: Routledge, 2006.

Gockel, Matthias. " 'Be Not Overcome by Evil, but Overcome Evil with Good': An Orientational Approach to Suffering and Evil." *Modern Theology* 25.1 (2009): 97–105.

Grant, Ruth Weissbourd, ed. *In Search of Goodness*. Chicago: U of Chicago P, 2011.

Hare, Richard M. *The Language of Morals*. Oxford: Clarendon, 1952.

Harris, George. "Pessimism." *Ethical Theory and Moral Practice: An International Forum* 5.3 (2002): 271–86.

Hazlett, Allan. "Possible Evils." *Ratio: An International Journal of Analytic Philosophy* 19.2 (2006): 191–8.

Hsieh, Nien-hê. "Value: Incommensurable." *Stanford Encyclopedia of Philosophy*. Stanford U, n.d. Web. 12 May 2011.

Hume, David. *Dialogues Concerning Natural Religion and Other Writings*. Cambridge: Cambridge UP, 2007.

Judt, Tony. *Reappraisals: Reflections on the Forgotten Twentieth Century*. New York: Penguin, 2008.

Kinneging, Andreas A. M. *The Geography of Good and Evil: Philosophical Investigations*. Trans. Ineke Hardy. Wilmington: ISI, 2009.

Kraut, Richard. *What Is Good and Why: The Ethics of Well-Being*. Cambridge: Harvard UP, 2007.

Langtry, Bruce. *God, the Best, and Evil*. Oxford: Oxford UP, 2008.

Law, Stephen. "The Evil-God Challenge." *Religious Studies: An International Journal for the Philosophy of Religion* 46.3 (2010): 353–73.

Lewis, Clarence I. *An Analysis of Knowledge and Valuation*. La Salle: Open Court, 1947.

Mendola, Joseph. *Goodness and Justice: A Consequentialist Moral Theory*. New York: Cambridge UP, 2006.

Mill, John Stuart. *Three Essays on Religion*. Amherst: Prometheus, 1999.

_____. *Utilitarianism*. Peterborough: Broadview, 2011.

Moore, George E. *Principia Ethica*. Rev. ed. Cambridge: Cambridge UP, 1993.

Nadler, Steven M. *The Best of All Possible Worlds: A Story of Philosophers, God, and Evil*. New York: Farrar, 2008.

Nash-Marshall, Siobhan. "Is Evil Really an Ontological 'Primitive'?" *Proceedings of the American Catholic Philosophical Association* 79 (2005): 157–71.

Needleman, Jacob. *Why Can't We Be Good?* New York: Penguin, 2007.

Nietzsche, Friedrich. *Beyond Good and Evil*. Trans. Judith Norman. New York: Cambridge UP, 2002.

Otte, Richard. "Evidential Arguments from Evil." *International Journal for Philosophy of Religion* 48.1 (2000): 1–10.

Perrett, Roy. "Evil and Human Nature." *Monist: An International Quarterly Journal of General Philosophical Inquiry* 85.2 (2002): 304–19.

Peters, Karl. "Understanding and Responding to Human Evil: A Multicausal Approach." *Zygon: Journal of Religion and Science* 43.3 (2008): 681–704.

Ricœur, Paul. *Evil: A Challenge to Philosophy and Theology*. Trans. John Stephen Bowden. London: Continuum, 2007.

_____. *The Symbolism of Evil*. Trans. Emerson Buchanan. New York: Harper, 1967.

Royce, Josiah. *Studies of Good and Evil: A Series of Essays upon Problems of Philosophy and Life*. New York: Appleton, 1899.

Said, Edward. *Culture and Imperialism*. New York: Knopf, 1993.

Scarre, Geoffrey. "The 'Banality of Good'?" *Journal of Moral Philosophy: An International Journal of Moral, Political and Legal Philosophy* 6.4 (2009): 499–519.

_____. "Can Evil Attract?" *Heythrop Journal: A Bimonthly Review of Philosophy and Theology* 41.3 (2000): 303–17.

Schopenhauer, Arthur. *Essays from the Parerga and Paralipomena*. Trans. Thomas B. Saunders. London: Allen, 1951.

Schott, Robin M. *Feminist Philosophy and the Problem of Evil*. Bloomington: Indiana UP, 2007.

Schrift, Alan D. *Modernity and the Problem of Evil*. Bloomington: Indiana UP, 2005.

Stone, Michael H. *The Anatomy of Evil*. Amherst: Prometheus, 2009.

Svendsen, Lars H. *A Philosophy of Evil*. Trans. Kerri A. Pierce. Champaign: Dalkey Archive, 2010.

Tooley, Michael. "Evil: Problem of." *Stanford Encyclopedia of Philosophy*. Stanford U, n.d. Web. 12 May 2011.

Wolfe, Alan. *Political Evil: What It Is and How to Combat It*. New York: Knopf, 2011.

Zimmerman, Michael J. "Value: Intrinsic vs. Extrinsic." *Stanford Encyclopedia of Philosophy*. Stanford U, n.d. Web. 12 May 2011.

Žižek, Slavoj. *Living in End Times*. New York: Verso, 2010.

_____. *Violence: Six Sideways Reflections*. New York: Picador, 2008.

CRITICAL
INSIGHTS

About the Editor _____

Margaret Sönser Breen is a professor of English and women's, gender, and sexuality studies at the University of Connecticut. She specializes in LGBT literature and, more broadly, gender and sexuality studies. Her publications include *Narratives of Queer Desire: Deserts of the Heart*; *Butler Matters: Judith Butler's Impact on Feminist and Queer Studies*, coedited with Warren J. Blumenfeld; and *Genealogies of Identity: Interdisciplinary Readings on Sex and Sexuality*, coedited with Fiona Peters. She has also edited or coedited four collections on evil and wickedness.

Contributors _____

Margaret Sönser Breen is a professor of English and women's, gender, and sexuality studies at the University of Connecticut. She specializes in LGBT literature and gender and sexuality studies. Her publications include *Narratives of Queer Desire: Deserts of the Heart*; *Butler Matters: Judith Butler's Impact on Feminist and Queer Studies*, coedited with Warren J. Blumenfeld; and *Genealogies of Identity: Interdisciplinary Readings on Sex and Sexuality*, coedited with Fiona Peters. She has also edited or coedited four collections on evil and wickedness.

Mena Mitrano holds PhDs in American literature from Rutgers and the University of Rome; she specializes in American literature, modernism, and theory. Her publications include *Gertrude Stein: Woman without Qualities* and *Language and Public Culture*, as well as the coedited volume *The Hand of the Interpreter: Essays on Meaning after Theory*. She is at work on a book on Susan Sontag and the public intellectual.

Sherri Olson is an associate professor in the Department of History and codirector of the Medieval Studies Program at the University of Connecticut. Her research focuses on medieval social and cultural history, with a special interest in the history of the peasantry, rural society, and monasticism. In addition to a number of articles and book reviews, her publications include two books, *A Chronicle of All That Happens: Voices from the Village Court in Medieval England* and *A Mute Gospel: The People and Culture of the Medieval English Common Fields*. She is working on a book entitled *Daily Life in a Medieval Monastery* and is planning another volume on monastic estate administration and the "interface" between monks and peasants in the thirteenth and fourteenth centuries.

Robert Deam Tobin is the Henry J. Leir Chair in Foreign Languages and Cultures at Clark University, where he teaches courses on literature, especially German literature, with a particular interest in sexuality and human rights. Long interested in the Age of Goethe, he is the author of *Warm Brothers: Queer Theory and the Age of Goethe* and *Doctor's Orders: Goethe and Enlightenment Thought* as well as coeditor of *A Song for Europe: Popular Music and Politics in the Eurovision Song Contest*. He is working on a book on the emergence of modern sexual discourses in nineteenth-century German-speaking central Europe.

Frederick S. Roden is an associate professor of English at the University of Connecticut. He is author of *Same-Sex Desire in Victorian Religious Culture* and editor of *Palgrave Advances in Oscar Wilde Studies*. He has also edited collections on Catholicism/queer narrative and Jewish/Christian intersections and written a commentary to the medieval Christian mystic Julian of Norwich. His research concerns Holocaust literature, and he is at work on a monograph about the borders of modern Jewish identity.

Gregory Kneidel is an associate professor of English at the University of Connecticut, where he specializes in Renaissance poetry and prose and the history of rhetoric. Author of *Rethinking the Turn to Religion in Early Modern English Literature*, he is a contributing editor to the *Variorum Edition of the Poetry of John Donne* and is working on a book on John Donne and the law.

Mitchell M. Harris is an assistant professor of English at Augustana College, where he teaches courses on early modern British literature and critical theory. His essays have appeared in *Christianity and Literature* and *Intersections in Christianity and Critical Theory*. A contributing writer to *The Oxford Guide to the Historical Reception of Augustine* and a contributing commentary editor to the *Variorum Edition of the Poetry of John Donne*, he is coediting a volume titled *Resurrecting the First "Five Hundred": The Church Fathers in Early Modern England* and finishing a monograph on Augustinian ethics in Tudor-Stuart literature.

Mark Kipperman is a professor of English at Northern Illinois University. He is the author of *Beyond Enchantment: German Idealism and English Romantic Poetry* and numerous articles on Shelley, Byron, and Keats.

Katie R. Peel is an assistant professor at the University of North Carolina Wilmington, where she teaches courses in young adult, children's, queer, and Victorian literatures. Her recent publications include an essay on Charlotte Brontë's Lucy Snowe as a queer character in *Villette* and an essay exploring the use of Julius and Ethel Rosenberg in interactive narratives for young readers.

Karen J. Renner is a lecturer in American literature at Northern Arizona University. Her work has appeared in *Nineteenth-Century Literature*, and she has edited a special double issue of *LIT: Literature Interpretation Theory* titled "Evil Children in Film and Literature." Her book project is titled *Perverse Subjects: Drunks, Gamblers, and Prostitutes in Antebellum America*.

Tom Hubbard is a Scottish novelist, poet, and itinerant literary scholar whose permanent home is in Fife, Scotland. His publications include *Seeking Mr. Hyde: Studies in Robert Louis Stevenson, Symbolism, Myth, and the Pre-Modern*; *The Integrative Vision: Poetry and the Visual Arts in Baudelaire, Rilke and MacDiarmid*; *Marie B.*; and *The Chagall Winnocks*. He has served as Lynn Wood Neag Distinguished Visiting Professor at the University of Connecticut and Professeur invité at the Université Stendhal–Grenoble 3 in France.

Pnina Rosenberg is an art historian specializing in the art and legacy of the Holocaust. She lectures on those subjects in the Department of Arts and Humanities of Technion (the Israel Institute of Technology) in Haifa, Israel. She has presented papers at international conferences and published books, articles, and exhibition catalogues on various aspects of art and the memory of the Holocaust, including *Salon des* *refuses: The Art of the Holocaust*, "The Memorials of Berlin: Bystanders and Remembrance," "Mickey Mouse in Gurs: Graphic Novels in a French Internment Camp," and *L'art des indésirables: L'art dans les camps d'internement français 1939–1944*. She is also art editor of *Prism: An Interdisciplinary Journal for Holocaust Educators*.

Patrick Colm Hogan is a professor in the Department of English and the Program in India Studies at the University of Connecticut. He is the author of fourteen books, including *Colonialism and Cultural Identity* and *Empire and Poetic Voice*. He has also edited four books, including *Literary India* and *Rabindranath Tagore: Universality and Tradition* (both coedited with Lalita Pandit).

Katharine Capshaw Smith is an associate professor of English at the University of Connecticut, where she teaches courses in children's literature and African American literature. Her monograph *Children's Literature of the Harlem Renaissance* won the Children's Literature Association's award for best scholarly book. The editor of the *Children's Literature Association Quarterly*, she is working on a project that examines photographic books about black childhood.

Erin Hollis is an assistant professor in the Department of English, Comparative Literature, and Linguistics at California State University, Fullerton. Her research focuses on modernist authors, including James Joyce, Mina Loy, and Virginia Woolf, and on popular culture, especially the work of Joss Whedon, creator of *Buffy the Vampire Slayer*, *Angel*, and *Firefly*. She has published an article examining *Buffy the Vampire Slayer* through the lens of Joyce's Leopold Bloom and is working on articles on *True Blood* and fan fiction and on James Joyce and Mina Loy's shared ecological concerns.

Vera J. Camden is a professor of English at Kent State University and a training and supervising analyst at the Cleveland Psychoanalytic Center in Cleveland, Ohio. She is also coeditor of the journal *American Imago*. She publishes widely in the fields of early modern English literature, psychoanalysis, and women's studies. She has taught the Harry Potter books since their first publication.

Richard J. Bleiler is humanities librarian at the University of Connecticut. His books include *Reference and Research Guide to Mystery and Detective Fiction* as well as the edited volumes *Science Fiction Writers* and *Supernatural Fiction Writers: Contemporary Fantasy and Horror*. He is also associate editor of *The Greenwood Encyclopedia of Science Fiction and Fantasy: Themes, Works, and Wonders*.

Index

good and evil
  duality of, 23
  gothic genre and, 240–41
  individual interpretation of, 126–27
  nature of, vii
  paradigms of, 207
  relationship between, 1
gothic genre, 238–51
Gottliebova-Babbitt, Dina, 192
governesses, societal role of, 148
Gray, Dorian (*The Picture of Dorian Gray*), 85–90
Gretchen (*Faust*). *See* Margarete (*Faust*)

Hallward, Basil (*The Picture of Dorian Gray*), 85–89
happy fall. *See* felix culpa
Harry Potter and the Prisoner of Azkaban (Rowling), 253, 259–68
Harry Potter and the Sorceror's Stone (Rowling), 254–56
Harry Potter generation, trauma of, 270
Harry Potter series (Rowling), 253–71
Hawthorne, Nathaniel, 159–73
Hay, John MacDougall, 186–87
hero-villain, 240
He Who Must Not Be Named (Harry Potter series). *See* Voldemort (Harry Potter series)
history, bias in, 44
Hogg, James, 176
Holocaust, the, 2–8, 24, 190–205
homosexuality, 12–14, 84–93
"Horror's Twin" (Gilbert), 36–37
House of the Seven Gables, The (Hawthorne), 160
House with the Green Shutters, The (Brown), 185–86
human trafficking. *See* slavery
Huysmans, Joris-Karl, 80

Hyde, Edward (*The Strange Case of Dr. Jekyll and Mr. Hyde*), 179–82

Ideal Husband, An (Wilde), 83
If This Is a Man (Levi). *See Survival in Auschwitz* (Levi)
imperialism, 144–58
Importance of Being Earnest, The (Wilde), 83
Inferno (Dante), 6–7
"In Search of Our Mothers' Gardens" (Walker), 16–19
internment camp. *See* concentration camp
inversion, 79
Iqbal (*Train to Pakistan*), 210–11

Jakobson, Roman, 28–29
Jane Eyre (Brontë), 144–58
Janet, Pierre, 258
Jean (*Survival in Auschwitz*), 6
Jekyll, Henry (*The Strange Case of Dr. Jekyll and Mr. Hyde*), 178–82
Jugga (*Train to Pakistan*), 209–12
justice, duties of, 104

Kailyard school, 185
Kidnapped (Stevenson), 177
King Lear (Shakespeare), 98–111
Kongo (*The Farming of Bones*), 225, 230
kout kouto. *See* Parsley Massacre
Kristeva, Julia, 38

labor, exploitation of, 225
language, 4–6, 226
Lear (*King Lear*), 98, 105–11
Leverkühn, Adrian (*Doctor Faustus* [Mann]), 72–75
Levi, Primo, 2–8, 24